POEMS
IN PROGRESS

To Geraldine – for inspiring my love of literature
Laura

For Milo – who already loves books as much as I do
Alexandra

First published in 2022 by
The British Library
96 Euston Road
London NW1 2DB

Cover image: 'Insomniac' by Sylvia Plath, reproduced by courtesy of Faber and Faber Ltd.

British Library Cataloguing-in-Publication Data
A catalogue record is available from the British Library

ISBN 978 0 7123 5466 0

Designed and typeset by Karin Fremer
Picture research by Sally Nicholls
Project editing by Abbie Day

Printed in the Czech Republic by Finidr

Alexandra Ault & Laura Walker

POEMS IN PROGRESS

Drafts from Master Poets

CONTENTS

My lip the secret Well of Life to learn;
And lip to lip it murmured, While you live
Drink, for once dead you never shall return.

35

I think the vessel that with fugitive
Articulation murmured once did live,
And merry-make, and that cold lip I kissed,
How many kisses might it take — and give!

36

For in the market-place one dawn of day
I watched the potter thumping his wet clay,
And with its all obliterated tongue
It murmured, Gently brother, gently pray!

37

Ah, fill the cup! what boots it to repeat
That time is slipping underneath our feet;
Unborn Tomorrow and dead Yesterday;

INTRODUCTION

There is something quite special, almost magical, about manuscript poems. Messy, complicated and sometimes illegible, these handwritten or typescript drafts hold a unique connection to their creator. These are the very pages which embody the spark of an idea, the flourish of a pen and the creation of a verse. While readers and audiences typically experience poetry through print or performance, manuscript poems show this art form at a moment before publication, often as a work in progress. Some manuscripts reveal much about the poet, their creative process and how they prepared a poem for publication. Others show how writing was often a collaborative process, with translators, friends, editors or scribes helping to shape the words on the page. Contained within this anthology are manuscript drafts and copies of poems, from verses scribbled on the backs of letters to beautiful calligraphic and illustrated stanzas. These are varied and surprising documents, which have their own complicated histories. How they survived, sometimes over a thousand years, is a story in itself.

Most of the manuscripts in this book are drawn from the collections of the British Library. It has been challenging to choose from the thousands of drafts, fair copies and proofs of poems found within the Library's diverse and global collections. They contain numerous works by famous writers such as William Blake, Charlotte Brontë, William Wordsworth, Samuel Taylor Coleridge, Christina Rossetti, Elizabeth Barrett Browning and T. S. Eliot. In addition, there are many works by poets and writers whose verses have particular resonance today, such as suffragettes, enslaved persons and political campaigners. Manuscripts have also been included from institutions in North America to broaden the selection. From the early modern period these include the seventh sonnet from *Pamphilia* by Lady Mary Wroth and the draft of the first book of Milton's *Paradise Lost*. Further manuscripts have been sought to capture the works of key American poets, including Phillis Wheatley, Emily Dickinson, Walt Whitman and Maya Angelou.

This volume is enriched by commentaries from some of the world's most important contemporary poets, each exploring one of their own manuscript drafts. It has been a privilege to be able to work with these poets and include their poems alongside historic manuscripts.

Poems in Progress is not a typical anthology as its focus is on the manuscript rather than the published poem. Historically, poetry anthologies were often divided thematically into miscellanies, with poems on similar subjects grouped together. This volume follows a similar approach, grouping poems broadly by theme rather than by author or time period.

All of the poems in this book are complex and dynamic and many would fit under more than one theme. For example, Alexander Pope's translation of *The Illiad* is found in the chapter on 'Conflict' as it fits with modern themes of loss and war, rather than in the 'Epics' section. Similarly, while much of Oscar Wilde's work might fit in 'Imbalance and Inequality' or 'Love', his poem 'Rome Unvisited' sits more obviously under the theme of 'Place'. In some instances poets appear more than once in the book with Christina Rossetti in 'Friendship and Family' as well as 'The Senses' and William Wordsworth in 'Place' and 'The Natural World'. Poetry often evokes shared experiences and feelings. Addressing discomfort, horror and injustice is as much a reason for the existence of poetry as elation and celebration. Some of the poems contained in the volume tackle traumatic, disturbing and challenging subjects.

This book includes a wide variety of different poetical formats, from sonnets and ballads to *ghazals* (Middle Eastern or Indian lyric poems) and *waka* (Japanese poems). The material used for writing poetry is diverse and there is a range of medium and formats represented here, from a single sheet of prison toilet paper to a word-processed document. A range of terms are used in the text to describe these characteristics and these are defined in the glossary on page 278.

Compiling this anthology has been an exciting journey into the poetry collections at the British Library and beyond. As curators it has provided us with the opportunity to share many of the Library's manuscript treasures and the stories behind them. We hope that you will enjoy exploring the manuscripts, poems and stories in this book as much as we have enjoyed writing about them.

A note on the text

TRANSCRIPTIONS

The transcriptions in this book were created by the authors unless otherwise stated. They correspond as closely to the original manuscript text as is feasible in the medium of type and are designed to help the reader interpret the handwritten poems. Spelling, capitalisation, contractions, punctuation, line breaks, deletions and underlining have been presented as they appear in the manuscripts. In a few cases it has been necessary to select the closest standard form of punctuation for unusual punctuation used in the manuscript. The thorn symbol, regularly used in the early modern period but now obsolete, has been transcribed as 'y' but is pronounced 'th' as in 'ye' ('the'). A number of poems have not been transcribed due to the condition of the manuscript, the legibility of the text or because it was not possible to clear copyright. In some cases a transcription of the published poem has been included instead. For poems in languages other than English a translation of the poem in English has been provided in place of, or as well as, a transcription. The name of the translator and source of the translation are given on page 274. In some cases this is the first time a poem has been translated into the English language.

PROVENANCE

A substantial number of the poems in this book derive from the Ashley Manuscripts at the British Library. These manuscripts were originally collected by Thomas James Wise (1859–1937), a bibliophile, literary scholar and forger, who named his collection after the street in which he lived. The manuscripts were purchased by the British Museum Library from his widow, Frances Wise (née Greenhaigh, 1871–1939), in 1937 and are catalogued under the prefix Ashley MS. Wise was particularly interested in the Romantic and Pre-Raphaelite poets, whose works form a large part of the collection.

Contained within this book are several literary manuscripts from the collection of the writer Stefan Zweig (1881–1942). Zweig's collection was donated to the British Library by his heirs in 1986 and is catalogued under the prefix Zweig MS. The collection reflects Zweig's interests in European history, music and literature.

The book also includes one poem from the collections of Sir Hans Sloane (1660–1753). Sloane's collections of manuscripts helped form the British Museum and subsequently the Natural History Museum and the British Library. He travelled to Jamaica as physician to the English governor in 1687 and, on his return, married an heiress to sugar plantations in Jamaica. The profits from these plantations, which were worked by enslaved people, contributed substantially to his income and financed his collecting. Sloane's collections are mostly associated with science, but also contain some significant literary items. Information on the history and provenance of the other manuscripts included in this book is given in the commentary for each poem.

chapter 1
EPICS

Poetry has been used to tell stories for thousands of years. The rhythms endemic in verse when spoken and sung have helped poets to remember and recite religious or historical tales. Epic poetry often looks back to a time beyond living memory to describe the exploits of a hero against the overwhelming force of supernatural enemies such as Ravana, king of the demons in Valmiki's *Rāmāyana*, or the monster Grendel in the Anglo-Saxon poem *Beowulf*.

In the early modern period, poets often looked back to earlier times for inspiration. The Italian poet Ludovico Ariosto brought to life the ideals of medieval chivalry in his epic poem *Orlando Furioso*. John Harington's translation popularised this epic in England in the sixteenth century. Tales of knights and their noble quests were a popular feature in medieval and early modern literature up until the early seventeenth century, when they fell out of fashion. John Milton, aware of the shift in literary tastes, changed course from writing an epic poem based on King Arthur to write a Christian story, which became the enduring classic poem *Paradise Lost*.

In the eighteenth and nineteenth centuries the literary ballad, which drew on the oral tradition of anonymous folk ballads, became a popular form of narrative poem. Shorter than epic poems, ballads usually employ more colloquial language and often have a tragic focus. Samuel Taylor Coleridge's *The Rime of the Ancient Mariner* and Robert Louis Stevenson's 'Ticonderoga' both contain themes of revenge and fate.

Traditional stories can also be re-worked by later poets to take on new forms and meanings. Lord Byron turns the legendary Spaniard Don Juan from womaniser into a man easily seduced. Over a century later Stevie Smith put her own interpretation on *The Illiad* in her poem 'A Dream', in which she imagines herself as Helen of Troy and explores the events of the poem from a modern feminist perspective. In translating *Sir Gawain and the Green Knight* Simon Armitage intended to bring the classic story to a modern audience. In his commentary Armitage discusses his creative process in translating the epic poem and the importance of the handwritten draft as a way of exploring and revising his work.

Epic poetry has and will inspire poets for generations – for as much as we love their classic tales of adventure, valour and sacrifice, we also desire to make them our own.

Mewar Rāmāyaṇa

VALMIKI (*fl. c.*500 BC)

1649–53, British Library, Add MS 15296(1), ff.70r–70v, folio 23 × 39 cm, black and red ink on slightly burnished paper; opaque watercolours on slightly burnished paper.

The *Rāmāyaṇa* is one of India's best-loved and most enduring stories. First told some 2,500 years ago in the Sanskrit epic poem ascribed to the sage Valmiki, it has been retold in different forms in many regional languages of India and beyond.

The story follows Prince Rama of Ayodhya, who has to go into exile as a result of his stepmother's plotting; his wife Sita and brother Lakshmana accompany him. When Sita is abducted by the wicked demon-king Ravana, armies of monkeys and bears help Rama and Lakshmana in their frantic search for her, until she is discovered by the devoted monkey Hanuman in Ravana's stronghold of Lanka. After an epic battle, in which Ravana perishes, Sita is rescued and returns with Rama in triumph to Ayodhya.

A text of great literary and religious significance, the *Rāmāyaṇa* enshrines the Hindu idea of *dharma* and continues to have an incomparable and lasting influence on culture and society in India and beyond. It has inspired countless artistic expressions in all fields.

This manuscript was commissioned in 1649 by Maharana Jagat Singh (1607–1652), the ruler of Mewar in Rajasthan. Five of its seven books are now in the British Library, while other parts of the manuscript remain in India, where they are held by three separate institutions and a private collection.

Originally in the traditional unbound *pothī* format, consisting of loose leaves, the Sanskrit text consists of 24,000 verses copied by the Jain scribe Hirananda (*fl.* seventeenth century). Over 400 lavish, full-page paintings depicting episodes from the story accompany the text.

This scene shows Rama, Sita and Lakshmana in the Citrakuta forest. It was painted by Sahib Din (*fl.* seventeenth century), a Muslim master artist who illustrated two books of the manuscript. Sahib Din used various narrative techniques in his paintings: here a sequence of events is presented on one page through multiple appearances of the same characters.

Over the centuries, the Sanskrit text of Valmiki's *Rāmāyaṇa* developed and underwent change, giving rise to different versions. The scribe of the Mewar *Rāmāyaṇa* manuscripts drew on several of these 'recensions', producing a text with some variations of its own. The English translation shown here is taken from *The Rāmāyaṇa of Vālmīki: An Epic of Ancient India, Volume II, Ayodhyākāṇḍa* (1986); although it does not match the Mewar recension word for word, it follows the same narrative and includes several of the details captured with great artistry in Sahib Din's painting.

Sarga 50

5. As Rāma set out in the early morning with Saumitri, he began to speak to lotus-eyed Sītā.
6. 'Look, Vaidehī, the *kiṃśuka* trees are in full blossom now that winter is past. Garlanded with their red flowers they almost seem to be on fire.
7. 'Look at the marking-nut trees in bloom, untended by man, how they are bent over with fruit and leaves. I know I shall be able to live.
8. 'Look at the honeycombs, Lakṣmaṇa, amassed by honey bees on one tree after another. They hang down as large as buckets.
9. 'Here a moorhen is crying, and in answer to it a peacock calls through delightful stretches of forest richly carpeted with flowers.
10. 'And look, there is Citrakūṭa, the mountain over there with the towering peak, teeming with herds of elephants and echoing with flocks of birds.'
11. So the brothers and Sītā proceeded on foot and reached the delightful mountain, charming Citrakūṭa.
12. And on reaching the mountain, where birds of every description came flocking, he said, 'This will be our dwelling for now. We shall enjoy ourselves here, dear brother.
13. 'Fetch wood, dear Lakṣmaṇa, good, hard wood and build a place to live, for my heart is set on living here.'
14. Hearing his words Saumitri, tamer of foes, went and brought different kinds of trees and built a leaf hut.

॥रा०१७०
श्रुतं नदीतीरवरूं समुच्छ्रितं॥ ॥इत्यार्षे श्री अयोध्याकांडे यमुनापारनिवासः॥ अथ रात्र्यां व्यतीतायामवसुप्तमनं
मं रामप्रत्यापयामास लक्ष्मणं ज्ञानकेऽन्तदा स्वगानीशृणु सौमित्रे वल्गुव्याहरतां वचः संप्रतिष्ठामहे ह्यत्रो
यदि लक्ष्मण मन्यसे स सुप्तः समुपबोध्यात्र लक्ष्मणः प्रतिबोधितः अहो निद्रां क्रमं चैव तं चैवाध्वपरिश्रमं ततस्त्या सम
हिताः स्नात्वा च सलिलं स्वच्छं उपास्य च सुसंध्यां तत्रैवाभिप्रतिस्थिरे चित्रकूटस्य पंथानमासाद्य कृतनिश्चयाः
तत्र वासं समुद्दिश्य ययुः श्री अपराक्रमाः अचिरेण समासाद्य ततः स चित्रपादपं चित्रकूटवनं रामः सीतां वचन
मब्रवीत यज्ञपात्राननुपश्यतां स्त्रीनेमालिनी मरितंप्रति शिशिरात्यये दीर्घाङ्घ्रि प्रदीप्तानिव किंशुकान् कर्णि
कारवनं चापि प्रयमंदाकिनी मनु वापितं रूपवैरैः प्रख्यैः प्रदीप्तैः कांचनैरिव पत्रपत्राज्ञातकान् विल्वान् पलाशां
स्तिलकांस्तथा फलभाराननतांश्चैव तथान्यान् फलयादयान् आकामव फलैरेव जीवितुं तनुमध्यमे अहो स्वर्गो
पमं प्राप्तश्चित्रकूटमिमं वनं पत्रपडोण प्रमाणानि लंवमानानि लक्ष्मण विताभिचित्रकूटेस्मिन्नस्य निमधुपैः
खगैः असौ कूजति दात्यूहस्तं शिखीप्रतिकूजति तं चोपहसतीवायं कूजंतं जलकुक्कुटः यत्र पुष्टरुतं श्रव
गायंत इव कानने भ्रमरा विचरंत्येते पुष्पपानकलस्वनाः पत्रपमंदाकिनीतीरे कुसुमप्रकरैः प्रिये रचिता
दुमे ३ नीव कुम्भश्रोणिश्यामानि द्रुमैः शिलातलानि चैमानि विमलानि शुचिस्मिते लतावतानसंछन्नानि पत्रपरम्याणि
त्वाविनि मातंगयूथानि चितेनानाविहगनादिते नानामृगगणाकीर्णे शैलेस्मिन् रम्यकानने वैदेहि विच
रिष्यामः सुखमत्र वयं प्रिये इह प्राप्यामि वैदेहि मयामहरतिं शुभां अवेक्षमाणां एवं ते रम्यां मंदाकिनीं नदीं वि

Paradise Lost

JOHN MILTON (1608–1674)

c.1665, The Morgan Library & Museum, MA 307, f.2r, volume 19.5 × 19.9 cm, iron gall ink on laid paper.

The publication of the epic *Paradise Lost* was delayed because of events including the Great Plague (1665), the Second Anglo-Dutch War (1665) and the Great Fire of London (1666). Milton composed the ten books of *Paradise Lost* between 1658 and 1663. The poem's narrative concerns the intertwined fates of Adam, Eve and Lucifer, and is widely regarded as one of the most important works of English literature. It has influenced the work of poets such as William Blake, Lord Byron and John Keats.

Having completely lost his sight by 1652, Milton relied heavily on scribes, both professional and from his family. He drafted in his mind, committing the words to memory, and then dictated sections of his work to his scribes. Only one surviving draft of *Paradise Lost* exists, and it is this thirty-three-page manuscript for Book 1 held at the Morgan Library & Museum. The manuscript is written in a single hand, probably that of a professional scribe, but is likely to have been copied from several earlier manuscripts. Milton corrected his work as it was read back to him, and this manuscript includes at least five different correcting hands. It probably survived because it became the printer's copy. The second folio, which contains the opening scene, is shown and transcribed here.

Paradise Lost was sold to the printer Samuel Simmons for £5, and the original contract is held at the British Library. Dated 27 April 1667, it bears Milton's seal and a signature probably written by an amanuensis (literary assistant). The signatures were witnessed by John Fisher and Benjamin Greene, a servant to Milton. The contract states that Milton will receive another £5 once 1,300 copies have sold. Milton might have earned a further £10 had two more editions been published, but he died soon after the second edition was printed.

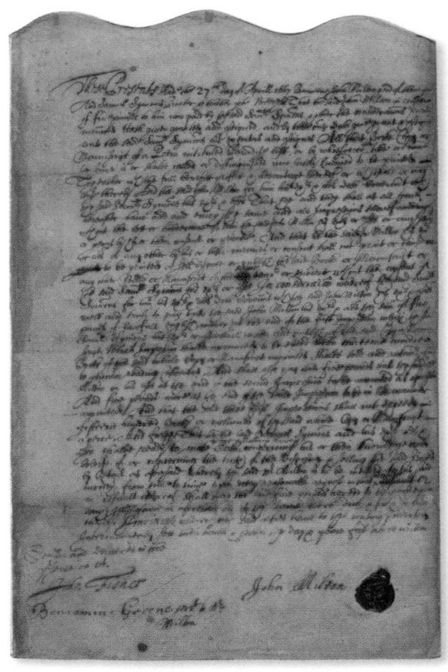

Contract for *Paradise Lost*, 27 April 1667, British Library, Add MS 18861.

Paradise Lost.
ffirst book.

Of mans first disobedience, & the fruit
Of that forbidd'en tree, whose mortall tast
Brought death into the world, & all our woe,
With losse of Eden, till one greater Man
Restore us, & regaine the blisfull seate,
Sing heav'nly Muse, that on the secret top
Of Oreb or of Sinai didst inspire
That shepheard, who first taught the chosen seed,
In the beginning how the Heav'ns & Earth
Rose out of Chaos: Or if Sion hill
Delight thee more, and Siloa's brooke that flow'd
Ffast by the Oracle of God; I thence
Invoke thy aide to my adventrous song,
That with no middle flight intends to soare
Above th' Aonian Mount; while it persues
Things unattempted yet in prose or rhime.
And cheifly thou O Spirit that dost prefer
Before all temples th' upright heart & pure
Instruct me, for thou know'st; thou from the first
Wast present, & with mighty wings outspread
Dove-like satst brooding on the vast Abysse,
And mad'st it pregnant: What in me is darke

Paradise lost.
First book.

Of mans first disobedience, & the fruit
Of that forbidden tree, whose mortall tast
Brought death into the worlde, & all our woe,
With losse of Eden, till one greater Man
Restore us, & regaine the blisfull seate,
Sing heav'nly Muse, that on the secret top
Of Oreb or of Sinai didst inspire
That shepheard, who first taught the chosen seed,
In the beginning how the Heav'ns & Earth
Rose out of Chaos: Or if Sion hill
Delight thee more, & Siloa's brooke that flow'd
Fast by the Oracle of God; I thence
Invoke thy aide to my adventrous song,
That with no middle flight intends to soare
Above th' Aonian Mount, while it persues
Things unattempted yet in prose or rhime.
And chiefly thou O Spirit, that dost prefer
Before all temples th' upright heart & pure,
Instruct me, for thou know'st; thou from the first
Wast present, & with mighty wings outspread
Dove-like satst brooding on the vast Abysse
And mad'st it pregnant: What in me is darke

semninga to sele comon frome fyrd
166
hwate feowertyne geata gongan gu
dryhten mid modig on gemonge meodo
wongas træd · ða com in gan ealdor
ðegna dæd cene mon dome gewurþ
hæle hilde deor hroðgar gretan · þa
wæs be feaxe on flet boren grend le
heafod þær guman druncon egeslic
eorlum ⁊ þære idese mid wlite seon
lic weras onsawon ·

XXIIII

BEOWULF maþelode bearn ecgþeo
hwæt we þe þas sælac sunu healfdenes
leod scyldinga lustū brohton tires
to tacne þe þu her to locast · ic þæt un
softe ealdre gedigde wigge under
wætere weorc geneþde earfoðlice
ætrihte wæs guð getwæfed nymðe
mec god scylde · ne meahte ic æt hil
de mid hruntinge wiht gewyrcan
þeah þæt wæpen duge ac me geuðe
ylda waldend þæt ic on wage geseah wlitig

Beowulf

UNKNOWN

c.1000, British Library, Cotton MS Vitellius A XV, f.169r, volume 24.5 × 18.5 cm, parchment leaves approximately 20.2 × 12 cm, black ink on parchment.

This copy of *Beowulf* is remarkable, as it is the only surviving manuscript of the story. The manuscript is thought to be approximately 1,000 years old, and dates from the late tenth or early eleventh century. Some believe that the story, which was originally told orally, harks back to the sixth century and that it was first written down in the eighth century. It is thought to have been composed by more than one person and has been added to and revised over the centuries.

The manuscript of *Beowulf* was part of the collection of Sir Robert Cotton (1571–1631), which was bequeathed to the nation by his grandson Sir John Cotton (1621–1702) in 1702. Under state ownership, the collection was moved to Ashburnham House in Westminster for safekeeping. However, a fire broke out on 23 October 1731 which damaged many manuscripts and completely destroyed a few. *Beowulf* escaped the fire relatively intact, but suffered greater loss through handling in the following years, as letters crumbled away from the outer portions of its pages. In 1753 the Cotton library formed one of the foundation collections of the newly established British Museum.

At more than 3,000 lines, *Beowulf* is the longest poem in Old English, the language spoken in Anglo-Saxon England. The story follows the feats of Beowulf, a prince of the Geats, who battles the monster Grendel and Grendel's vengeful mother. In this extract, Beowulf returns with Grendel's head and begins a speech to Hrothgar, high lord of the Scyldings, about his battle with Grendel's mother.

Fierce, keen in the hosting, a fourteen of men
Of the Geat-folk a-ganging; and with them their lord,
The moody amidst of the throng, trod the mead-plains;
Came then in a-wending the foreman of thanes,
The man keen of his deeds all beworshipp'd of doom,
The hero, the battle-deer, Hrothgar to greet.
Then was by the fell borne in onto the floor
Grendel's head, whereas men were a-drinking in hall,
Aweful before the earls, yea and the woman.
The sight wondrous to see the warriors there look'd on.

XXV (XIIII in original text) CONVERSE OF HROTHGAR WITH BEOWULF

Spake out then Beowulf, Ecgtheow's bairn:
What! we the sea-spoils here to thee, son of Healfdene,
High lord of the Scyldings, with lust have brought hither
For a token of glory, e'en these thou beholdest.
Now I all unsoftly with life I escaped,
In war under the water dar'd I the work
Full hard to be worked, and well-nigh there was
The sundering of strife, save that me God had shielded.
So it is that in battle naught might I with Hrunting
One whit do the work, though the weapon be doughty;
But to me then he granted, the Wielder of men,
That on wall I beheld there all beauteous hanging
An ancient sword might-endow'd (often he leadeth right
The friendless of men); so forth I drew that weapon.

A Dream.

I had a dream I was Helen of Troy
In looks, age and circumstance,
But otherwise I was myself.

It was the ninth year of the siege
And I did not love anybody very much
Except perhaps Cassandra,
It was those peculiar eyes she had
As if she were short-sighted
That made me feel I could talk to her, ~~I would love anybody I could talk to.~~
I suppose you know how it's going to end,
As well as I do? Dreams, dreams? They aren't dreams
You know. Do you know?

I used to walk on the walls
And look towards the Grecian tents,
It's odd, I said (to Cassandra, of course) how
Everything one has read about Troy
As they have always been such splendid writers who were writing
Naturally gets into one's conversation
'Where Cressid lay that night'. So there we were
On the walls of Troy. But what I did not know
And I could not get Cassandra to say either,
Was which of the Helen legends I was,
The phantom, with the real Helen in Egypt,
Or the flesh-and-blood one here
That Menelaus would take back to Sparta.

Remembering this, that there was still some uncertainty,
Raised my spirits. I must say
Dispiritedness was what we were all sunk in,
And though the Royal Family may have seemed spectral
Their dispiritedness was substantial enough, and I dare say
The Greeks were in much the same case, dispirited;
Well, nine years there had been of it, and now
The heavy weather, and the smells
From the battlefield, when the wind was in that direction.
And the spirit of the men, too, on both sides,
This was substantial enough; it seemed to me
Like the spirit of all armies on all plains in all wars, the men
No longer thinking why they were there
Or caring, but going on; like the song the English used to sing
In the first world war: We're here, because we're here, because
We're here, because we're here. This was the only time
I heard Cassandra laugh, when I sung this to her. I said:
There you are, you laugh; that shows you are not nearly so
Religious as you think. That's blasphemous, that laugh,
Sets you free. But then she got frightened. All right, I said,

except they did not notice
How beautiful Scamander looks under this sort of sky
And the black Greek ships piled up on the seashore beyond

A Dream

STEVIE SMITH (FLORENCE MARGARET SMITH) (1902–1971)

Before 1966, British Library, Add MS 53732, ff.2r–3r, folios 25.2 × 20 cm, typewritten with blue and black ink annotations and illustrations.

Epic poetry has often been altered, updated and reworked by later poets into their own original poetry. Sometimes reverential, often questioning and even critical, poets shed their own light and understanding on these universal epics. The poet Florence Smith, who published under her nickname Stevie, was one such poet. Her poem 'A Dream' reimagines Homer's (*fl.* ninth or eighth century BC) epic work the *Iliad* from the perspective of Helen of Troy.

Smith is known for the dark humour in her poetry and her accompanying quirky illustrations. Her typescript includes annotations, additional lines of poetry and a couple of drawings in ball-point pen, perhaps showing Helen of Troy herself. The four handwritten lines added to the bottom of the poem have been transcribed here. The British Library purchased this draft and four other poems from the Arts Council on 16 April 1966.

In 'A Dream' Smith places a twentieth-century narrator in Helen of Troy's shoes. This allows her to retell the story from a modern feminist perspective. Helen's lack of voice in the traditional story means that we only have a story created by men that cites her as the cause of a major war. Here the modern Helen explores the futility of the war and the horrors that await the combatants. She compares the senselessness of the conflict vividly to the First World War as depicted by Wilfred Owen and Siegfried Sassoon.

Smith also incorporates different versions of the story of Helen of Troy into 'A Dream'. In Homer's story Helen's elopement with Paris leads to the Trojan War and her role in the story is primarily as the beautiful woman who caused a dispute between men. An alternative version, associated with the Greek poet Stesichorus (632/629–556/553 BC), suggests that Proteus, disguised as an Egyptian king, held Helen in Egypt while Zeus sent Paris to Troy with an *eidolon* (phantom or wraith) of Helen.

3

Dont be free, go along and finish up on Clytemnestra's sword-point,
Pinked like a good girl. I used to get so cross.
Paris was stupid, it was impossible to talk to him.
Hector might have been different, at least he understood enough
To be offended - fear of the gods again, I suppose - because
When I said: Well, you know what the Trojan Women
Are going to say about the sack of Troy, and being led away
Into captivity, they are going to say: If these things had not
Happened to us, we should not be remembered. I hope that
Will be a comfort to you, he was angry and said
I should bring bad luck to Troy by my impiety, so I laughed
But I felt more like crying. I went into our palace then
And into my own room. But the heaviness of the sky
Still oppressed me, and the sad colours of rust and blood
I saw everywhere, as Cassandra saw too. Oh, I thought,
It is an ominous eternal moment I am captive in, it is always
This heavy weather, these colours, and the smell of the dead men.
It is curious to be caught in a moment of pause like this,
As a river pauses before it plunges upon a great waterfall.
I was at home with these people at least in this - that we wished
It was over and done with. But oh, Cassandra, I said, catching hold of her,
For she was running away, I shall never make
That mischievous laughing Helen, who goes home with Menelaus
And over her needlework in the quiet palace laughs,
Telling her story, and says: Oh shameful me. I am only at home
In this moment of pause, where the feelings, the colours, and spirits
Are substantial, but the people are ghosts. When the pause finishes
I shall wake.

Transcription of four handwritten lines, bottom of f.2r:

except they did not notice
How beastly Scamander looks under this sort of sky
And the black Greek ships piled up on the seashore beyond
Like prison hulks, like slugs

SIMON ARMITAGE (b.1963)

Sir Gawain and the Green Knight

***c*.2005**, black ink on cream lined paper, Leeds University Library, BC MS 20c Armitage. First published in *Sir Gawain and the Green Knight* (Faber and Faber, 2009).

“

I find it very peculiar looking back at drafts of poems. The hurried scribbles and 'organic' spellings look very naïve in retrospect, and miles away from the finished poems with their manicured typography and livery of printed text. But it reminds me why I encourage students to write by hand, so they can see the archaeology of their efforts and recognise how much revision is necessary. This is one of the most famous passages in the original poem, Gawain's journey into the unknown as he searches for the Green Knight and the Green Chapel of his destiny. After several false starts at the beginning of the project I'd got some momentum going by this time, and was beginning to find a satisfying orchestration of rhyme, rhythm and alliteration. There are many moving parts in the poem, to do with its rules and formulas, and translating it occasionally felt like puzzling over a long, elaborate word game. The first version of each line would have been a literal translation of the Middle English, the second version an attempt to give it some meaning and grammatical cohesion, and the third version a hopeful stab at transforming lumps of raw language into the thing we call poetry.

”

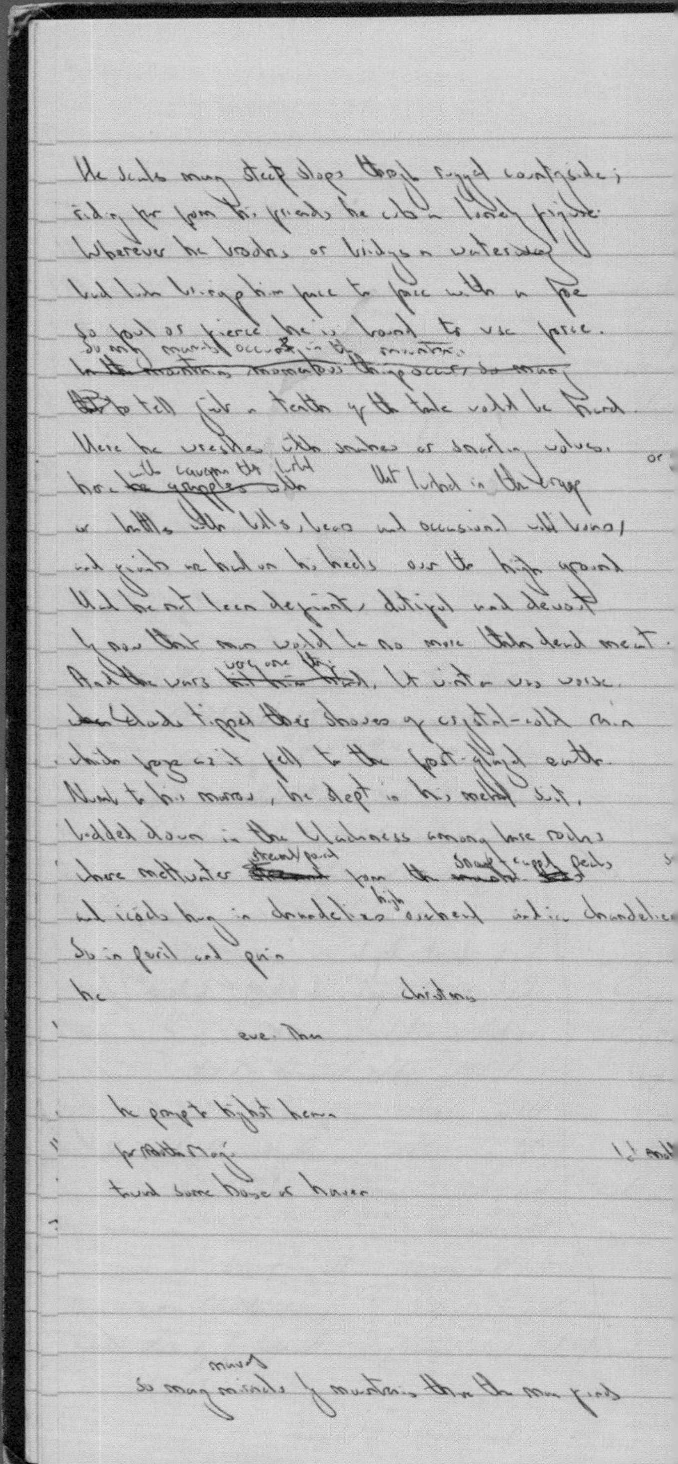

Now through the realm of England he rides and rides,
Sir Gawain, a servant of God on his grim quest,
passing many long nights unloved and alone,
foraging to eat, finding little to call food,
with no friend but his horse through forests and hills,
and no one to talk to but the Almighty Lord.
He wanders his way near to the north of Wales.
Away to his left are the Anglesey Isles.
He keeps to the coastal path, fording each watercourse,
crossing at Holy Head and coming ashore
in the wilds of the Wirral, whose wayward people
both God and good-hearted men have given up on.
But he cautiously asks those he comes across
whether or not, in this neck of the woods,
they talk of a green knight or green temple
No, they say, never. Never in their lives.
They know of neither a knight or a chapel
so strange.
He trails through bleak terrain.
His mood and manner change
at every twist and turn
towards that chosen church

tittle/tattle

Orlando Furioso

LUDOVICO ARIOSTO (1474–1533), TRANSLATED BY SIR JOHN HARINGTON (*c.*1560–1612)

Late sixteenth century, British Library, Add MS 18920, f.179r, volume 22 × 17 cm, iron gall ink on laid paper.

Orlando Furioso is an Italian epic poem that first appeared in 1516 and was printed in complete form in 1532. A chivalric romance featuring the knight Orlando, the story is set against a backdrop of fictional war between the Christian Emperor Charlemagne and Agramente (Agolant), a Saracen king from Africa. It was a highly influential poem, and parts of it are considered to have been a source for William Shakespeare's (1564–1616) *Much Ado about Nothing*, written between 1598 and 1599.

This translation is by Sir John Harington, courtier, godson of Queen Elizabeth I (1533–1603) and author. The manuscript was used for the first English print edition of the work, published by Richard Field (*c.*1561–1624) in 1591. It contains corrections and pasted alterations, together with instructions to the printer. While much of it is in Harington's hand, part of it is in the hand of his servant Thomas Combe. The translation contains details that pertain to Harington's own life and experience. On f.179, the text extols the virtues of earlier artists such as Giovanni Bellini (1430–1516) and Leonardo da Vinci (1452–1519). In the manuscript Harington had originally added the name of the English miniaturist Nicholas Hilliard (1547–1619), who painted portraits of Queen Elizabeth I and King James VI of Scotland and I of England (1566–1625): 'Allso owr Englyshe Hillyard by desart / Doe meryt in this prayse to have a part'. Harington crossed out these original lines and altered the text to 'with dyvers others that by due desart. / Doe meryt in this prayse to have a part'. The Argument and the first sixteen lines of canto 33 have been transcribed here.

This volume was owned by the bookseller Thomas Thorpe (1791–1851), who sold it at his auction in 1843. It was subsequently sold at Sotheby's on 24 April 1852, where the British Museum purchased it via the booksellers Messrs Boone of New Bond Street, London.

The Argument of ye xxxiij. Canto.

Bradamant sees engravn by passing art
the future warrs of fraunce uppon a screen.
Byardos flight the combat feers doth part
Renaldo and the Seryean between:

Astolfo having past the greater part
of all the world and many countryes seen.
Unto Senapos kyngdom last arryves
and from his boord the foul Harpias dryves.

Of theas famous drawers looke in the History of this booke.

Canto xxxiij
1

Tymagoras, Parrhasius Polygnote,
Tymant Protogenes Appollodore
Zewres, a man for ~~speciall note~~ skill of speciall note
Appelles eake, plaste all the rest before
whose skill in drawing all the world doth note
and talke of still (to wryters thanks thearfore)
whose works and bodyes tyme & deth did waste
yet spyte of tyme and death theyr formes doth last

2

with others that in thease our later ~~[present]~~ dayes
have lyvd, as Leonard and John Bellyne,
and hee theat carves and drawes with equall prayse,
Mychaell more then a man, Angell dyvyne,
And Flores whom the fflemings greatly prayse
and Raphaell and Titian passing fyne
~~Allso owr Englyshe Hillyard by desart~~ with dyvers others that by due desart.
Doe ~~that~~ meryt in this prayse to have ~~[illegible]~~ a part.

The Argument of ye xxxiij. Canto.

Bradamant sees engravn by passing art
the future warrs of fraunce vppon a screen.
Byardos flight the combat feers doth part
Renaldo and the Serycan between:

Astolfo having past the greater part
of all the world and many countryes seen.
vnto Senapos kyngdom last arryves
and from his boord the foul Harpias dryves.

Canto xxxiijo.

1
Tymagoras, Parrhasius Polygnote
Tymant Protogenes Appollodore
Zewres a man for ~~speciall note~~ skill of speciall note
Appelles eake plaste all the rest before
whose skill in drawing all the world doth note
and talke of still (to wryters thanks therefore)
whose works and bodyes tyme and deth did waste
yet spyte of tyme and death theyr fames doth last

Of theas famous drawers looke in the History of this booke.

2
with others that in theas our ~~present~~ later days
have lyvd, as Leonard and John Bellyne,
and hee that carvs and draws with equall prayse,
Mychaell more then a man Angell dyvyne,
And flores whome the fflemings greatly prayse
and Raphaell and Titian passing fyne
~~Allso our Englyshe Hillyard by desert~~ wth dyvers others that by due desert.
for ~~that~~ meryts in this prayse to have ~~his~~ a part.

3
Yet all theas cunning drawers with theyr skill,
could not attayn by picture to expresse,
what strange events should happen, well or yll,
In future tymes, no not so much as guesse:
this art ys proper vnto Magyke skill,
or to a prophet, or a prophetesse!
by this rare art, Merlin of England paynted,
storys wch which our age hath been acquaynted.

4
Hee made by magyke art that stately hall
and by the selfe same art hee caused to bee
strange historyes ingraved on the wall
which as I sayd the guests desyred to see
now when they were from supper rysen all
the pages lyghted torches two or three
Making the room to shyne as bryght as day
when to his guests the owner thus did say.

I would quoth he

Don Juan

GEORGE GORDON NOEL BYRON, SIXTH BARON BYRON (1788–1824)

1822, British Library, Ashley MS 5163, f.21v, volume 40.5 × 27.5 cm, folio 36.9 × 25 cm, iron gall ink on laid paper.

Don Juan is a legendary character who features in many literary and musical works. He is traditionally depicted as an arrogant and aggressive womanising libertine, but Byron's version of the character is very different: he is seduced by women rather than being a seducer himself.

Don Juan is divided up into sixteen cantos and was published serially, like a novel, between 1819 and 1824. Shown here is a folio from the original manuscript for cantos 6 and 7. The poem is written on different-sized sheets and wrapped and sewn into brown rag paper, with Byron's writing on the outside. That the sheets of paper in the volume vary in size shows that Byron used what was available to him at the time rather than working in notebooks. In this manuscript Byron has corrected his original draft using a different ink. The writing and corrections suggest that he was working at speed.

The image and transcription here show the beginning of the seventh canto, in which Don Juan takes part in the Russian siege of the Ottoman stronghold of Izmail in 1790.

Canto 7th

1.

Oh Love! Oh Glory! what are ye! who fly
 Around us ever – rarely to alight –
There's not a Meteor in the polar Sky
 Of such transcendent ~~and such~~ or more fleeting flight.
Chill~~ed~~ and chained to ~~the~~ cold earth we lift on high
 Our eyes in search of either lovely light –
A thousand and a thousand colours they
Assume, ~~and~~ then leave us ~~to a frozen day~~. on our freezing way.

2.

And such as they are, such my present tale is –
 A nondescript and ~~ever changing~~ often ~~changing~~ varying rhyme –
A ~~kind of~~ versified Aurora Borealis –
 Which ~~dazzles~~ flashes oer a waste and ~~so~~ icy clime,
~~Now~~ When we know what all are we must bewail us,
 But neer the less – I hope it is no crime –
To laugh at all things – for I wish to know –
What after all – are all things – but a Show?

3.

They accuse me – me the present writer of
 The present poem – of – I know not what –
A tendency to underrate and scoff
 At human ~~[thought]~~ Powers and Virtue and all that
And this they say in language rather rough;
Good God! I wonder what they would be at!

ABOVE: Lord Byron, engraving by Edward Finden, British Library, 1466.i.25.

Canto 7th

1.

Oh Love! Oh Glory! what are ye who fly
Around us ever—rarely to alight—
There's not a Meteor in the polar sky
Of such transcendant ~~and~~ or ~~such~~ more fleeting flight—
Chill'd and chained to ~~th~~ cold earth we lift on high
Our eyes in search of either lovely light—
A thousand and a thousand colours they
Assume, ~~and~~ then leave us ~~to a frozen day~~ on our freezing way.

2.

And such as they are, such my present tale is—
A nondescript and ~~ever changing~~ strange varying rhyme—
A ~~kind of~~ versified Aurora Borealis—
Which ~~dazzles~~ flashes o'er a waste and ~~s~~ icy clime,
~~Then~~ When we know what all are we must bewail us
But ne'ertheless—I hope it is no crime—
To laugh at all things—for I wish to know—
What after all—are all things—but a Show?

3.

They accuse me—Me—the present writer of
The present poem—of—I know not what—
A tendency to underrate and scoff
At human ~~Strength~~ Power and Virtue and all that—
And this they say in language rather rough;
Good God! I wonder what they would be at!

And cried to him for vengeance
On the man that laid him low;
And thrice the living Cameron
Told the dead Cameron, no.

"Thrice have you seen me, brother;
But now ~~ye~~ shall see me no more,
Till you meet your angry fathers
Upon the farther shore.
Thrice have I spoken and now,
Before the cock be heard,
I take my leave forever
With the naming of a word.
It shall sing in your sleeping ears,
It shall hum in your waking head:
The name – Ticonderoga –
And the warning of the dead."

Now when the night was over
And ~~all~~ the time of peoples fears,
The Cameron rose and walked abroad,
And the word was in his ears.
"Many a name I know," he thought
"But never a name like this:
O, where shall I find me a skeely man,
Shall tell me what it is?"

~~Many a league he footed,~~
~~In many a loch he sailed,~~
Where the ~~mowers sang in meadows~~
~~And where the eagle wailed.~~
With many a man he counselled

And the mighty of the ~~king~~ pipes   war-pipes.
Struck terror in Cathay

~~So~~ "Many a name have I heard," he thought,
"In all the tongues of men,
Full many a name both here and there
Full many both now and then:

Ticonderoga: A Legend of the West Highlands

ROBERT LOUIS STEVENSON (1850–1894)

1887, British Library, Ashley MS 5050, f.5r, folio 30 × 20.5 cm, black ink on blue/grey lined paper.

Robert Louis Stevenson is known primarily for his novels, which include *Treasure Island* (1883), *Kidnapped* (1886) and *Strange Case of Dr Jekyll and Mr Hyde* (1886). He was born in Edinburgh, and Scotland features in much of his literature. In the ballad 'Ticonderoga' Stevenson followed the tradition of earlier Scottish writers such as Robert Burns and Walter Scott in using elements apparently drawn from traditional stories. This is the original manuscript of 'Ticonderoga', which includes many revisions and changes by Stevenson.

Stevenson said that he based the poem on a story told to him by Alfred Nutt (1856–1910), a British publisher who studied and wrote about Celtic folklore. The poem is set in the mid-eighteenth century and tells the story of a man of the Cameron clan who gives shelter to a Stewart man on the run. Although he soon finds out that the man he is sheltering has killed his brother, the Cameron man decides not to turn him away. During the night his brother's ghost visits him and calls on him to take vengeance. On being refused, the ghost places a curse on his brother using the mysterious name Ticonderoga. The Cameron man is subsequently called up to fight for the British army against France and her allies in the Seven Years' War. After service in Germany and Asia he is sent to North America, where he is killed at the battle of Ticonderoga, the site of which is in present-day New York State.

In this extract, from the middle of the poem, the ghost speaks to impart the fatal word, Ticonderoga. The text is very similar to the published version apart from the four lines that Stevenson has crossed out at the bottom of the draft. Stevenson reused several sheets of the paper, for on the reverse of one page he has written a 'Family Prayer', while extracts from his manuscript of 'Thomas Stevenson: Civil Engineer' appear on others.

45

And cried to him for vengeance
    On the man that laid him low;
And thrice the living Cameron
    Told the dead Cameron, no.

'Thrice have you seen me, brother;
    But now ~~y~~ shall see me no more,
Till you meet your angry fathers
    Upon the farther shore.
Thrice have I spoken and now,
    Before the cock be heard,
I take my leave forever
    With the naming of a word.
It shall sing in your sleeping ears,
It shall hum in your waking head:
The name – Ticonderoga –
And the warning of the dead.'

Now when the night was over
And ~~all~~ the time of people's fears,
The Cameron rose and walked abroad,
And the word was in his ears.
'Many a name I know,' he thought
'But never a name like this:
O, where shall I find a skeely man,
Shall tell me what it is?'

~~Many a league he footed,~~
~~On many a loch he sailed,~~
~~Where the mowers sang in meadows~~
~~As where the eagle wailed.~~
With many a man he counselled

The Rime of the Ancient Mariner

SAMUEL TAYLOR COLERIDGE (1772–1834)

1806, British Library, Add MS 47508, f.5r, notebook 8.2 x 12 cm, folio 7.7 x 11.2 cm, pencil and iron gall ink on paper in a leather-bound notebook.

This is one of Samuel Taylor Coleridge's many notebooks, containing drafts, thoughts, notes and memoranda relating to an array of subjects. Of the seventy-two surviving Coleridge notebooks, the British Library cares for over fifty, spanning the years 1794 to 1833.

Notebook 11 was written between 6 September 1806 and 25 November 1810. It includes an ink autograph transcription of lines 201–12 of *The Rime of the Ancient Mariner*.[1] This poem and 'Kubla Khan' are probably Coleridge's best-known works. It is an epic story of a sailor who stops a wedding guest to tell him a story of an ill-fated and long voyage which was marred by his slaying of an albatross. Historically, albatrosses were considered to bring good luck if they were spotted flying over a ship, as it was believed that they held the soul of a deceased mariner and that they would protect the sailors on board. Why the mariner shoots the albatross is never explained, but the consequences are severe. Thus the symbol of good luck quickly turns into a terrifying burden.

The poem, which comprises seven parts, was begun in 1797 and first published in *Lyrical Ballads* in 1798. The small excerpt from the poem in this notebook was written around October 1806, about eight years after the poem was published. The excerpt contains significant changes and shows that Coleridge continued to revise the poem long after it had been committed to print.

Sic perit Ingenium,
Ingenii (<u>aliter Genii</u>) ni
pignora vitam Perpetuam
statuant –

==

With never a whisper in the main
Off shot the spectre ship:
And stifled words & groans of pain
Mix'd on each ~~trembling~~ murmering lip,
And We look'd round & we look'd up
And Fear at our hearts as at a cup
The Life-blood seem'd to sip
The Sky was dull & dark the Night,
The Helmsman's Face by his lamp gleam'd bright,
From the sails the Dews did drip,
Till ~~rose~~ clomb above the Eastern Bar
The horned moon, with one bright Star
Within its nether Tip.
One after one, by the star-dogg'd moon.

Cover of Samuel Taylor Coleridge's notebook, British Library, Add MS 47508.

Sic perit Ingenium,
Ingenii (alter Genii) ni
pignora vitam perpetuam
statuant ~

With never a whisper in the main
Off shot the spectre ship:
And stifled words & groans of pain
Mix'd on each ~~trembling~~ murmuring lip.

And We look'd round & we look'd up
And Fear at our hearts as at a cup
The Life-blood seem'd to sip
The Sky was dull & dark the Night,
The Helmsman's Face by his lamp gleam'd bright,
From the sails the Dews did drip,
Till ~~rose~~ clomb above the Eastern Bar
The horned moon, with one bright Star
Within its nether Tip.

One after one, by the star-dogg'd moon,
&c —

chapter 2

FANTASY

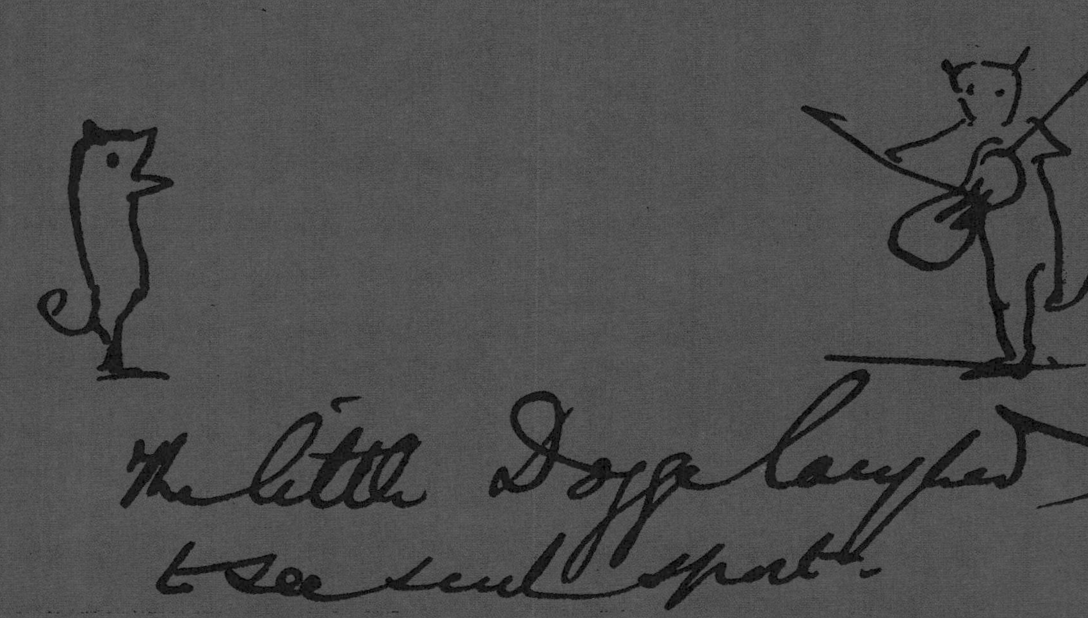

Loved by both adults and children, fantasy literature allows the reader to escape from everyday life into a world filled with magic, mythical creatures and adventure. Fantasy as a genre did not emerge until the nineteenth century, but it drew significantly on ideas and stories from classical mythology, medieval literature and more modern folk traditions. In his poem 'Song: Go and catch a falling star', John Donne used fantastical imagery to create a list of impossible tasks that he believed would be easier to achieve than finding a faithful woman.

From fairy tales to nonsense rhymes, the inventive and imaginative nature of fantasy literature often appeals to children. One of the earliest and most prominent works of the genre is Lewis Carroll's *Alice's Adventures in Wonderland*. The story includes a number of poems that are recited to Alice by the talking animals she encounters as she travels through Wonderland. Edward Lear wrote and illustrated nonsense stories, poems and nursery rhymes for the children of his literary friends, including his version of 'Hey diddle diddle'. Not always written for children, fantasy can also be written *by* children; the Brontë sisters Anne and Emily created the wonderful world of Gondal at the ages of 10 and 12 respectively.

Fantasy can also have a darker side. Gothic and horror literature uses fantastical elements to scare and shock the reader. Edgar Allan Poe was a master of this style and his poems and stories often include supernatural references. The world of 'Annabel Lee' is like a living nightmare, with jealous angels and demons trying to separate the narrator from his love. The Welsh poet Vernon Watkins drew on the terrifying custom of the Mari Lwyd (grey mare) as the subject for his ballad. The practice involved parading a horse's head or skull from house to house at night. To gain admittance to the house, the carriers of the horse's head challenged the residents to a battle of wits or exchange of rude rhymes known as *pwnco*.

Fantasy literature often blurs the distinction between dreams and reality. Derek Walcott's poem 'At Lampfall' uses memories, daydreams and references to classical literature to capture the essence of the sea. Hollie McNish, in her poem 'Recurring pregnancy nightmare number 2: the nights you were born a goat', describes the horror of giving birth to a furry goat. However, for Samuel Taylor Coleridge sleep itself acted as inspiration. He claimed that his wondrous journey to Xanadu and the pleasure dome of Kubla Khan appeared to him in an opium-addled dream.

Fantastical poems allow us to leave the real world behind and enter our imaginations, where anything is possible.

A Mouse's Tale

LEWIS CARROLL (CHARLES DODGSON) (1832–1898)

1862–4, British Library, Add MS 46700, f.15v, volume 19 × 12.3 cm, ink on paper, bound in dark green morocco covers, with gilt title.

The story of Alice and her adventures in Wonderland is one of the best-known and most loved examples of English fantasy literature. Its writer, the Reverend Charles Dodgson, was better known by his pen name Lewis Carroll. Like Edward Lear, he was a lover of all things nonsensical.

The story originated on a boat trip up the River Thames on 4 July 1862 when Dodgson, a mathematics tutor at Christ Church, Oxford, told the tale to Alice Liddell (1852–1934) and her sisters, the daughters of the dean of Christ Church. The sisters liked the story so much that Alice asked Dodgson to write it down for them. On 26 November 1864 Dodgson presented Alice with this manuscript, originally titled *Alice's Adventures Under Ground*, as 'A Christmas Gift to a Dear Child in Memory of a Summer's Day'. By this time, Dodgson no longer visited the sisters at the request of their parents. Some academic writers have since suggested Dodgson's enthusiasm for children may have had a sexual dimension, although others see it as reflecting the idealisation of childhood common in Victorian culture.

Lewis Carroll included several poems in his story. This poem is told by the mouse and is described as 'a long and sad tale'. Alice mistakes 'tale' for 'tail' and the poem takes the shape of a long curved tail. The manuscript poem differs significantly from the published version. In this poem dogs are the enemies of the mice as well as cats. Carroll greatly expanded the book when he prepared it for publication and the final version contained new additions including the Cheshire Cat and the Mad Hatter's tea party.

This manuscript was treasured by Alice Liddell for many years until, as a result of financial difficulties, she sold it at auction in 1928 to an American collector. In 1948 it was bought by a group of American benefactors as a gift to the British nation, 'as a measure of cultural reparation' and in recognition of the part played by Britain during the early part of the Second World War.

Illustration of Alice and a mouse swimming from *Alice's Adventures Under Ground*, Lewis Carroll, British Library, Add MS 46700, f.11r.

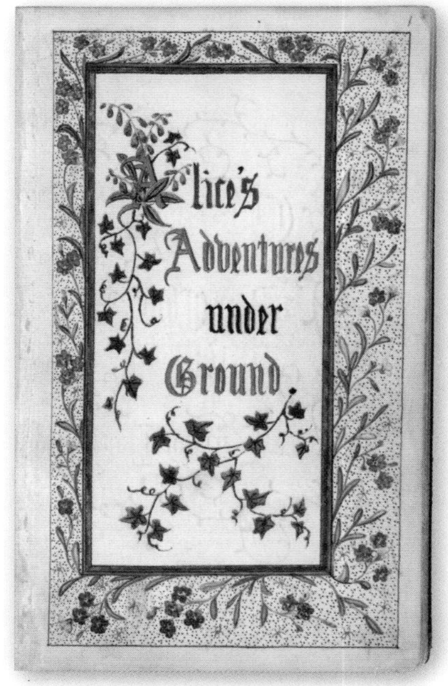

Portrait of Alice Liddell from *Alice's Adventures Under Ground*, Lewis Carroll, British Library, Add MS 46700, f.46v.

LEFT Title page of *Alice's Adventures Under Ground*, Lewis Carroll, British Library, Add MS 46700, f.1r.

We lived beneath the mat
Warm and snug and fat
But one woe, & that
Was the cat!
To our joys
a clog, In
our eyes a
fog, On our
hearts a log
Was the dog!
When the
cat's away,
Then
the mice
will
play,
But, alas!
one day, (So they say)
Came the dog and
cat, Hunting
for a
rat,
Crushed
the mice
all flat,
Each
one
as
he
sat
Underneath the mat,
Warm, & snug, & fat —
Think of that!

And nowe, Good Morrowe to our wakeing soules,
W^ch^ watch not one another out of Feare,
For love, All love of other sights controules,
And makes one little roome, an every where,
Lett sea discoverers to new worldes have gon,
Lett Mapps to others, worlds on worldes have showne
Lett us possesse one world, each hath one, and is One.

My Face in thyne Eye, thyne in myne appeares,
And true playne harts doe in the Faces rest
Where can wee fynde two better Hemispheres
W^th^out sharpe North, w^th^out declyning west,
What ever dyes, was not mixt equallye
If our two loves be one, or thou and I
Love so alike, that none doe slacken, none can dye.

Song:-

Goe, and catch a falling starr,
Gett wth chylde a Mandracke roote
Tell me where all past yeares are,
Or who cleft the Devills foote,
Teach mee to heare Mermaydes singing
Or to keepe of Envies stinging
And finde
what winde
Serves to advance an honest mynde.

If thou beest borne to strange sights
Things Invisible see
Ride ten thousand dayes, and nights,
Till age snowe white hayres on Thee,
Thou, when thou returnest, wilt tell mee
All strange wonders that befell thee,
And sweare,
Noe where
Lives a woman true, and fayre.

If thou fyndest One, lett mee knowe
Such a Pilgrimage were sweete,
Yett doe not, I would not goe
Though at next doore wee might meete,
Though shee were true, when you mett her
And last, till you write your letter,
Yett shee
Will bee
False, ere I come, to two, or three.

Song: Go and catch a falling star

JOHN DONNE (1572–1631)

1620–34, British Library, Harley MS 4955, f.113v, volume 37 × 27 cm, iron gall ink on laid paper.

This poem is part of a volume called the Newcastle Manuscript, a collection of poetry and drama compiled for William Cavendish, first duke of Newcastle (1593–1676), between 1620 and 1634. It is written in the hand of Cavendish's secretary, John Rolleston (1597?–1681), and includes works by Ben Jonson, John Donne and Dr Richard Andrewes (bap.1575–1634), among others. The volume is now part of the Harley Collection at the British Library. Very few manuscripts survive in Donne's hand and much of his poetry is known through contemporary copies such as the Newcastle Manuscript. 'Song: Go and catch a falling star' was first published in print in 1633.

Although this poem appears fantastical, as it asks the reader to undertake impossible tasks such as impregnating a mandrake root or hearing mermaids sing, its central theme is bitterness at the unfaithfulness of women. Donne asks the reader to let him know if they find a true woman after riding ten thousand days and nights, but suggests that she will probably have lost her faithfulness by the time he meets her. The fantastical imagery of falling stars and mermaids singing is strikingly at odds with the cynical message of the poem.

While the volume was expensively produced, the manuscript is showing signs of iron gall ink beginning to eat through the paper, so that text on the preceding folio can be seen though the page.

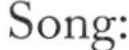

Song:
Goe, and catch a falling starr,
Gett wth chylde a Mandracke roote
Tell me where all past yeares are,
Or who cleft the Devills foote,
Teach mee to heare Mermaydes singing,
Or to keepe of Envies stinging,
And finde,
what winde,
Serves to advance an honest mynde.

If thou beest borne to strange sights
Things Invisible see,
Ride ten thouzand dayes, and nights,
Till age snowe white hayres on Thee,
Thou, when thou retornist, wilt tell mee
All strange wonders that befell thee,
And sweare,
No wheare
Lives a woman true, and fayre.

If thou fynd'st One, lett mee knowe
Such a Pilgrimage weare sweete,
Yett doe not, I would not goe,
Though at next doore, wee might meete,
Though she weare true, when you mett her
And last, till you write your letter,
Yett shee
Will bee
False, ere I come, to two, or three.

ABOVE: John Donne, engraving by Pierre Lombart, British Library, G.11415.

At Lampfall

DEREK WALCOTT (1930–2017)

1963–4, British Library, Add MS 52594, ff.39–41, folios 16 x 10.5 cm, black ink on three pages of lined notepaper.

'At Lampfall' was written by the playwright Derek Walcott in the early 1960s. It explores themes of folklore, myth, legend, empire and the sea. Originally published in *The Gulf and Other Poems* in 1969, the poem draws on classical and artistic references. The first verse refers to the artist Joseph Wright of Derby's (1734–1797) dramatic chiaroscuro painting of an astrological lecture called 'A Philosopher Lecturing on the Orrery'. Walcott uses the contrast of light and dark in this painting to conjure a similarly dramatic image of the sea in his poem. The last verse mentions Penelope, the wife of Odysseus, who deterred suitors by pretending to weave a shroud. Walcott likens the movement of the sea to Penelope's loom.

The poem is written on three sheets torn from a lined notebook and the manuscript displays some textual changes and corrections where Walcott has underlined or traced over some words.

Walcott, who was born in 1930 on the island of St Lucia in the Caribbean, described the region as a place of 'unfinished associations' born of slavery and indentureship[1]. He is considered by many to be one of the pre-eminent Caribbean voices of the twentieth century.

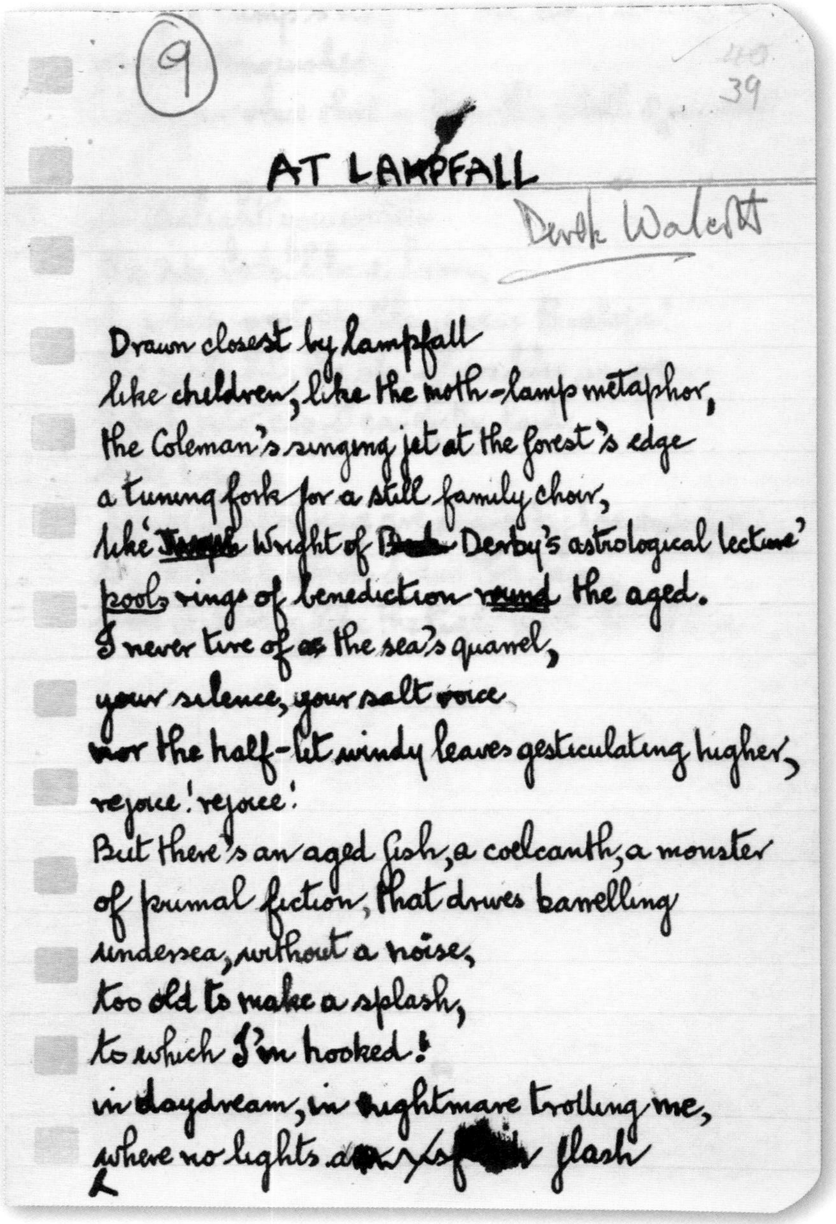

Derek Walcott, photograph by Brooks Kraft.

(9)

40
39

AT LAMPFALL

Derek Walcott

Drawn closest by lampfall
like children, like the moth-lamp metaphor,
the Coleman's singing jet at the forest's edge
a tuning fork for a still family choir,
like 'Wright of Derby's astrological lecture'
pools rings of benediction round the aged.
I never tire of the sea's quarrel,
your silence, your salt voice
nor the half-lit windy leaves gesticulating higher,
rejoice! rejoice!
But there's an aged fish, a coelacanth, a monster
of primal fiction, that drives barrelling
undersea, without a noise,
too old to make a splash,
to which I'm hooked!
in daydream, in nightmare trolling me,
where no lights [illegible] flash

but the plankton's constellation of lost stars.
I see through its aged eyes,
its dead green, glaucous stare,
and I'm elsewhere. As far as
I shall ever go whom I behold now,
dear family by the humming glow,
the gas lamp's ring that the sea's boiling rim's
never extinguished,
like your voice that curls in the shell of my ear.

At twilight you watch
the sea rock like a loom,
its white-wool shuttle, sheer Penelope!
The coals lit, the sky glows like an oven
heart into heart carefully laid
like bread.
This is the hour we are drawn by love and fear
by dread, which draws the same,
like children, like the tiger moth to flame.

(11) 42 41

At the road's edge the forest swallows its children
We belong here.
There's Venus. We are not yet lost.
Like you, I prefer
the firefly's electric, erratic little
lamp, mining.
to the highways hissing with bright iron beetles.

April 9th

Annabel Lee

EDGAR ALLAN POE (1809–1849)

c.1849, Harvard University, MS AM 233.6, folio 43 cm x 16.5 cm, ink on lined paper.

'Annabel Lee' was the last complete poem written by the American author Edgar Allan Poe. In it the narrator describes his love for Annabel Lee, which had begun when they were children in a 'kingdom by the sea'. Their love was so great that the angels were jealous and intervened to cause her tragic early death.

The death of a young woman is a common theme in Gothic literature. Coleridge created the ghostly wraith Geraldine in his poem 'Christabel', which was a significant influence on Poe's poetry. Poe called the death of a young woman 'the most poetical topic in the world'.[2]

Some scholars believe that Annabel Lee is based on Poe's wife, Virginia Clemm (b.1822), who had died two years earlier in 1847. Clemm was Poe's first cousin and was only 13 when the couple married, to the disapproval of her mother and wider society because of her young age. Poe and Clemm lied on the marriage certificate, which recorded that she was 21, not 13. A number of women, including a former childhood sweetheart, claimed to have been the inspiration for the poem, while others believed that Annabel Lee was a figment of Poe's vivid and melancholy imagination.

Poe ensured that the poem was published after his death by creating a number of fair copy manuscripts. Shown and transcribed here are the first four verses of the poem. The complete draft was sent to Poe's literary executor, Rufus Wilmot Griswold (1815–1857). It was published on 9 October 1849, two days after Poe's death, together with his obituary in the *New-York Daily Tribune*.

Annabel Lee.
By Edgar A. Poe.

It was many and many a year ago,
In a kingdom by the sea,
That a maiden there lived whom you may know
By the name of Annabel Lee; —
And this maiden she lived with no other thought
Than to love and be loved by me.

I was a child and she was a child,
In this kingdom by the sea;
But we loved with a love that was more than love —
I and my Annabel Lee —
With a love that the wingéd seraphs in Heaven
Coveted her and me.

And this was the reason that, long ago,
In this kingdom by the sea,
A wind blew out of a cloud, chilling
My beautiful Annabel Lee;
So that her high-born kinsmen came
And bore her away from me,
To shut her up in a sepulchre,
In this kingdom by the sea.

The angels, not half so happy in Heaven,
Went envying her and me —
Yes! —that was the reason (as all men know,
In this kingdom by the sea)
That the wind came out of the cloud by night,
Chilling and killing my Annabel Lee.

Annabel Lee.

By Edgar A. Poe.

It was many and many a year ago,
In a kingdom by the sea,
That a maiden there lived whom you may know
By the name of Annabel Lee; —
And this maiden she lived with no other thought
Than to love and be loved by me.

_I_ was a child and _she_ was a child,
In this kingdom by the sea;
But we loved with a love that was more than love —
I and my Annabel Lee —
With a love that the wingéd seraphs in Heaven
Coveted her and me.

And this was the reason that, long ago,
In this kingdom by the sea,
A wind blew out of a cloud, chilling
My beautiful Annabel Lee;
So that her high-born kinsmen came
And bore her away from me,
To shut her up in a sepulchre,
In this kingdom by the sea.

The angels, not half so happy in Heaven,
Went envying her and me —
Yes! — that was the reason (as all men know,
In this kingdom by the sea)
That the wind came out of the cloud by night,
Chilling and killing my Annabel Lee.

Hey diddle diddle

EDWARD LEAR (1812–1888)

February 1865, British Library, Add MS 47462, f.35r, folio 20.7 × 15 cm, black ink on wove paper.

Nonsense verse is a form of literature that is often fantastical and humorous and that, by definition, never makes sense. It originated in old folk tales and nursery rhymes and was also written by academics and intellectuals. Edward Lear, who was a landscape painter, illustrator and writer, was one of its main proponents, along with Lewis Carroll.

Lear used quick line drawings to illustrate this well-known nursery rhyme, usually called 'Hey diddle diddle'. He also illustrated other nursery rhymes including 'Sing a song of sixpence' and 'Goosy goosy gander'. His illustrations were highly influential and contributed to the development of the modern-day cartoon.

This illustrated copy is thought to have been made for Janet Symonds (1865–1887), the daughter of the poet John Addington Symonds (1840–1893). It was donated to the British Museum Library in 1951 in a volume that also included Lear's drafts of 'History of the Seven Families of the Lake Pipplepopple' and 'Nonsense Alphabet'.

The nursery rhyme 'Hey diddle diddle' dates back several centuries. Some scholars believe that it originated in the medieval period, as cats playing fiddles were popular illustrations in illuminated manuscripts. The earliest published record of the poem was in London in 1765, when it appeared in *Mother Goose's Melody*.

Many have sought to find meaning in the rhyme. Some of the theories are that it is a corruption of ancient Greek, that it has something to do with the constellations and that it describes Queen Catherine of Aragon (1485–1536). The proffered explanations, like the poem, appear to be largely nonsense.

Self-portrait of Edward Lear and his cat Foss, British Library, Add MS 61891, f.110r.

Heyh diddle diddle
The Cat & the fiddle

The Cow jumped over
the moon.

The little Dogge laughed
to see such sport.

And the Dish ran away
with the Spoone.

High diddle diddle
The Cat & the fiddle

The Cow jumped over the moon.

The little Dogge laughed to see such sport.

And the Dish ran away with the Spoone!

35

The Ballad of the Mari Lwyd

VERNON WATKINS (1906–1967), WITH EDITORIAL COMMENTS BY T. S. ELIOT (1888–1965)

1936–40, British Library, Add MS 54157, f.1r, folio 33 × 20.5 cm, typewritten with pencil annotations on paper and f.163r, folio 23.5 × 18 cm, black ink on lined paper, in a school exercise book with a picture of Robert Burns on the front.

This poem by Vernon Watkins was inspired by the Welsh folk tradition called the Mari Lwyd ('grey Mari' or 'grey mare'). On the last day of the year, a wooden horse's head painted white or grey and covered in ribbons, or a horse's skull, would be carried from house to house. The carriers were a group of singers or impromptu poets who would challenge the occupiers of each house to a rhyming contest. If the householder was unable to produce a rhyme or reply, the carriers would enter the house, lay the horse's head on the table and eat with the losers.

Like many folk traditions, the origins of the Mari Lwyd are not known. The tradition was popular across much of South Wales, where Vernon Watkins grew up and lived for most of his life. It was most popular during the nineteenth century and was revived in the twentieth century. In his poem Watkins attempted to bring together those who are separated across the mortal divide on the 'last breath' of the year.

Watkins wrote a rough draft of the poem in this notebook before typing it up for publication. The typescript was submitted to Faber & Faber, where it was annotated by T. S. Eliot, who was an editor and board member. On the first page Eliot remarks that the title of the poem is too 'forbiddingly Welsh' for a broader English-language audience. Nevertheless, his overall verdict is positive as is shown in the transcription to the right.

Watkins collated the drafts of his poems before presenting his archive to the British Library through the Arts Council on 11 February 1967.

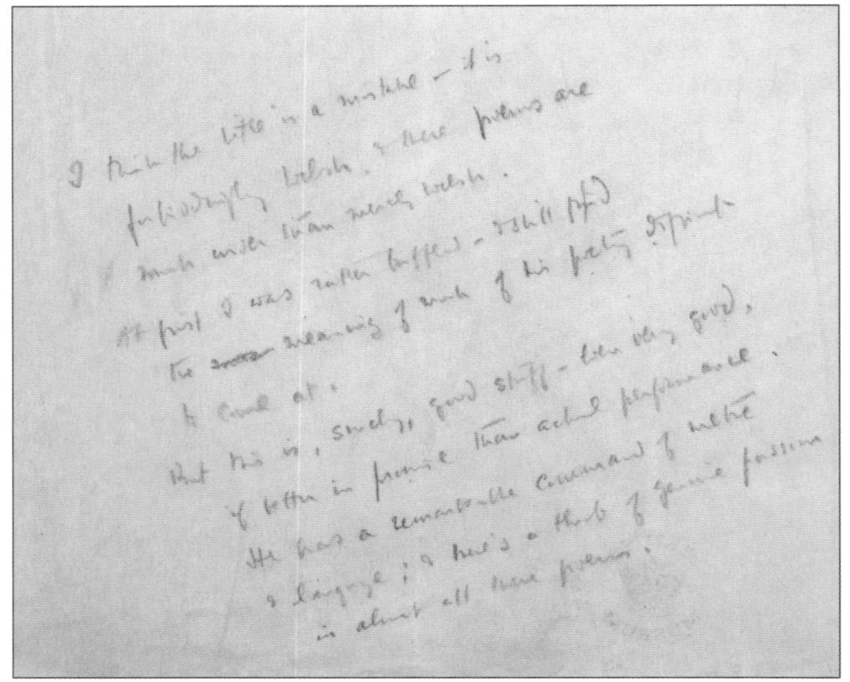

Detail of British Library, Add MS 54157, f.163r.

I think the title is a mistake – it is forbiddingly Welsh, & these poems are much wider than merely Welsh.

At first I was rather baffled - & still find the [illegible] meaning of much of his poetry difficult to come at.

But this is, surely, good stuff – even very good, if better in promise than actual performance. He has a remarkable command of metre & language; & there's a throb of genuine passion in almost all these poems.

BALLAD OF THE MARI LWYD

& OTHER POEMS

by

Vernon Watkins.

The Collier.
Sonnet. (Pit-Boy).
Elegy on the Heroine of Childhood.
Griefs of the Sea.
Old Triton Time.
From My Loitering.
Empty Hands.
Indolence.
The Turning of the Leaves.
The Sunbather.
Sycamore.
The Room of Pity.
Yeats' Tower.
After Sunset.
The Fountain.
The Age-Changers.
Two Decisions.
Portrait of a Friend.
A Prayer Against Time.
The Dead Words.
The Keen Shy Flame.
The Mummy.
Mana.
Earth-Dress.
Thames Forest.
Spring Song.
Autumn Song.
The Shooting of Werfel.
Stone Footing.
Atlas On Grass.
Sonnet. (Infant Noah).
A Lover's Words.
Three Epitaphs:
The Miser.
The Touch-Typist.
In Memory of Elizabeth Corbett Yeats.
The Safe Soul.
The Windows of Breath.
The Mother and Child.
Ballad of the Mari Lwyd.

Rough Draft

Ballad of the Mari Lwyd.

Midnight. Midnight. Midnight. Midnight.
Hark at the hands of the clock.
Now ~~[illegible]~~ dead men rise in the frost of the stars
And fists on the coffins knock.
They dropped in their graves without a sound;
Then they were steady and stiff;
But now they ~~[illegible]~~ tear through the frost of the ground
As heretic, drunkard and thief.

Sinner and saint, sinner and saint:
A horse's head in the frost.

Fasten the yard-gate; bolt the door,
And let the great fat drip.
The roar that we love is the frying-pan's roar
On the flames like a floating ship.
Shut out that wind that would steal our sheep
That blast that would brand our cows.
Fish out the flagons. Uncork the deep
Beer of this bolted house.

Midnight. Midnight. Midnight. Midnight
Hark at the hands of the clock.

Rough Draft

Ballad of the Mari Lwyd.

Midnight. Midnight. Midnight. Midnight.
Hark at the hands of the clock.
Now ~~squatters~~ dead men rise in the frost of the stars
And fists on the coffins knock.
They dropped in their graves without a sound;
Then they were steady and stiff;
But now they ~~spring~~ tear through the frost of the ground
As heretic, drunkard and thief.

Sinner and saint, sinner and saint:
A horse's head in the frost.

Fasten the yard-gate; bolt the door,
And let the great fat drip.
The roar that we love is the frying-pan's roar
On the flames like a floating ship.
Shut out that wind that would steal our sheep,
That blast that would brand our cows.
Fish out the flagons. Uncork the deep
Beer of this bolted house.

Midnight. Midnight. Midnight. Midnight.
Hark at the hands of the clock.

HOLLIE McNISH (b.1983)

January 2021, typewritten with black ink annotations on white paper. Previously unpublished poem.

I love editing poems. When I write poems down for the first time, it's normally a bit rushed, panicked even. I get worried that what I'm thinking of won't stay in my head unless I scribble it down really quickly: like dreams in the morning slowly dissipating and disappearing into the day. So I rush write at first. I don't think about layout or punctuation or spacing or even really the choice of words, because I don't want those thoughts to get in the way of me managing to get down the poem's idea before I forget it entirely or, more likely, before life interrupts it with other tasks that fill my head. I enjoy the rush writing of an idea or an image but I enjoy the editing more. The slowness of it all, once I have that first skeletal thought on the page and I can just sit with it and play around with it and take my time working out the words and spacing and structure that matches it best. The title normally comes last. I mainly finish on the title.

”

Recurring pregnancy nightmare number 2!
the night^*s* you were born a goat

the pushing ^*part* was
^*quicker*^*slicker*^*swifter* easier than ~~i imagined~~, *expected //*
but when ~~the midwife~~ ~~*she*~~ *they*
wrapped you ~~up~~ *in that blanket*
~~and~~ placed you in my arms //
your face a ~~face~~ ^*full* of goat fur ;
your purrs ~~purrs~~ ^*full?* of bleets ;
teeth the teeth of goat teeth ;
your feet full of ~~hoofs~~ *hooves //*
~~an arc of~~ *a thousand* smiling midwives *arc of grinning?*
cooing at your ~~newborn bloom~~ / *by my bedside* *congratulating me?* ~~*cuddles*~~
as if you weren't a goat at all // *the annoying 'mummy' speak?*
stifling cries muffling my ~~mouth panic~~ *screams* ~~*that*~~
~~as i shouted out in panic~~
this is not ~~*a*~~ ^*my baby girl!*
this is not ~~*a*~~ *baby girl!*
~~*this is a goat this is a goat*~~
~~with repeated denial~~ *with calm, concurred denial*
their heads nodding ~~*in sync*~~ *in slow motion*

~~a chorusing command~~
hands reaching forwards to *idea of not loving immediately??*

as they ~~smirked and~~ stroked
my sweating ~~mother's hair~~ *mother's head /* ~~*head*~~ */ hair*

be good and take your child ~~*home*~~, *hollie*
be good and take your child

~~*don't worry*~~ *not all mothers love ^at first* ~~*immediately*~~ *immediately*
it ~~*sometimes takes it*~~
time don't worry if you don't
and i sob into my
and their ~~*smile, silent*~~ ^*head tilt to the side*
~~*and they ska*~~ *and they look at me and smile*
be good and take your child x 2

Recurring pregnancy nightmare number 2!

the night you were born a goat

the pushing part was
easier than ~~i imagined;~~ expected //
but when ~~the midwife~~ they
wrapped you ~~up~~ in that blanket -
~~and~~ placed you in my arms //
face a ~~face~~ of goat fur;
purrs ~~purrs~~ of bleets;
teeth the teeth of goat teeth;
feet full of hoofs hooves //
~~an arc of~~ smiling midwives
cooing at ~~your newborn bloom~~
as if you weren't a goat at all //
muffling my ~~mouth~~ ~~panic~~ ~~that~~ //
~~as i shouted out in panic~~
this is not a baby girl!
this is not a baby girl!
~~*this is a goat this is a goat*~~
~~with repeated denial~~ with calm, concurred denial
heads nodding in slow motion sync
~~a chorusing command~~
as they ~~shirked and~~ stroked
my sweating, ~~mother's hair~~ head hair
be good and take your child ~~home~~, hollie
be good and take your child
~~don't worry,~~ not all mothers love ~~immediately~~ immediately at first
it ~~sometimes~~ takes time
don't worry if you don't

and I sob into my
and they smile, stroke
and they look at me and smile
be good and take your child v 2

Final Draft

the pushing part was
easier than expected;
but when they

wrapped you in that blanket -
placed you in my arms:
your face full of goat fur;

your purrs full of bleet;
teeth full of goat teeth;
your feet full of hooves

one hundred, zombie midwives
cooing at my bedside
as if you weren't a goat at all

heads nodding synced slow motion
with calm, concurred denial
silent to my screams, that

this is not my baby girl!
this is not a baby girl!
gloved hands opened out

to soothe my sweating hair
assuring me in unison
not all mothers love at first

sometimes it takes time, so
be good and take your child now
be good and take your child

The Gondal Poems

EMILY BRONTË (1818–1848)

1844–8, British Library, Add MS 43483, f.4v, folio 10.3 x 16.5 cm, iron gall ink on lined wove paper.

This autograph poem is from a volume of childhood writings by Emily Jane Brontë. The volume includes pencil notes and headings throughout by her sister Charlotte. Emily copied out forty-five poems relating to the imaginary world of Gondal. The poems were transcribed in February 1844 and additions made later in the same year. Further additions were made as late as 13 May 1848, just a few months before Emily's death at the age of 30. The first poem in the volume is dated 6 March 1837. Shown here is one page from the manuscript that contains an extract from the longer poem. The transcription ends mid-stanza and the poem continues on the following folio. This particular section focuses on the imaginary Aspin Castle, which is inhabited by a phantom.

Gondal was a fictional North Pacific island invented in the 1830s by Emily and her sister Anne. Gondal's landscape included elements drawn from the Brontës' native Yorkshire, as well as from the Scottish Highlands, which Emily encountered through her favourite author, Sir Walter Scott. Like much of the Brontë juvenilia, the writing on this manuscript is minute and mimics printed text. Augusta Geraldine Almeda was the heroine of the Gondal saga and her initials feature throughout the manuscript.

Five of the poems from this notebook were published in *Poems by Currer, Ellis and Acton Bell* in 1846. Currer, Ellis and Acton Bell were the pseudonyms for Charlotte, Emily and Anne Brontë.

The manuscript was inherited by Charlotte's husband, the Reverend Arthur Bell Nicholls (1819–1906). It remained in Nicholls' possession until his death in December 1906. The manuscript was purchased at auction by Elizabeth Smith (née Blakeway, 1825–1914), wife of the publisher George Smith. She later bequeathed it to the British Museum Library.

Written in Aspin Castle. E. August 20th 1842
February 6th 1843

Anne (pencil)

How do I love on summer nights
To sit within this Norman door
Whose sombre portal hides the lights
Thickening above me evermore!

How do I love to hear the flow
Of Aspins water murmuring low
And hours long listen to the breeze
That sighs in Beckden's waving trees

To night, there is no wind to wake
One ripple on the lonely lake.
To night the clouds subdued and grey
Starlight and moonlight shut away

'Tis calm and still and almost drear
So utter is ~~the~~ the solitude;
But still I love to linger here
And form my mood to nature's mood.

There's a wild walk beneath the rocks
Following the bend of Aspins side
'Tis worn by feet of mountain-flocks
That wander down to drink the tide

Never by ~~glen~~ cliff and gnarled tree
[gnarled tree (in pencil)]
Wound fairy path so sweet to me
Yet of the native shepherds none
In open day and cheerful sun
Will tread its labyrinths alone.

~~For round their hearths they'll tell the tale~~
~~And every listener swears it true~~
~~How wanders there a phantom pale~~

Far less, when evening's pensive hour
Hushes the bird and shuts the flower
And gives to Fancy magic power
O'er each familiar tower.

For round their hearths they'll tell this tale
And every listener swears it true
How wanders there a phantom pale
With spirit-eyes of dreamy blue –

It always walks with head declined
Its long curls move not in the wind

Kubla Khan

SAMUEL TAYLOR COLERIDGE (1772–1834)

1797–1804, British Library, Add MS 50847, folio 29.5 × 18.5 cm, ink on blue tinted paper.

This is an autograph copy, with corrections and revisions, of Coleridge's famous poem 'Kubla Khan'. The text is different in places to the version first published by Coleridge in his book *Christabel: Kubla Khan, a vision; The Pains of Sleep* (1816).

In 1797 Coleridge was staying at Nether Stowey in Somerset. Dorothy and William Wordsworth were living nearby, and the three writers frequently took walking tours around the Quantock Hills and the North Somerset and North Devon coastlines. Coleridge said that 'Kubla Khan' was composed during a tour in 1797, when he visited Lynton and the nearby Valley of the Rocks in North Devon.[3] He recited the poem to friends, but it was not published until some twenty years after it had been written.

Coleridge claimed to have written the poem after taking a dose of opium and reading *Purchas his Pilgrimage*, an epic religious geography first published in 1613 in which the author describes Xanadu, the summer palace built by Kublai Khan.[4]

In Xannadù did Cubla Khan
A stately Pleasure-Dome decree;
Where Alph, the sacred River, ran
Thro' Caverns measureless to Man
Down to a sunless Sea.
So twice six miles of fertile ground
With Walls and Towers were compass'd round:
And here were Gardens bright with sinuous Rills
Where blossom'd many an incense-bearing Tree,
And here were forests ancient as the Hills
Enfolding sunny spots of Greenery.
But o! that deep romantic Chasm, that slanted
Down a green Hill athwart a cedarn Cover,
A savage Place, as holy and inchanted
As e'er beneath a waning Moon was haunted
By Woman wailing for her Daemon Lover:
[~~illegible~~] From forth this chasm with hideous Turmoil seething,
As if this Earth in fast thick Pants were breathing,
A mighty Fountain momently was forc'd,
Amid whose swift half-intermitted Burst
Huge Fragments vaulted like rebounding Hail,
Or chaffy Grain beneath the Thresher's Flail.
And mid these dancing Rocks at once & ever
It flung up momently the sacred River.
Five miles meandering with a mazy Motion
Thro' wood and Dale the sacred River ran,
Then reach'd the Caverns measureless to Man
And sank in Tumult to a lifeless Ocean;
And mid the Tumult Cubla heard from [~~illegible~~] far
Ancestral Voices prophesying War.
  The shadow of the Dome of Pleasure
   Floated midway on the wave
   Where was heard the mingled Measure
   From the Fountain and the Cave.
It was a miracle of rare Device,
A sunny Pleasure-Dome with Caves of Ice!

A Damsel with a Dulcimer

ABOVE: Samuel Taylor Coleridge, mezzotint by Samuel Cousins, British Library, c.126.C.10.

In Xannadù did Cubla Khan
A stately Pleasure-Dome decree;
Where Alph, the sacred River, ran
Thro' Caverns measureless to Man
Down to a sunless Sea.
So twice six miles of fertile ground
With Walls and Towers were compass'd round:
And here were Gardens bright with sinuous Rills
Where blossom'd many an incense-bearing Tree,
And here were Forests ancient as the Hills
Enfolding sunny Spots of Greenery.
But o! that deep romantic Chasm, that slanted
Down a green Hill athwart a cedarn Cover,
A savage Place, as holy and inchanted
As e'er beneath a waning Moon was haunted
By Woman wailing for her Dæmon Lover:
~~And here~~ From forth this Chasm with hideous Turmoil seething,
As if this Earth in fast thick Pants were breathing,
A mighty Fountain momently was forc'd,
Amid whose swift half-intermitted Burst
Huge Fragments vaulted like rebounding Hail,
Or chaffy Grain beneath the Thresher's Flail.
And mid these dancing Rocks at once & ever
It flung up momently the sacred River.
Five miles meandring with a mazy Motion
Thro' wood and dale the sacred River ran,
Then reach'd the Caverns measureless to Man
And sank in Tumult to a lifeless Ocean;
And mid this Tumult Cubla heard from far
Ancestral Voices prophesying War.
The Shadow of the Dome of Pleasure
Floated midway on the Wave
Where was heard the mingled Measure
From the Fountain and the Cave.
It was a miracle of rare Device,
A sunny Pleasure-Dome with Caves of Ice!

A Damsel with a Dulcimer

In a Vision once I saw:
It was an Abyssinian Maid,
And on her Dulcimer she play'd
Singing of Mount Amara.
Could I revive within me
Her symphony & song,
To such a deep Delight 'twould win me,
That with Music loud and long
I would build that Dome in Air,
That sunny Dome! those Caves of Ice!
And all, who heard, should see them there,
And all should cry, Beware! Beware!
His flashing Eyes! his floating Hair!
Weave a circle round him thrice,
And close your Eyes in holy Dread:
For He on Honey-dew hath fed
And drank the Milk of Paradise.

This fragment with a good deal more, not recoverable, composed, in a sort of Reverie brought on by two grains of Opium, taken to check a dysentery, at a Farm House between Porlock and Linton, a quarter of a mile from Culbone Church, in the fall of the year, 1797.

S. T. Coleridge

In a Vision once I saw:
It was an Abyssinian Maid,
And on her Dulcimer she play'd
Singing of Mount Amara.
Could I revive within me
Her Symphony & Song,
To such a deep Delight 'twould win me,
That with Music loud and long
I would build that Dome in Air,
That sunny Dome! those Caves of Ice!
And all, who heard, should see them there,
And all should cry, Beware! Beware!
His flashing Eyes! his floating Hair!
Weave a circle round him thrice,
And close your Eyes in holy Dread.
For He on Honey-dew hath fed
And drank the Milk of Paradise.——

This fragment with a good deal more, not recoverable, composed, in a sort of Reverie brought on by two grains of Opium, taken to check a dysentery, at a Farm House between Porlock & Linton, a quarter of a mile from Culbone Church, in the fall of the year, 1797.——

S. T. Coleridge

Sent by Mrs Southey as an Autograph of Coleridge.

53

chapter 3

THE SENSES

Poetry can be employed to evoke touch, sight, smell, sound and even taste. Describing the senses is something that has occupied writers and poets for centuries, as can be seen in the diverse collection of poems in this section.

Poetry, with its rhythms and rhymes, naturally lends itself to being spoken or performed. Stories told through poetry have been part of oral culture from the earliest epic poems through to works performed at modern 'open mic' events. Some poems, such as Walter Scott's 'Glencoe', have been specifically written and set to music for public performance. In the twentieth century the performance poet Bob Cobbing experimented with the underlying sounds in the English alphabet to create what he called 'visual noise'.

Poets from Geoffrey Chaucer to Sylvia Plath have used imagery evoking the senses to add depth to their work. In *The Canterbury Tales*, Chaucer's characters exist in a rich, ripe and sensual world, filled with taste, sound and smells. Similarly, in her poem 'Insomniac', Sylvia Plath uses colours, taste and touch to describe the extreme emotional and physical discomfort caused by sleeplessness.

Some poets have consciously seen their work as a rival to other art forms. Henry Savile's poem 'Advice to a Painter' is part of a broader tradition known as *ut pictura poesis* (as is painting so is poetry), in which the work of the poet was argued to be analogous to that of the artist, depicting a scene using words and paper rather than brush and canvas. While Savile's poem was also used to convey a political message, it takes pains to provide grandiose advice to a painter on how best to paint a portrait.

Other poems in this chapter evoke the senses in different ways to heighten the impact of their message. In William Cowper's poem 'The Bee and the Pine Apple', the sweet scent of a pineapple behind a gardener's protective screen attracts the attentions of a bee, becoming a metaphor for the error of striving for worldly riches beyond reach. Christina Rossetti's description of an apple tree is a metaphor for virginity and its subsequent loss, a modern echo of the Christian story of the Garden of Eden. The Persian poet Shams al-Din Muhammad Hafiz Shirazi wrote about the effects of visiting a tavern in the early morning and described a singing head, drawing together sound, taste and pain into one experience. The *ghazal* (sonnet/ode) is shown alongside a poem by Johann Wolfgang von Goethe, which was inspired by Hafiz and extols the virtue of intoxication.

The Canterbury Tales

GEOFFREY CHAUCER (*c.*1340–1400)

Mid-fifteenth century, British Library, Harley MS 1758, f.1*v and f.1r, folios 34 × 22.6 cm, volume 35 × 26 cm, ink, colour and gold on parchment.

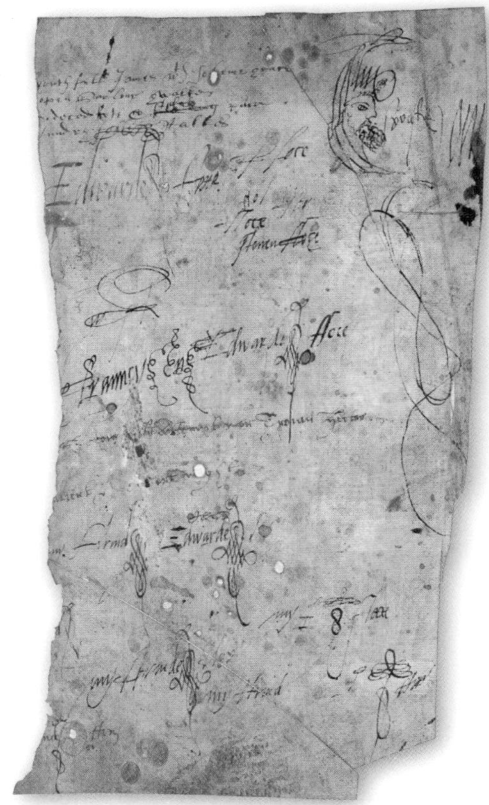

Geoffrey Chaucer's *Canterbury Tales* was so popular that over ninety manuscript copies of it survive today, most of which date from the fifteenth century. Written in Middle English, the poem brings together thirty-one pilgrims travelling from the Tabard Inn in Southwark, London, to Canterbury Cathedral to visit the shrine of Thomas Becket (b.1120), the archbishop of Canterbury who was murdered in 1170. The owner of the Tabard Inn suggests that each pilgrim tell two tales on their way to Canterbury and one on their return to help pass the time, and that the best story be rewarded with a free supper at the inn.

Only twenty-four stories were produced in the end and the return journey, with its corresponding tales, was not written. The stories that do exist are told by a broad cross-section of society, drawing on satire, wit and reality to evoke a rich, ripe and ribald world. Chaucer engages us through our senses: wet weather, sweet breath and melodies draw us into his world from the first verse of the Prologue.

This manuscript was probably written by three different hands, likely those of professional scribes, and then corrected by a supervisor. The flyleaf (the blank leaf in the front cover, pictured above) shows inscriptions from former owners. These include Francis Atterbury (1663–1732), bishop of Rochester and Jacobite conspirator, and the politician Robert Harley (1661–1724), first earl of Oxford and Mortimer, to whom Atterbury, as dean of Christ Church, Oxford, presented this manuscript sometime between 1711 and 1713. Robert Harley and his son, Edward Harley (1689–1741), amassed what is now known as the Harley Collection, which was sold to the nation in 1753 by an Act of Parliament that also established the British Museum.

<H>ere begynneth the book of tales of Caunterburye compiled by
Geffraie Chaucers of Brytayne chef poete:
Whan that aprill with his shoures swote
The drought of Marche hath perced to the rote
And bathed every veyne in suche licoure
Of whiche vertue engendred ys the floure
And Zephirus eke with his swete breth
Enspired hath in every holt and heth
The tendre croppes, and the yong sonne
Into the Ram his half cours ronne
And smale fowles maken melodye,
That slepen all the nyght with open eye
So priketh hem nature in here corages,
Than longen folk to gon in pilgrymages,
And palmers for to seke straunge strondes,
To ferne halwes, couthe in sondry londes;
And specialy, from everie schires ende
Of Englond, to Caunterburye thei wende,
The holy blissfull martyr for to seke,
That hem hath holpen whan that thei were seke.

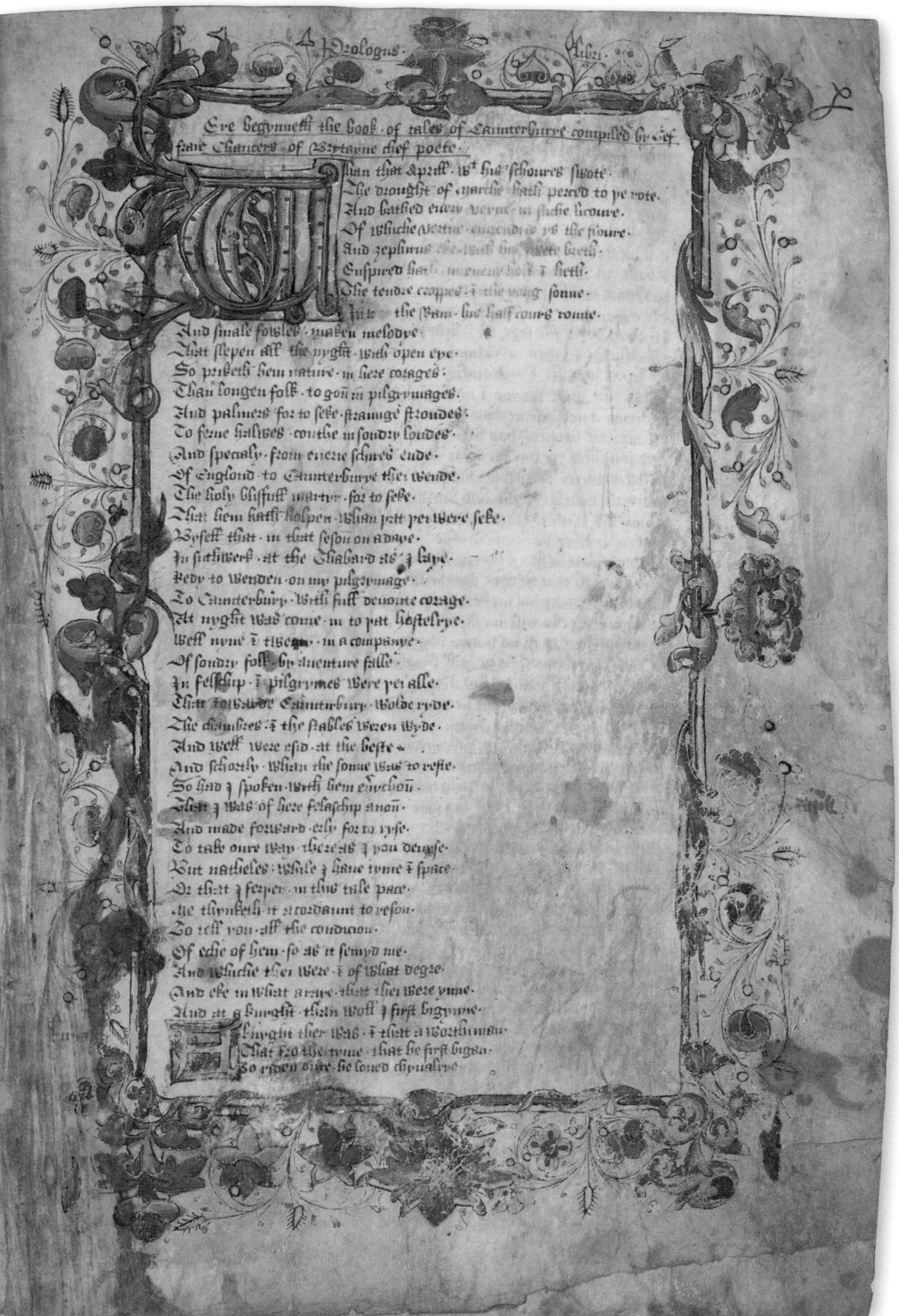

Here begynneth the book of tales of Caunterburye compiled by Geffray Chaucers of Brytayne chief poete.

Whan that Aprill wt his schoures swote
The drought of marche hath perced to þe rote
And bathed euery veyne in suche licoure
Of whiche vertue engendred ys the floure
And zephirus eke with his swete breth
Enspired hath in euery holt & heth
The tendre croppes & the yong sonne
Hath in the Ram his half cours ronne
And smale fowles maken melodye
That slepen all the nyght with open eye
So priketh hem nature in here corages
Than longen folk to gon in pilgrymages
And palmers for to seke straunge strondes
To ferne halwes couthe in sondry londes
And specialy from euery schires ende
Of England to Caunterburye they wende
The holy blisfull martyr for to seke
That hem hath holpen whan þat þei were seke
Byfell that in that seson on a daye
In Suthwerk at the Tabard as I laye
Redy to wenden on my pilgrymage
To Caunterbury with full deuoute corage
At nyght was come in to þat hostelrye
Well nyne & twenty in a companye
Of sondry folk by auenture falle
In felschip & pilgrymes were þei alle
That toward Caunterbury wolde ryde
The chambres & the stables weren wyde
And well were esid at the beste
And schortly whan the sonne was to reste
So had I spoken with hem euerychon
That I was of here felaschip anon
And made forward erly for to ryse
To take oure way there as I you deuyse
But natheles while I haue tyme & space
Or that I ferper in this tale pace
Me thynketh it acordaunt to reson
To tell you all the condicion
Of eche of hem so as it semyd me
And whiche they were & of what degre
And eke in what araye that they were ynne
And at a knyght than woll I first bigynne
A knyght ther was & that a worthi man
That fro the tyme that he first bigan
To riden oute he loued chyualrye

Riddle of Life

SHAMS AL-DIN MUHAMMAD HAFIZ SHIRAZI (715/*c.*1325–792/1389)

Solang man nüchtern ist (As long as a man's sober)

JOHANN WOLFGANG VON GOETHE (1749–1832)

AH **855** / AD **October 1451**, British Library, Add MS 7759, ff.115v–116r, volume 17.1 x 10.8 cm, black, gold and red ink on coloured Chinese paper. **1814**, British Library, Zweig MS 153, f.1r, folio 31.2 × 20 cm, ink on paper.

Shams al-Din Muhammad Hafiz Shirazi was a fourteenth-century Persian poet best known as Hafiz. His lyric poetry included *ghazals* (sonnets/odes), which explore the traditional subjects of love and loss, as well as sensual pleasures and politics. This poem is narrated by Hafiz and describes his trip to a tavern in the early morning. Hafiz's descriptions of drinking to excess and the pursuit of love can be taken literally as the joys of hedonism, but they can also be viewed as a metaphor for the search for truth and God within the Sufi tradition.

The poem forms part of a larger manuscript of Hafiz's *Divan* (*Collection of Poems*), which was copied by Sulayman al-Fushanji (*fl.* Ramazan 855/October 1451), possibly in Herat, Afghanistan. The poems are written on imported Chinese paper, which is unusually heavy and coloured various shades of orange, pink, blue, yellow/green, grey and purple.

Hafiz's *ghazals* are regarded as some of the best of Persian poetry in Iran and are widely read and quoted today. Well-known enthusiasts included Goethe, Arthur Conan Doyle (1859–1930), Queen Victoria and Friedrich Nietzsche (1844–1900). Goethe translated many works by Hafiz and declared that 'Hafiz is peerless'. He was so inspired by Hafiz that he based a collection on Hafiz's poetry called *West-östlicher Divan* (*West–Eastern Divan*, 1819), which was well received in Europe.

The second poem is a fair or presentation copy of the poem often referred to as 'Sober' or 'As long as a man's sober', which comes from Goethe's *West-östlicher Divan*. The poem calls on Hafiz to teach Goethe the fruits of his wisdom and extolls the virtues of intoxication. Its lyrics were used by the composer Carl Friedrich Zelter (1758–1832) for a four-part song. Zelter's autograph score can be seen below Goethe's poem and continues on the verso. Beneath the staves Zelter has written out the text of the first of the two verses by Goethe.

This translation of Hafiz's text into English by Richard Le Gallienne (1866–1947), published in 1903, uses poetic licence and differs significantly from the original Persian text. It does not replicate the full beauty of the original poem and is slightly old-fashioned in its phrasing, but nevertheless conveys the sense of Hafiz's original. The translation of Goethe's poem is closer to the original text and retains the humour and liveliness of the poem.

Whatever language we read Hafiz and Goethe in, it is clear that for both poets the loss of their senses was the pathway to God, love and happiness.

سحرگاهان که مخمور شبانه   گرفتم باده با چنگ و چغانه

نهادم عقل را ره توشه از می   ز شهر هستیش کردم روانه

نگار می فروشم عشوهٔ داد   که ایمن گشتم از مکر زمانه

ز ساقی کمان ابرو شنیدم   که ای تیر ملامت را نشانه

نبندی زان میان طرفی کمروار   اگر خود را ببینی در میانه

برو این دام بر مرغی دگر نه   که عنقا را بلندست آشیانه

که بندد طرف وصل از حسن شاهی   که با خود عشق بازد جاودانه

ندیم و مطرب و ساقی همه اوست   خیال آب و گل در ره بهانه

بده کشتی می تا خوش برانیم   از این دریای ناپیدا کرانه

وجود ما معمائیست حافظ   که تحقیقش فسونست و فسانه

Riddle of Life / Ode 487
With last night's wine still singing in my head,
I sought the tavern at the break of day,
Though half the world was still asleep in bed;
The harp and flute were up and in full swing,
And a most pleasant morning sound made they;
Already was the wine-cup on the wing.
'Reason,' said I, ''t is past the time to start,
If you would reach your daily destination,
The holy city of intoxication.'
So did I pack him off, and he depart
With a stout flask for fellow-traveller.
Left to myself, the tavern-wench I spied,
And sought to win her love by speaking fair;
Alas! she turned upon me, scornful-eyed,
And mocked my foolish hopes of winning her.
Said she, her arching eyebrows like a bow:
'Thou mark for all the shafts of evil tongues!
Thou shalt not round my middle clasp me so,
Like my good girdle – not for all thy songs! –
So long as thou in all created things
Seest but thyself the centre and the end.
Go spread thy dainty nets for other wings –
Too high the Anca's nest for thee, my friend.'

Then took I shelter from that stormy sea
In the good ark of wine; yet, woe is me!
Saki and comrade and minstrel all by turns,
She is of maidens the compendium
Who my poor heart in such a fashion spurns.
Self, HAFIZ, self! That thou must overcome!
Hearken the wisdom of the tavern-daughter!
Vain little baggage – well, upon my word!
Thou fairy figment made of clay and water,
As busy with thy beauty as a bird.

Well, HAFIZ, Life's a riddle – give it up:
There is no answer to it but this cup.

Buchstabe Nun
Gazele XXV

Solang man nüchtern ist
Gefällt das Schlechte,
Wie man getrunken hat
Wais man das Rechte,
Nur ist das Übermass
Auch gleich zu handen
Hafis o lehre mich
Wie du's verstanden.
Denn meine Meynung ist
Nicht übertrieben:
Wenn man nicht trinken kann
Soll man nicht lieben,
Doch sollt ihr Trinker euch
Nicht besser dünken:
Wenn man nicht lieben kann
Soll man nicht trinken.

26 Jul 1814

As long as a man's sober,
Badness pleases;
When he's imbibed,
He knows what's right;
Yet excess too
Is imminent;
Teach me, O Hafiz,
The fruits of your wisdom!
Because what I think
Is no exaggeration:
If one can't drink,
One shouldn't love;
But you drinkers
Shouldn't think yourselves better,
If one can't love,
One shouldn't drink

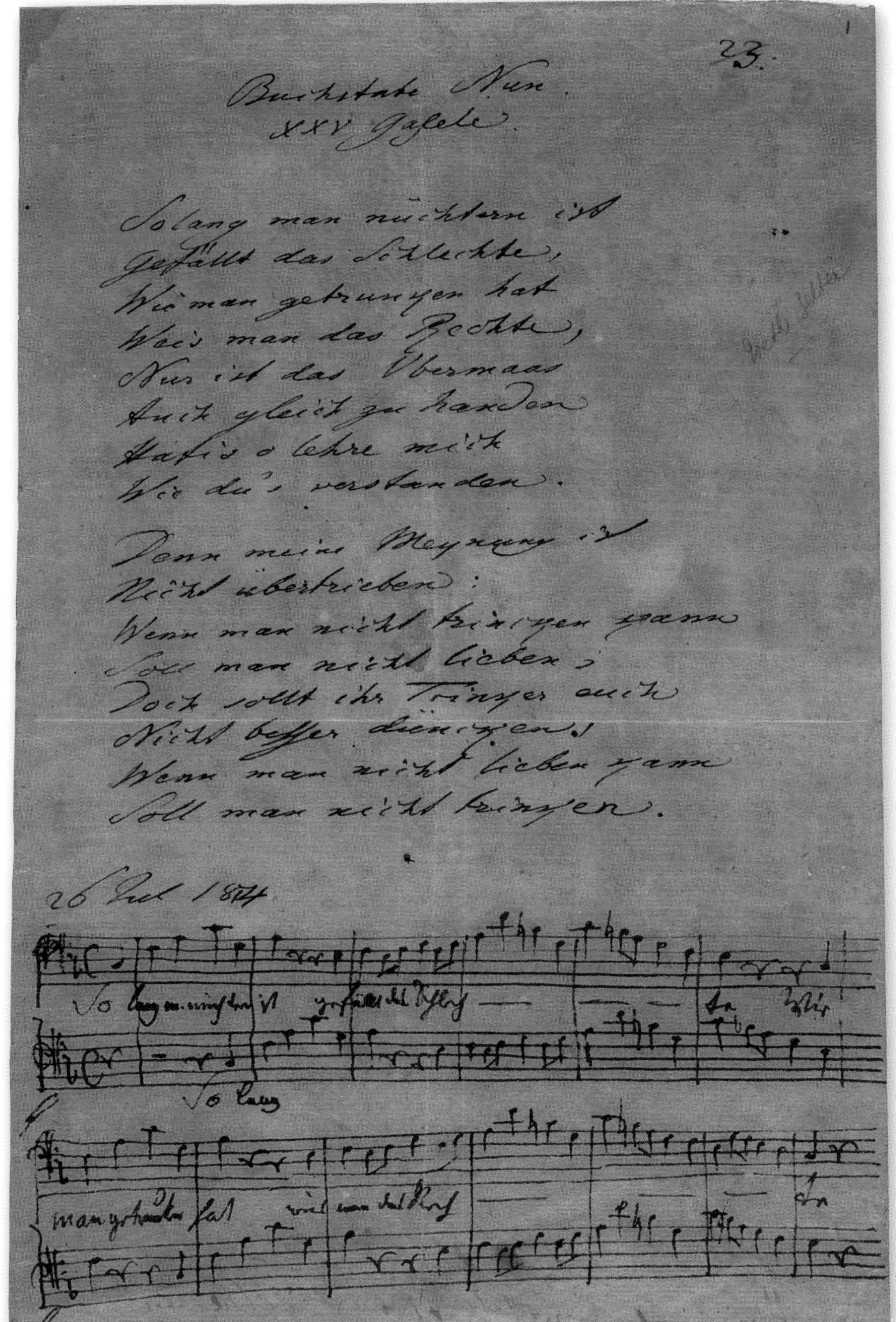

23.

Buchstabe Nun.
XXV Gasele.

Solang man nüchtern ist
Gefällt das Schlechte,
Wie man getrunken hat
Weis man das Rechte,
Nur ist das Übermaas
Auch gleich zu handen
Hafis o lehre mich
Wie du's verstanden.

Denn meine Meynung ist
Nicht übertrieben:
Wenn man nicht trinken kann
Soll man nicht lieben;
Doch sollt ihr Trinker euch
Nicht besser dünken:
Wenn man nicht lieben kann
Soll man nicht trinken.

26 Jul 1814

'Meditation on WORMS', 'Snow' and an extract from 'Transcript for a new sound poem'

BOB COBBING (1920–2002)

1954–c.1975, British Library, Add MS 88909/46, f.1v, folio 22.5 × 17.5 cm, blue ink on lined notebook paper. Add MS 88909/48, folio 25.5 × 20.5 cm, typewritten on yellow paper.

Bob Cobbing's abiding interest in the sound of poetry was awakened during his English lessons in the sixth form at Enfield Grammar School. He was particularly inspired by Vachel Lindsay's 'The Congo', a sonorous poem for which Lindsay gave explicit performance instructions in the right margin (from 'a rapidly piling climax of speed and racket' to 'a penetrating, terrified whisper').[1] Such terms can be happily applied to the inventive exploration of rhythm and sound in Cobbing's performance poetry.

Among Cobbing's earliest works are 'Two Experiments', both written in 1954 and subsequently copied into a notebook. Each is a lexical exercise structured as four columns. The first, 'Meditations on WORMS', is an earth poem concerned with 'decay and discovery'.[2] The second, 'Snow', is a poem of the air which uses present participles to describe snow's 'fluttering' and 'drifting' fall, in contrast to its 'deadening', 'frigid' and 'entombing' character.

As Cobbing's sound and visual poetry developed, he explored both the emotive power of the phoneme (the smallest unit of spoken language) and the communicative power of graphic expression and visual noise. Creatively exploiting a Gestetner ink duplicator and, later, a Canon photocopier, Cobbing morphed and warped text into new shapes to create forms of suggestive notation or 'scores' for recital. This innovative approach to poetry combined design, print and oral performance into a continuous creative act.

The archive of Bob Cobbing at the British Library is a comprehensive collection spanning his long career as an artist, teacher, poet and publisher, and includes some 300 reel-to-reel recordings of his poetry in performance. The collection was acquired from his wife, the artist Jennifer Pike Cobbing (1920–2016), on 1 June 2005.

Two Experiments.

1 Meditation on WORMS.

Rust	moth	fungus	mildew
Dryrot	canker	maggott	WORM
Wriggle	coil	roll curl	buckle
Twine	twirl twist	wind spiral	WORM
Hunt fish	ferret	root out	fathom
Unearth	disinter	grub up	WORM
Ingratiate	insinuate	intrude	invade
Permeate	interpenetrate	infiltrate	WORM
Crumbling	mouldering	rotted	blighted
Decayed	corrupted	tainted	WORM
Corpse	carcass	cadaver	carrion
Dust earth	ashes	mummy	WORM.

2 Snow

Chill	frigid	gelid	algid
Keen fresh	bleak raw	biting	snow
Icy	glacial	boreal	brumal
Arctic	hibernal	siberial	snow
Rain sleet	hailstones	snowflakes	crystals
Rime	hoar frost	icicle	snow
Bobbing	floating	reeling	fluttering
Dawdling	dwindling	drifting	snow
Settling	filming	carpeting	entombing
Muffling	deadening	death-white	snow
Drear	drowsy	engulfing	numbness
Further	can't go	end here	snow

Two Experiments.

(1) Meditation on WORMS.

Rust	moth	fungus	mildew
Dryrot	canker	maggott	WORM
Wriggle	coil	roll curl	buckle
Twine twirl	twist wind	spiral	WORM
Hunt fish	ferret	root out	fathom
Unearth	disinter	grub up	WORM
Ingratiate	insinuate	intrude	invade
Permeate	interpenetrate	infiltrate	WORM
Crumbling	mouldering	rotted	blighted
Decayed	corrupted	tainted	WORM
Corpse	carcass	cadaver	carrion
Dust earth	ashes	mummy	WORM.

(2) SNOW

Chill	frigid	gelid	algid
Keen fresh	bleak raw	biting	SNOW
Icy	glacial	boreal	brumal
Arctic	hibernal	siberial	SNOW
Rain sleet	hailstones	snowflakes	crystals
Rime	hoar frost	icicle	SNOW
Bobbing	floating	reeling	fluttering
Dawdling	dandling	drifting	SNOW
Settling	filming	carpeting	entombing
Muffling	deadening	death-white	SNOW
Drear	drowsy	engulfing	numbness
Further	cant go	end here	SNOW

1954

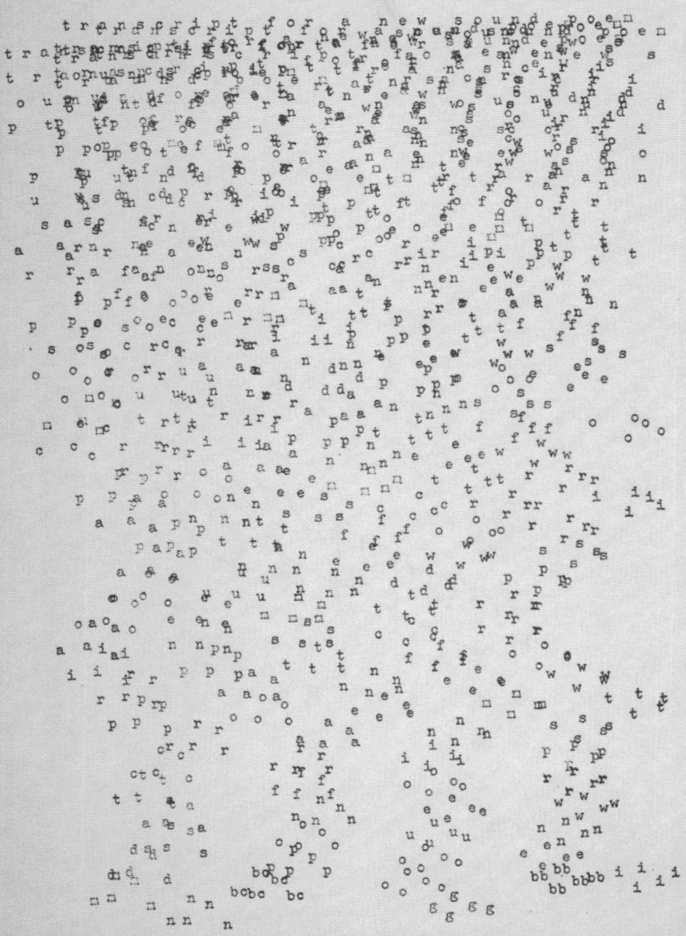

No 3. 3

The Bee & the Pine Apple.

A Bee allur'd by the Perfume,
Of a rich Pine Apple in Bloom,
Found it within a Frame inclos'd,
And Lick'd the Glass yt interpos'd.
Blossoms of Apricot & Peach,
The Flow'rs yt Blow'd within his Reach,
Were arrant Drugs compar'd with That,
He strove so Vainly to get at.
No Rose could yield so Rare a Treat,
Nor Jessamine was half so Sweet.
The Gardner saw this Much-Ado,
(The Gardner was the Master too)
And thus he said — Poor restless Bee!
I Learn Philosophy from Thee,
I Learn how Just it is and Wise,
To Use what Providence supplies,
To Leave fine Titles, Lordships, Graces,
Rich Pensions, Dignities & Places,
Those Gifts of a Superior Kind,
To those for whom they were design'd.
I Learn yt Comfort dwells alone,
In that which Heav'n has made our Own.
That Fools incurr no greater Pain,
Than Pleasure Coveted in Vain.

This must have been written so long ago as the year 1778, because it was, of course, anterior to the piece entitled "Another on the Same", which immediately precedes the Lines "On the Trial of Adml. Keppel" upon the same half sheet of paper.

The Bee and the Pine Apple

WILLIAM COWPER (1731–1800)

c.1778, British Library, Add MS 37059, f.3r–3v, folio 18.5 × 11.5 cm, pen and iron gall ink on laid paper, single sheet written on both sides.

William Cowper was considered one of the most important writers of his generation. His poetic depictions of rural life contributed to the evolution of writing about the natural world and are now seen as a precursor to the work of Romantic poets such as William Wordsworth. Cowper penned the powerful anti-slavery poem 'The Negro's Complaint' in 1788, which was later quoted by Martin Luther King (1929–1968). Cowper was an evangelical Christian and much of his work reflects his religious beliefs.

'The Bee and the Pine Apple', published as 'The Pineapple and the Bee', is one of Cowper's lesser-known poems. A note written in a different hand at the bottom of this manuscript suggests it was written in around 1778. Cowper was sent pineapple seeds by his friend Sarah Hill (née Matthews, *fl.*1771–after 1811), and in a letter to her husband, the lawyer Joseph Hill (1733–1811), he mentioned hoping to have pineapple plants sent from Jamaica, as he had already prepared beds and a frame for them.[3] This poem warns against the pursuit of worldly goods and honours. It describes highly fragranced plants and flowers and shows that Cowper had an understanding of the process of growing rare fruit. The manuscript is part of a bound volume of letters and drafts by Cowper, many of which were not published until some time after his death. The volume also contains a second, different version of the poem.

The provenance of the manuscript is explained in a letter at the end of the volume, which states that it came to Edward Philip Ash (1842–1909) as heir to his aunt, Miss Anna Ash, the daughter of Dr Edward Ash (1764–1829), physician-in-ordinary to George III (1738–1820). Ash believed that his grandfather or aunt must have received it from Sarah Hill. She had been a great friend of their family and, at her death, bequeathed them a cottage in Wargrave, Berkshire.

The Bee & the Pine Apple

A Bee allur'd by the Perfume,
Of a rich Pine Apple in Bloom,
Found it within a frame inclos'd,
And Lickd the Glass y^t interpos'd.
Blossoms of Apricot & Peach,
The Flowr's y^t Blowd within his Reach,
Were arrant Drugs compar'd with That,
He strove so Vainly to get at.
No Rose could yield so Rare a treat,
Nor Jessamine was half so sweet.
The Gard'ner saw this Much: Ado,
(The Gard'ner was the Master too)
And thus he said – poor restless Bee!
I Learn Philosophy from Thee,
I Learn how Just it is and Wise,
To use what Providence supplies,
To Leave fine Titles, Lordships, Graces,
Rich Pensions, Dignities & Places,
Those Gifts of a Superior Kind,
To those for whom they were designd.
I Learn y^t Comfort dwells alone,
In that which Heav'n has made our Own.
That fools incurr no greater pain,
Than Pleasure coveted in Vain!

This must have been written so long ago as the year 1778, because it was, of course, [illegible] =rior to the piece entitled 'Another on the Same', which immediately precedes these Lines 'On the Trial of Adm^l Kepple' upon the same half sheet of paper.

Insomniac

SYLVIA PLATH (1932–1963)

1961, British Library, Add MS 52617, f.78r, folio 25.4 × 20.1 cm, black ink on paper.

The inability to drift off is an unpleasant feeling and lack of sleep can muddle the senses. In the poem 'Insomniac', Sylvia Plath explores the torturous experience of trying to fall asleep. She describes reliving past 'embarrassments' and memories that replay through the mind like an 'old, granular movie'.

Plath suffered from insomnia so severely that it led to self-harm and a mental breakdown. She was living with her mother at the time and they sought help together. Her psychiatrist recommended sleeping pills and also suggested she find a job to take her mind off things. Neither worked and Plath continued to be unable to write. She was diagnosed with severe depression and underwent electroconvulsive therapy. The treatment was so traumatic that Plath tried to end her own life by taking sleeping pills.

This is a working draft of 'Insomniac', the prize-winning poem that Plath submitted to a poetry competition at the Cheltenham Festival in 1961. On the first page of the draft the first and third verses show extensive changes, with whole lines crossed out and rewritten. The second verse is largely as it appears in the published version.

This poem and the accompanying letter have been bound into a volume with drafts of the other poems entered into the competition. The volume was presented to the British Library by Eric Walter White (1905–1985) through the Arts Council of Great Britain.

Insomniac
The night sky is ~~a sheet~~ only a sort of carbon paper,
Blueblack, with the much-poked periods of stars
letting in / light, peephole after peephole –
A bonewhite ~~the~~ light the ~~past [lies]~~, like death, behind all thing's.
~~He has~~ under the eyes of the stars & the ~~bony~~ moon's rictus
~~of a moon that carries her light into the world~~
~~Of the aluminum-coloured moon, he suffers~~
He suffers his desert silence~~s~~; sleeplessness
Stretching ~~like~~ as a fine, irritating, ~~fine~~ sand in all directions

Over & over the old, granular movie
Exposes embarrassments—the mizzling days
Of childhood & adolescence, sticky with dreams,
Parental faces on tall stalks, alternately stern & tearful;
A garden of buggy roses that made him cry.
His forehead is bumpy as a sack of rocks
[~~illegible~~] Memories jostle each other for face-room like obsolete film stars.

He is immune to ~~the~~ pills: ~~are useless now,~~ red, purple, blue —
~~They bloomed like~~
~~The elegant pellets of oblivion~~
How they lit the tedium of the ~~vacuous void~~ protracted evening!
~~Powerful low-hanging~~ Those sugary planets ~~promising [illegible]~~ under whose ~~[expert solar]~~ influence ~~promised~~ win for him
~~And A science fiction life~~ & a A life ~~[illegible]~~ baptized in no-life ~~at all~~ for a while,
~~And a~~ & the sweet, drugged wakening, ~~like~~ of a forgetful baby.
He ~~has grown is immune to them~~ Their poppy-cheerful colors do him no good.

Insomniac

The night sky is only a sort of carbon paper,
Blueblack, with the much-poked periods of stars
Letting in light, peephole after peephole —
A bone-white light, like death, behind all things.
Under the eyes of the stars & the moons' rictus
He suffers his desert silences, sleeplessness
Stretching its irritating sand in all directions
as a fire,

Over & over the old, granular movie
Exposes embarrassments, the mizzling days
Of childhood & adolescence, sticky with dreams,
Parental faces on tall stalks, alternately stern & tearful;
A garden of buggy roses that made him cry.
His forehead is bumpy as a sack of rocks.
Memories jostle each other for face-room like obsolete film stars.

He is immune to pills: red, purple, blue —
How they lit the tedium of the protracted evening!
Those sugary planets whose influence won for him
A life baptized in no-life for a while,
& the sweet, drugged waking of a forgetful baby.
Then poppy-cheerful colors do him no good.

(1) 901. XXII C

Aduice to a Painter

Spread a large Canuas painter to Contain
the Great Assembly and the numerous train
who all about him shall in Councill Sit
Abiuring wisdom and Despising wit
Hating all Justice and resolued to fight
to rob its Natiue Country of its Right
First Draw him ~~prostrate~~ falling to the South
Adoring Rome this libel in his Mouth
Most Holy Father being Joyn'd in League
with Father patrick Darby and with ~~Leauge~~ Teague
Thrown at your Sacred foot I humbly Bow
I and the wise Assosiates of my vow
I Swear not fire nor Sword shall euer end
Till all this Nation to your foot Stool bend
Arm'd with bold Zeal and Blessings from your hand
Ile raise my Irish and my Popish band
And by a Noble well Contriued plott
Manag'd by wise Fitz Gerrard and by Scot
proue to the world Ile haue ould Engl^d know
That Common Sence is my Eternall fo
I nere Can fight in a more Glorious Cause
then to Destroy their liberties and lawes

Advice to a Painter (Advice to a Painter to Draw the Duke by)

HENRY SAVILE (1642–1687)

Seventeenth century, British Library, Sloane MS 901, f.2, volume 20 × 17.5 cm, pen and iron gall ink on laid paper.

This poem was at one time attributed to Andrew Marvell (1621–1678). While Marvell was associated with other poems that were part of the 'Advice to a Painter' trope, these lines are now thought to be by Henry Savile. The notion of a poet giving advice to a painter was part of a wider discussion about the competing merits of painting and poetry – or *ut pictura poesis* (as is painting so is poetry) – that went back to ancient Greece. Many poems in the seventeenth century in particular described artworks and galleries and, as in this poem, deigned to offer advice to artists.

The first 'Advice to a Painter' poem was written by Edmund Waller (1606–1687) to flatter King Charles II (1630–1685) and the monarchy. The genre quickly developed into satire and was at the centre of royal, political and religious manoeuvring. Marvell developed the 'Advice to a Painter' trope for political ends, which led to further versions of the theme, including Savile's poem. By 1700 there were nearly forty different poems using this theme. This particular poem attacks the Duke of York, later King James II (1633–1701), and is anti-Catholic and anti-Irish in sentiment, reflecting the prevailing prejudices in English politics and society at the time. When these lines were written, James had yet to ascend the throne and there was significant unrest at the prospect of a Catholic king. James was crowned in 1685, but deposed after the 'Glorious Revolution' in November 1688.

This manuscript reproduces only the first forty lines of the original poem and is written by an unknown hand. It is part of a volume of manuscripts on different subjects. The first folio of the poem is shown and transcribed here.

Advice to a Painter

Spread a large Canvas painter to Contain
The Great Assembly and the numerous train
who all about him shall in Councill sit
Abjuring wisdom, and Despising wit
Hating all justice, and resolvd to fight
to rob its native Country of its Right
First Draw him falling prostrate to the south
Adoring Rome this libel in his Mouth
Most Holy Father being joyn'd in Leauge
with Father Patrick Darby and with Teague
Thrown at your sacred feet I humbly Bow
I, and the wise Assosiates of my vow
I swear not fire nor sword shall ever end
Till all this Nation to your foot stool bend
Armd with bold Zeal and Blessings from your hand
Ile raise my Irish and my Popish bands
And by a Noble well contrived plott
Manag'd by wise Fitz Gerrard and by Scot
prove to the world Ile have ould Engl know
That Common Sence is my Eternall fo
I nere can fight in a more Glorious Cause
then to Destroy their liberties and lawes

Glencoe

WALTER SCOTT (1771–1832)

1811, British Library, Add MS 35264, ff.52v–53r, folios 36 × 26 cm, black ink on paper.

Poetry can be read aloud, but it can also be set to music and sung as lyrics. Walter Scott wrote the poem 'Glencoe' at the request of the Scottish music collector and publisher George Thomson (1757–1851). Thomson had been so impressed by the castrato Ferdinando Tenducci's (1735–1790) renderings of traditional Scottish songs at a concert organised by the Edinburgh Musical Society that he decided to create his own collection.

Thomson commissioned writers including Robert Burns, Walter Scott, Alexander Boswell (1775–1822), James Hogg (*c.*1770–1835), Joanna Baillie (1762–1851), Amelia Opie (1769–1853), Anne Grant (1755–1838), William Smyth (1765–1849) and Lord Byron to collect and compose traditional Scottish, Welsh and Irish poetry that he could use as lyrics. He sought out an equally impressive list of musicians to set the lyrics to music, including Ignaz Pleyel (1737–1831), Leopold Koželuch (1747–1818), Joseph Haydn (1732–1809), Ludwig van Beethoven (1770–1827), Johann N. Hummel (1778–1837), Carl Maria von Weber (1786–1826), George Farquhar Graham (1789–1867), Henry Bishop (1787–1855) and Thomson's son-in-law, the music critic George Hogarth (1783–1870).

'Glencoe' was written to commemorate the massacre in 1692 of around thirty members of Clan MacDonald for failing to take the pledge of allegiance to King William III (1650–1702) and Queen Mary (1662–1694).

This is a manuscript copy of the poem and includes a note from the editor at the top of the page in which he reveals that the poem was chosen for the collection as it is both 'beautiful' and 'touching'. Included here are the first three verses of the poem, which have been marked up for use by Beethoven. The note in red ink, which runs down the side of the page, contains information for the musician on where the emphasis is to be placed. In this poem the emphasis should fall on the second part of each first line.

Page 11
Glencoe- O tell me Harper
written for this work
By Walter Scott Esq

This air (no.5) was communicated by a friend in Ireland, is so like the next ~~air~~ in this Collection, that the one, seems to have sprung from the other: yet there is some difference and both are so beautiful & so touching, that the Editor could not allow himself to suppress either.

O tell me, ~~grays~~ Harper wherefore flow
Thy wayward notes of wail and woe
Far down the desert of Glencoe,
    Where none may list their melody?
Say, harp'st thou to the mists that fly,
Or to the dun deer glancing by,
Or to the eagle that from high
    Screams chorus to thy minstrelsy.

No, not to these, for they have rest –
The mist wreath has the mountain crest,
The stag his lair, the erne her nest,
    Abode of lone security.
But those for whom I pour the lay,
Not wild-wood deep nor mountain grey,
Not this deep dell that shrouds from day
    Could screen from treacherous cruelty.

Their flag was furl'd, and mute their drum,
The very household dogs ~~lay~~ were dumb,
Unwont to bay at guests that come
    In guise of hospitality.
His blythest notes the piper plied,
Her gayest snood the maiden tied,
The dame her distaff flung aside,
    To ~~ply~~ tend her kindly housewifery.

Left side

Glencoe — O tell me Harper

Written for this work

By Walter Scott Esq

(No. 5)

This air, which was communicated by a friend in Ireland, is so like the next ~~air~~ in this Collection, that the one seems to have sprung from the other: yet there is some difference, and both are so beautiful & so touching, that the Editor could not allow himself to suppress either.

O tell me ~~grey~~ Harper wherefore flow
Thy wayward notes of wail and woe
Far down the desert of Glencoe,
    Where none may list their melody?
Say harpst thou to the mists that fly,
Or to the dun deer glancing by,
Or to the eagle that from high
    Screams chorus to thy minstrelsy.

No, not to these, for they have rest—
The mist wreath has the mountain crest,
The stag his lair, the erne her nest,
    Abode of lone security.
But those for whom I pour the lay,
Not wild-wood deep nor mountain grey,
Not this deep dell that shrouds from day
    Could screen from treachrous cruelty.

Their flag was furl'd, and mute their drum,
The very household dogs ~~lay~~ were dumb,
Unwont to bay at guests that come
    In guise of hospitality.
His blythest notes the piper plied,
Her gayest snood the maiden tied,
The dame her distaff flung aside,
    To ~~ply~~ tend her kindly housewifery.

~~Poet has thrown the emphasis upon the second of the first line in every stanza except the first so, it would be well for the Singer if it were so in first stanza also, for example, "O tell me Harper, Alas grey harper &c."~~

Page 11

33
1

An Apple-gathering.

—

I plucked pink blossoms from mine apple tree
And wore them all that evening in my hair:
Then in due season when I went to see
I found no apples there.

With dangling basket all along the grass
As I had come I went the selfsame track:
My neighbours mocked me while they saw me pass
So empty-handed back.

Lilian and Lilias smiled in trudging by,
Their ~~piled~~ heaped-up basket teazed me like a jeer;
Sweet-voiced they sang beneath the sunset sky
Their mother's home was near.

Plump Gertrude passed me with her basket full,

34

A stronger hand than hers helped it along;
A voice talked with her thro' the shadows cool
More sweet to me than song.

Ah Willie Willie, ~~was~~ my love less worth
Than apples with their green leaves piled above?
I counted rosiest apples on the earth
Of far less worth than love.

So once it was with me you stooped to talk
Laughing and listening in this very lane:
To think that by this way we used to walk
We shall not walk again! —

I let my neighbours pass me, ones and twos
And groups; the latest said the night grew chill
And hastened: but I loitered, while the dews
Fell fast I loitered still.

— 23rd November 1857

An Apple-Gathering

CHRISTINA ROSSETTI (1830–1894)

23 November 1857, British Library, Ashley MS 1365, ff.1r–1v, folios 16 × 10 cm, black ink on loose leaf paper.

In Victorian Britain female sensuality was seen as something to be repressed and confined to marriage. Women who had sex outside marriage could be abandoned by their families and were vilified and shunned by society. The fate of the fallen woman was explored in novels such as George Eliot's *Adam Bede* (1859) and Thomas Hardy's *Tess of the d'Urbervilles* (1891).

Christina Rossetti's concern with the fate of women who had escaped prostitution or who had had sex outside marriage led her to volunteer, between 1859 and 1870, at the St Magdalen House refuge for women. The charity sought to provide shelter for and to rehabilitate these women, as well as to help them earn a living.

The fallen woman features in Rossetti's poems 'Maude Clare' and 'Cousin Kate'. 'An Apple-Gathering' can also be read as the tale of a fallen woman. The apple tree in the poem is more than it first appears. It can be seen as representing the narrator's virginity. Instead of waiting for marriage, as was expected in Victorian society, the narrator has sex with her lover and suffers for her impatience. Because she had plucked the blossom, the fruit would not grow and so 'in due season' she 'found no apples there'.

In losing her virginity before marriage, the narrator has lost her reputation and her chance of a good marriage. The poem continues as the narrator's neighbours pass her by, their baskets full of apples and their reputations intact. The poem ends with the narrator alone and her lover, Willie, unconcerned with her fate.

This manuscript is a fair copy of the poem Rossetti had originally written on 23 November 1857. It is exactly the same as the published version, which first appeared in *Goblin Market and Other Poems* in 1862. The manuscript was acquired by Thomas James Wise and was purchased by the British Library as part of the Ashley Library.

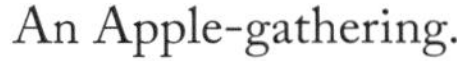
An Apple-gathering.

I plucked pink blossoms from mine apple tree
And wore them all that evening in my hair:
Then in due season when I went to see
I found no apples there.

With dangling basket all along the grass
As I had come I went the selfsame track:
My neighbours mocked me while they saw me pass
So empty-handed back.

Lilian and Lilias smiled in trudging by,
Their heaped-up basket teazed me like a jeer;
Sweet-voiced they sang beneath the sunset sky
Their mother's home was near.

Plump Gertrude passed me with her basket full,
A stronger hand than hers helped it along;
A voice talked with her thro' the shadows cool
More sweet to me than song.

Ah Willie Willie, was my love less worth
Than apples with their green leaves piled above?
I counted rosiest apples on the earth
Of far less worth than love.

So once it was with me you stooped to talk
Laughing and listening in this very lane:
To think that by this way we used to walk
We shall not walk again! —

I let my neighbours pass me, ones and twos
And groups; the latest said the night grew chill
And hastened: but I loitered, while the dews
Fell fast I loitered still.

— 23rd November 1857

ABOVE: Christina Rossetti, engraving after a drawing by Dante Gabriel Rossetti, British Library, 010920.f.20.

chapter 4

PLACE

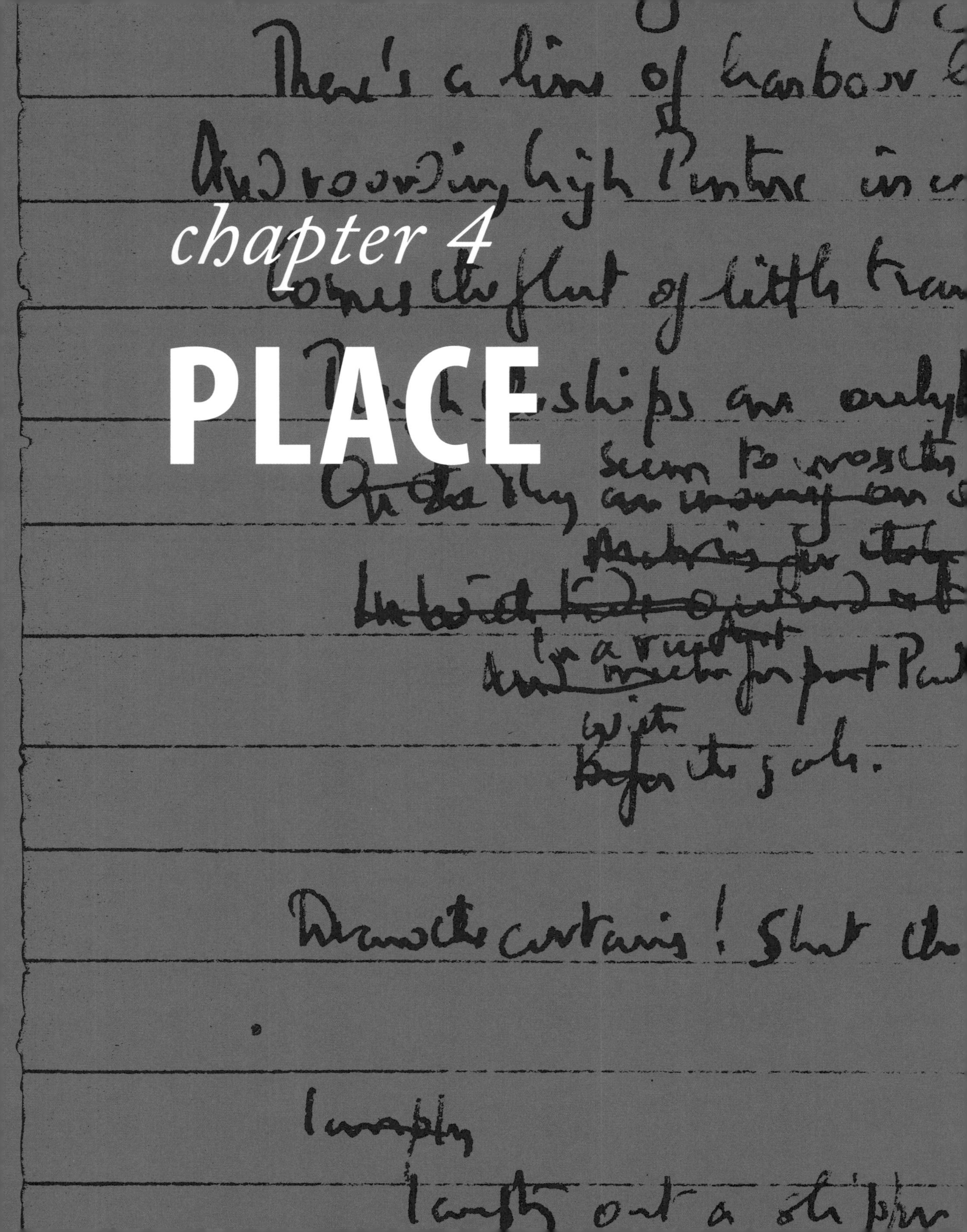

Poetry draws audiences through cities and across landscapes. It can reflect a crowded and intimidating urban environment or describe the majesty and beauty of a place.

In some poems the urban landscape offers opportunity and entertainment; in others it is oppressive and overwhelming. William Blake's poem 'London' depicts the city as dark and threatening, whereas William Wordsworth's metropolis, as seen from Westminster Bridge on a sunny morning, is bright and joyous. In 'Les petites vieilles' ('The little old ladies') Charles Baudelaire captures the popular pastime of people-watching in Paris, the city in which he lived most of his life. Jean Follain's poem 'Broken Bottle', translated by David Gascoyne, uses an unnamed urban environment as a backdrop for close reflection on a scene. John Betjeman contrasts urban and rural in his poem 'Harrow-on-Hill', while Evelyn Waugh's description of Crystal Palace makes the building appear almost heavenly and at odds with the lives of people in the foggy city below. In 'Rome Unvisited' Oscar Wilde describes an unfulfilled pilgrimage after he was unable to visit the city due to insufficient funds. Despite Wilde's journey being curtailed, the poem depicts Rome as a glittering and holy city after which the poet yearns.

Travel is a means of exploring and describing place. Composed on a train from Paris to Grenoble, Lee Harwood and John Ashbery's 'Train Poem – A Collaboration' is a contrast to other works in this section which focus on a single location. Liz Berry's poem 'Princes End' is set in the Black Country and explores the tender moment of first cradling a tippler hen. While Berry uses a single space to harness movement, open skies and seas are evoked by the mention of the bird's young who are flying from Scotland to Ireland. The importance of home is explored by Frances Cornford, who paints an idyllic and romantic image of Cambridge in autumn, while in his poem 'Jamaica' Andrew Salkey explores the story of his homeland, from its early history as the home of the indigenous Arawak people to its discovery by European explorers and subsequent colonisation. The poem explores the legacy of colonialism and slavery on the island and its people.

The experience of a place can be threatening, elevating, unsettling, safe, permanent or fleeting. It is a theme that draws readers into widely differing spaces though the medium of poetry.

London

WILLIAM BLAKE (1757–1827)

***c*.1792**, British Library, Add MS 49460, f.56r, volume 15.9 × 19.7 cm, iron gall ink and pencil on laid paper.

Cover of William Blake's notebook, British Library, Add MS 49460.

This notebook originally belonged to William Blake's brother Robert (b.1763), who died in 1787. The notebook contained only a few sketches until Blake began using it after Robert died. Blake used the notebook intermittently over a period of thirty years. He began at the front, recording ideas relating to good and evil which he explored by looking at the journey of man from birth to death. On completing the notebook, Blake turned it upside down and began working from the other end, drafting poems and ideas for his book *Songs of Innocence and of Experience* (1794). Other notes and ideas relate to a planned illustrated edition of *Paradise Lost* by John Milton, which Blake did not complete.

This page shows Blake's draft of his famous poem 'London', which was published in *Songs of Experience*. The poem forces the reader to follow narrow, dark and unfriendly London streets while contemplating the brutal nature of the city. Blackened churches loom while palace walls run with blood. Soldiers sigh, harlots curse and babies cry. Blake's London is a near-apocalyptic vision of the rotting heart of a nation. Like Baudelaire's Paris in 'Les petites vieilles', Blake's London is a city to be walked, its streets trodden. This draft shows changes to words, such as the word 'dirty' which Blake amended to 'chartered' in the published edition, to describe the streets and the River Thames. That even the river was controlled or chartered reveals the impact of humans on the city. The manuscript shows that Blake returned to and corrected the draft at a later date, as the ink is different in the corrections. This notebook was once owned by the poet Dante Gabriel Rossetti (1828–1882).

The image opposite shows a detail of f.56r. The folio can be seen in full on page 111.

London

I wander thro' each dirty street
Near where the dirty Thames does flow
And ~~[illegible]~~ mark in every face I meet
Marks of weakness marks of woe

In every cry of every man,
In ~~every voice of every child~~ every infants cry of fear
In every voice in every ban
The ~~german~~ mind forgd ~~links I hear~~ manacles I hear

~~Between~~ How the chimney sweepers cry
~~Blackens oer the churches walls~~ Every blackning church appalls
And the hapless soldiers sigh
Runs in blood down palace walls

~~But most thro' midnight harlots curse~~
~~From every dismal street I hear~~
~~Weaves around the marriage hearse~~
~~And blasts the new born infants tear~~
But most ~~from~~ thro' ~~every~~ [wintry streets] I hear
How the midnight harlots curse
Blasts the new born infants tear
And [~~hangs~~] [illegible] with plagues the marriage hearse
But most the shrieks of youth
I hear
But most thro midnight &
How the youthful

London

I wander thro each dirty street
Near where the dirty Thames does flow
And ~~see~~ mark in every face I meet
Marks of weakness marks of woe

In every cry of every man
In ~~every voice of every child~~ every infants cry of fear
In every voice in every ban
The ~~german~~ mind forgd ~~links I hear~~ manacles I hear

~~But most~~ How the chimney sweepers cry
~~Blackens oer the churches walls~~ Every blackning church appalls
And the hapless soldiers sigh
Runs in blood down palace walls

~~But most the midnight harlots curse~~
~~From every dismal street I hear~~
~~Weaves around the marriage hearse~~
~~And blasts the new born infants tear~~

But most ~~from every~~ thro' wintry streets I hear
How the midnight harlots curse
Blasts the new born infants tear
And hangs with plagues the marriage hearse

But most the ~~streets of youth~~ shrieks of youth

But most thro midnight ~~&~~ I hear
How the youthful ~~hear~~

I ~~wept~~ slept in the dark
In the silent night
I murmurd my fears
And I felt delight

In the morning I went
As rosy as morn
To seek for new Joy
But I met with scorn

To Nobodaddy

Harrow-on-Hill
JOHN BETJEMAN (1906–1984)

The Crystal Palace
EVELYN WAUGH (1903–1966)

c.1935–75, British Library, Add MS 71645, f.18r, folio 20.5 × 16 cm, blue ink and pencil on lined paper and f.70r, folio 25.5 × 23 cm, black ink on lined paper.

A sketch by John Betjeman of his teddy bear, British Library, Add MS 71645, f.110r.

John Betjeman was fascinated by the concept of place and it formed the foundation for many of his poems. He had recently returned from holiday in Cornwall when he wrote the poem 'Harrow-on-Hill'. In the poem, Betjeman compares the suburbia of Harrow on the Hill to the picturesque seascape of Cornwall. This page contains the last verse of the poem. It is a working draft and differs considerably from the published version. Betjeman has drawn three suburban houses alongside the poem in blue ink.

The second poem, also found in Betjeman's papers, was handwritten by his friend, the writer Evelyn Waugh, a contemporary at Oxford University. The two friends took inspiration from one another. Betjeman brought his teddy bear, Archibald Ormsby Gore, with him to university and Archie became the model for Sebastian Flyte's teddy bear, Aloysius, in Waugh's novel *Brideshead Revisited* (1945). In this poem Waugh invokes Betjeman's poetic style to describe a visit to the Crystal Palace, a cast iron and plate glass construction originally built in Hyde Park in 1850–1 to house the Great Exhibition. It was moved to Penge Place in 1854 and stood in that location until it was destroyed by fire in 1936. In the mid-1950s a television mast was built on the site. Like Betjeman, Waugh has illustrated his poem, and a cheerful sketch of the palace sits above the poem.

Waugh shared Betjeman's interest in architecture and the built environment. Betjeman used his popularity to campaign for the survival of old buildings, including St Pancras station, just across the road from the British Library in London. His interest in architecture dated back to his school days and is a strong feature of his poetry.

These two poems are part of a larger archive of the poems, letters and sketchbooks of John Betjeman that was purchased by the British Library from his daughter Candida Lycett Green (1942–2014) in May 1992.

Harrow-on-Hill
Collected Poems

A ~~mackerel sky is~~ thunder cloud is ~~hanging~~ [rising] -over Kenton
There's a line of harbour lights at Perivale
And rounding high Pentire in a flood of sunset fire
Comes the fleet of little trawlers under sail
Though the ships are only hours
On the sky ~~are moving on~~ seem to [cross the] skyline
~~Motoring for the harbour~~
~~In with tide o wind & birds behind them~~
In a run for it
~~And make~~ for ~~port~~ Padstow harbour
With ~~Before~~ the gale.

Draw the curtains! Shut the casement
I [~~imply~~]
I empty out a slipper full of sand

Draw the curtains! Shut, the window
And still my bedroom slipper's full of sand

18

Harrow-on-the-Hill
Collected Poems

A ~~mackerel~~ thunder cloud ~~sky~~ is ~~hanging~~ frying over Kenton
There's a line of harbour lights at Perivale
And roaring high Pinner in a flood of sunset fire
Comes the fleet of little trawlers under sail

Though the ships are only houses   gale / Pale
On the sky ~~are moving~~ seem to cross the sky line
~~Anchoring for the harbour~~
~~In which high winds behind them~~
~~And~~ ~~making~~ for a riper port ~~for port~~ Padstow harbour
~~Before~~ with the gale.

Draw the curtains! Shut the casement

I empty
I empty out a slipper full of sand

Draw the curtains! Shut the window
And still my bedroom slipper's full of sand

The Crystal Palace.

When to that shining palace oft I go
The minarets above, the fog below,
And when fair <u>Penge</u> betrays the lovely sight
Of villas, trams and gaslight ~~railways~~; from that height
Of which raised o'er ~~or~~ the ~~petty~~ lives of little men
I stand, viceregal, - then, my muse, Ah then,
Then, Betjeman, I see your brow and eyes
Raised like these gleaming towers to the skies,
While, on the nether chin, unshaven, grow
The muddy hairs, like Penge's fog, below.
Your thoughts are trams that roar, loud, low and near,
Your eye a nonconformist gasolier.

The Crystal Palace.

When to that shining palace oft I go
The minarets above, the fog below,
And when fair <u>Penge</u> betrays the lovely sight
Of villas trams and ~~railways~~ gaslight, from that height
On which raised o'er the ~~paltry~~ lives of little men
I stand, viceregal, — then, my muse, Ah then,
Then, Betjemen, I see your brow and eyes
Raised like these gleaming towers to the skies,
While, on the nether chin, unshaven, grow
The muddy hairs like Penge's fog, below.
Your thoughts are trams that roar, loud, low and neat,
Your eye a nonconformist gasolier.

Rome Unvisited

OSCAR WILDE (1854–1900)

1876, British Library, Add MS 81628, f.1r–v, folio 17.6 × 13.5 cm, pencil on paper.

This manuscript contains the final three stanzas from the poem 'Rome Unvisited' on the verso of a letter to an unknown recipient, possibly the poet Aubrey de Vere (1814–1902). The poem was published in *The Month and Catholic Review* in September 1876. There is a fourth stanza at the bottom of the manuscript, but it was not published as part of the poem. Wilde often wrote several successive drafts of his poetry and playscripts, and many different manuscripts and typescripts have survived from his prolific output. This manuscript differs significantly to the final published poem.

Oscar Wilde travelled to Italy in 1875, visiting Florence, Bologna, Venice and Milan. Inspiration in Venice yielded works such as 'San Miniato', a poem written in praise of the artist Fra Angelico (1395–1455) after visiting the church of San Miniato on 15 June. Ten days later Wilde had to curtail his trip because of insufficient funds and was unable to visit Rome. In response, and perhaps as a way of channelling his disappointment, he wrote 'Rome Unvisited', arguably one of his most religious poems.

Oscar Wilde, photograph by Napoleon Sarony, British Library, Add MS 81785 1.

Thanks – I agree with you about my last verse. but not on your grounds.
I don't think the words are beautiful enough for the thought
I think of these three – subject to your decision – I think that would wind it up better. What do you say?

Yours ever
Oscar.

And yet what changes time can bring!
The cycles of revolving years
May free my heart from all its fears
And teach my tongue / lips a song to sing –

Before yon field of troubled / ruined / gold
Is garnered into yellow sheavs
Or ere the autumns scarlet leavs
Flutter like birds a-down the wold

I may have won the bitter race
And set my fingers on the goal,
And ~~looked upon~~ looking though the Auriole
Beheld the Father face to face –

My limbs are overfaint to win
Or pass beyond the sacred gate,
Sleep, sleep, O troubled soul & wait
Till Gods own hand shall lead thee in.

I think that verse
wind it up better.
What do you
say?

Yours ever

Oscar

Magdalen College,
Oxford.

Thanks – I agree
with you about
my last verse – but
not on your grounds.
I don't think the
words are beautiful
enough for the thought.
I think of these
three – subject to
your decision –

And yet what change time can bring! –
The cycles of revolving years
May free my heart from all its fears
And teach my {tongue / lips} a song to sing –

Before yon field of {troubled / ruined} gold
Is garnered into yellow sheaves
Or ere the autumn's scarlet leaves
Flutter like birds adown the wold

I may have won the better race
And set my fingers on the goal,
And ~~looked upon~~ looking through the aureole
Behold the Father face to face –

My limbs are overfaint to win
Or pass beyond the sacred gate,
Sleep, sleep, O troubled soul & wait
Till God own hand shall lead thee in

Jamaica

ANDREW SALKEY (1928–1995)

***c.*1973**, British Library, Deposit 10310, folio 33 × 20.3 cm, typewritten on paper with pencil annotations.

Born in Panama in 1928 and raised in Jamaica, Andrew Salkey moved to Britain in the 1950s to further his education. He later described how, to learn more about his home island of Jamaica and its people, he 'got a British Museum reading card, and I went to the Public Record Office nearby'.[1] Through his research he:

> started learning about me and home and the history, because I damn well wanted to talk to Jamaicans about Jamaica … And therefore for the first time I began to realise myself as a colonial and us as a colony, and our history and the way that we were forever at somebody else's beck and call.

Salkey's research formed the basis of his 1955 prize-winning poem 'Jamaican Symphony', which he later reworked into the poem 'Jamaica', published in 1973. In the blurb for the first edition Salkey describes the poem as being 'about Jamaica, about the experience of the slave trade and of colonisation and about a struggle for freedom and for identity which still rages today among Caribbean peoples. It deals with political issues, but is not simply a political poem. Rather it conjures up the swirling colours, the music, the moods, the atmosphere of a bustling, suffering, vital island community.'[2]

This typescript version of the poem consists of fifteen parts. Part 1, titled 'Caribbea', contains the single poem 'Xaymaca' (the Taíno name for Jamaica). 'Caribbea' and 'Xamayca' are personified as female beings with the capacity to feel human emotions such as sorrow, loss, pain and shame. The poem 'Xamayca' asserts the history of the island while it was inhabited by the Arawak and Taino peoples, long before the arrival of Europeans and its subsequent colonisation. It emphasises the island's strength and resilience, and addresses the impact of colonialism. In writing this poem, Salkey attempts to redress the gap in knowledge left by colonial rule and to inspire Jamaicans to explore their history.

The pencil annotations on the first page of the draft are comments on the layout of the poem for publication. This typescript poem is part of Salkey's archive, which was acquired by the British Library in 2005.

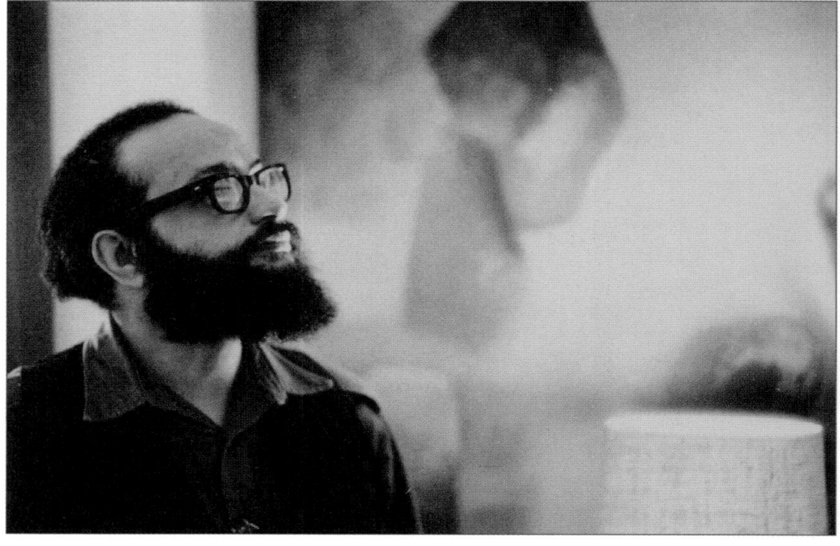

Andrew Salkey, photograph by Vanessa Stamford, British Library, Deposit 10310.

Part One CARIBBEA

Xaymaca

(i)

Caribbea,
knowledgeable,
patient,

raise your emancipated arms;
give your breasts,

maternal,
absolute,
elegant,
malachite eyes.

Caribbea,
moving in the morning,
shift your pearls;
bolster Xaymaca.

Our Sea,
prepare a path.

When the Doctor Breeze
and the Undertaker Wind
guess your age,
I see you wince;
I feel the shame you bear;
I, too, shudder,
knowing your age,
banded as the coconut palm.

I remember you aging like the coffee bean,
when the Arawaks screamed your name;
when, through the swift, slanting arbaletes
stinging the palpitating ground,
Port Maria bared her cocoa brown teeth
and Columbus found a wall of ghosts;
when, after scratches from lobster-claw,

LIZ BERRY (b.1980)

Princes End

April 2015, black ink on cream lined notebook paper.
First published in *Tipton Tales* (Multistory, 2017).

“

Princes End is an area of Tipton in the Black Country, near to where I grew up. It’s a deprived area, but one where there’s still a strong sense of tradition and community.

When my first son was a baby I was invited to spend the morning at a homing pigeon loft there. Bill, the loft owner, allowed me to hold one of his birds, a beautiful tippler hen. I’d never held a bird before and it reminded of the time I’d first held my son in the hospital: that mix of fear and wonder.

I wrote about the experience in my notebook, the place a poem always begins for me. As in so many of my messy early drafts, the bones of the poem are already present: the hen ‘lifted from her throne of straw’; the feathers she would slip; how the pigeon becomes both mother and child (‘she was you, she was me’), vulnerable and tender after the storm of the first year.

”

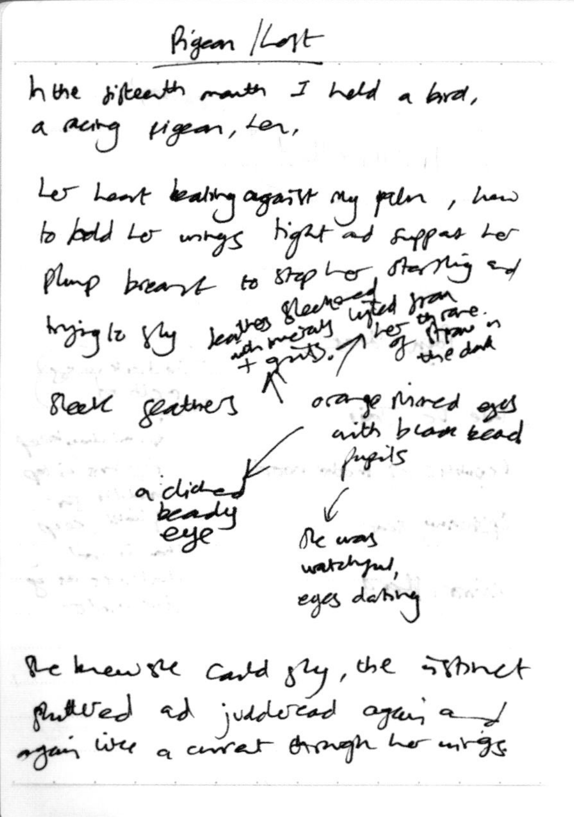

Pigeon/Loft

In the fifteenth month I held a bird, a racing pigeon, hen,

her heart beating against my palm, how to hold her wings tight and support her plump breast to stop her startling and trying to fly

sleek feathers > feathers sleekened with minerals and grit
> lifted from her throne of straw in the dark

orange rimmed eyes with black bead pupils > a cliched beady eye
> she was watchful, eyes darting

She knew she could fly, the instinct fluttered and juddered again and again like a current through her wings.

My hands were gentle but firm. I held her as I held you, a little fearful, wanting to seem calm, sooting (soothing), the life in her jimmucked as yours did.

I had known rage and fury and terror this year. I had known grief and loss and my fists had pummelled pillows and my own body but now I knew how to hold all that within me, to keep it within me, to know it was within me and still be gentle. I had seen the darkest part of my own heart.

Bill held up her wings to the sunlight and we looked at each feather, each feather she would slip in order to grow the next, the new wing…

hidden beneath the old.

I knew you. I knew her. I knew her brittle egg. Her chicks winging their way (now) from her to Scotland and Ireland. I knew her wings, her fear, her plump and tender and vulnerable breast, her watchfulness, her.

I held her as I first held you > an amateur, afraid to do it wrong, to frighten her
She was you, she was me. She was us both. > the shell, egg, the chick, the wing, the watchful eye, the flight, the feather slipped and forgotten on the loft floor.

Her little heart, as small as the working of a clock, I could (almost) see it, red and pulsing, glowing like the sweet raw heart of Mary, a little ruby, a jewel,

Broken Bottle

JEAN FOLLAIN (1903–1971), TRANSLATED BY DAVID GASCOYNE (1916–2001)

After 1978, British Library, Add MS 89011/2/12, folio 21 x 15 cm, blue ball-point pen on white paper.

Jean Follain studied law in Caen, France, and subsequently moved to Paris to practise as a lawyer. He first published poetry in 1933 and began to gain critical recognition. Follain's work is seen as marking an important moment at the end of Surrealism. Much of it explores themes of morality and the impermanence of life, often using everyday objects. Follain's contrasting of the seemingly mundane with the philosophical and existential is evidenced in 'Broken Bottle'. The quick move from the description of a broad urban environment to the broken bottle in splinters functions, in poetic terms, like a camera rapidly zooming in on an object for close contemplation.

David Gascoyne was a British poet, critic, writer, translator and Surrealist. As well as his own poetry and novels, he published translations of French Surrealist writers. *Man's Life Is This Meat* (1936) is his best-known work, bringing together his translations and his own writing. Gascoyne learned French reading and deciphering texts with a dictionary. His earliest piece of journalism, written while he was still a teenager, was an article on French poetry in *Everyman* magazine. By the time he was 17 he was fluent in the language, spending his birthday that year in Paris. Just before the outbreak of the Second World War Gascoyne lived in Paris, where he became friends with artists and writers such as Salvador Dalí (1904–1989) and Max Ernst (1891–1976). He was very much at the centre of twentieth-century writing, especially poetry. In an interview in 1991 he recalled attending a party thrown by T. S. Eliot and Faber, to mark the last issue of the *Criterion*, in which he had written a review of a book on Arthur Rimbaud.

This folio is part of a series of manuscripts in Gascoyne's archive entitled 'Some poems from *Présent Jour*'. *Présent Jour* was published by Galanis in 1978.

Jean Follain
Broken Bottle

Buildings close in the landscape
in the foreground are piles of wood
seated dreamers
and on the ground
the dark splinters
of a bottle lying there broken since a year ago
when a sudden disturbance
made someone drop it after singing a love-song.

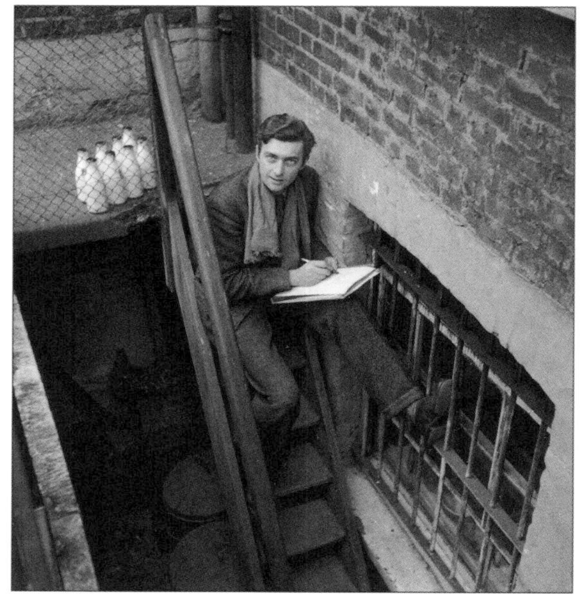

David Gascoyne, photograph by George Douglas.

Jean Follain

Broken Bottle

Buildings close in the landscape
in the foreground are piles of wood
seated dreamers
and on the ground
the dark splinters
of a bottle lying there broken since a year ago
when a sudden disturbance
made someone drop it after singing a love-song.

Composed upon Westminster Bridge, September 3, 1802

WILLIAM WORDSWORTH (1770–1850)

1806, British Library, Add MS 47864, f.30v, folio 18.5 × 11 cm, iron gall ink on laid paper.

This is a manuscript copy of William Wordsworth's 'Composed Upon Westminster Bridge'. It was sent to the publishers Longman, Rees, Hurst and Orme, along with other poems such as 'I Wandered Lonely as a Cloud' (see page 100), for inclusion in Wordsworth's book *Poems in Two Volumes* (1807). This copy of the poem was transcribed in 1806, although according to Wordsworth the original version was composed in 1802 when crossing Westminster Bridge 'on the roof of a coach, on my way to France'.[3] Wordsworth made changes to the poem before sending this manuscript to the publishers in 1806, including replacing the word 'heart' with 'soul' in line 11.

In the short poem, Wordsworth shows his ability to glorify the built environment as much as the natural one. Wordsworth's London is 'bright & glittering' in the 'smokeless air'. The image of the city contrasts with that of William Blake, whose London is dark, smoky and foreboding (see page 76). While Wordsworth's River Thames 'glideth at his own sweet will', Blake's flows dirty. Wordsworth's London contains temples which 'lie open unto the fields & to the sky' whereas Blake's has blackened churches which 'appal'.

Although this draft gives the original date of the poem as 1803, Wordsworth later corrected it to 1802. This manuscript and the others in the same volume were owned by Thomas Norton Longman (1771–1842), one of the publishers of *Poems in Two Volumes*, and were passed down through his family.

Composed upon Westminster Bridge
September 3rd 1803

Earth has not anything to shew more fair:
Dull would he be of ~~heart~~ soul who could pass by
A sight so touching in it's majesty:
This City now doth like a ~~G~~garment wear
The beauty of the morning; silent, bare,
Ships, towers, domes, theatres, & temples lie
Open unto the fields, & to the sky;
All bright & glittering in the smokeless air.
Never did Sun more beautifully steep
In his first splendor valley, rock, or hill;
Ne'er saw I, never felt, a calm so deep!
The River glideth at his own sweet will:
Dear God! the very houses seem asleep;
And all that mighty heart is lying still.

14

Composed upon Westminster Bridge
September 3rd 1803

Earth has not any thing to shew more fair:
Dull would he be of ~~heart~~ soul who could pass by
A sight so touching in its majesty:
This City now doth like a garment wear
The beauty of the morning; silent, bare,
Ships, towers, domes, theatres, & temples lie
Open unto the fields, & to the sky;
All bright & glittering in the smokeless air.
Never did Sun more beautifully steep
In his first splendor valley, rock, or hill;
Ne'er saw I, never felt, a calm so deep!
The River glideth at his own sweet will:
Dear God! the very houses seem asleep;
And all that mighty heart is lying still.

N. B. next Sonnet begins
Beloved Vale &c See No 15

XI

Autumn Morning at Cambridge.

I ran out in the morning, & the air was clean & new
And all the grass was glittering & gray with autumn dew
And I ran out to the apple-tree & pulled an apple down
And all the bells were ringing in the old gray town.

Down in the town, off the bridges & the grass
They are sweeping up the leaves to let the people pass
Sweeping up the old leaves, golden-reds & browns,
While the men go to lecture, with the wind in their gowns.

Autumn Morning at Cambridge

FRANCES CORNFORD (1886–1960)

1908, British Library, Add MS 56332, f.11r, folio 17.6 × 11 cm, black ink on lined paper in a blue-card-bound notebook with a black spine.

Frances Cornford (née Darwin) was born in the city of Cambridge in 1886 and died there in 1960. Both of her parents taught at the university. Her father, Francis Darwin (1848–1925), the third son of Charles Darwin (1809–1882), was a lecturer in botany, while her mother, Ellen Wordsworth Crofts (1856–1903), was a lecturer in English at Newnham College.

Cornford met her husband Francis Cornford (1874–1943) in Cambridge when he played the lead role in the Marlowe Society's 1908 performance of Milton's *Comus*. Francis was a student at Trinity College and later Laurence Professor of Ancient Philosophy. They married in 1909.

Cornford began to write poetry at the age of 16 and soon became distinguished among the poets of her age. Unswayed by the Modernist techniques of poets such as Ezra Pound (1885–1972) and T. S. Eliot, her poetry is marked by a quiet humour. She became well known for the poem 'To a Fat Lady Seen from a Train' (1910), which caused her some embarrassment.

Cornford drafted her poetry in notebooks, and poems often appear more than once. Ten of her notebooks are held as part of her archive at the British Library. This notebook was dedicated to her father and contains ten poems that appear in her first collection, *Poems*, which was published in 1910. 'Autumn Morning at Cambridge' presents an affectionate view of the town, which was her home for most of her life.

Autumn Morning at Cambridge.

I ran out in the morning, & the air was clean & new
And all the grass was glittering & gray with autumn dew
And I ran out to the apple-tree & pulled an apple down
And all the bells were ringing in the old gray town.

Down in the town, off the bridges & the grass
They are sweeping up the leaves to let the people pass
Sweeping up the old leaves, golden-reds & browns,
While the men go to lecture, with the wind in their gowns.

Cover of Frances Cornford's poetry notebook, British Library, Add MS 56332.

Train Poem – A Collaboration

LEE HARWOOD (1939–2015) AND JOHN ASHBERY (1927–2017)

1965, British Library, Add MS 88998/6/3, folios 25.5 × 18.5 cm, black ink on paper; black ink with pencil annotations on paper.

'Train Poem' was written during a rail journey between Paris and Grenoble in 1965. It was a collaboration between the English poet Lee Harwood and the American poet John Ashbery, whose work was enormously influential on Harwood in the 1960s. At the time the poem was written, Harwood and Ashbery were lovers. Spontaneously composed, the poem not only captures the passing French scenery framed by the window but also conveys an internal emotional landscape of veiled eroticism, as the two poets counter and encounter one another.

It is difficult to distinguish between the handwriting of the two poets in the original manuscript. Harwood has written on the back: 'Both our script – so alike: & this by chance & a real though pleasant surprise'.

Readers have often speculated about who wrote which words. The archive of Lee Harwood, acquired by the British Library in 2012, includes not only the original joint manuscript but also a subsequent typescript copy (hitherto unpublished), in which Harwood has underlined Ashbery's words. As the typescript 'key' reveals, the pattern of their poetic exchange is not a simple arrangement in which each poet wrote a single line before passing pen and paper across to the other. The authorship switches playfully within lines, as the poem, which has a restless, surreal quality, abruptly shifts grammatically and tonally.

'Train Poem – A Collaboration' was first published in Harwood's limited edition collection *The Man with Blue Eyes* (New York, 1966) and subsequently reprinted in *The White Room* (London, 1968).

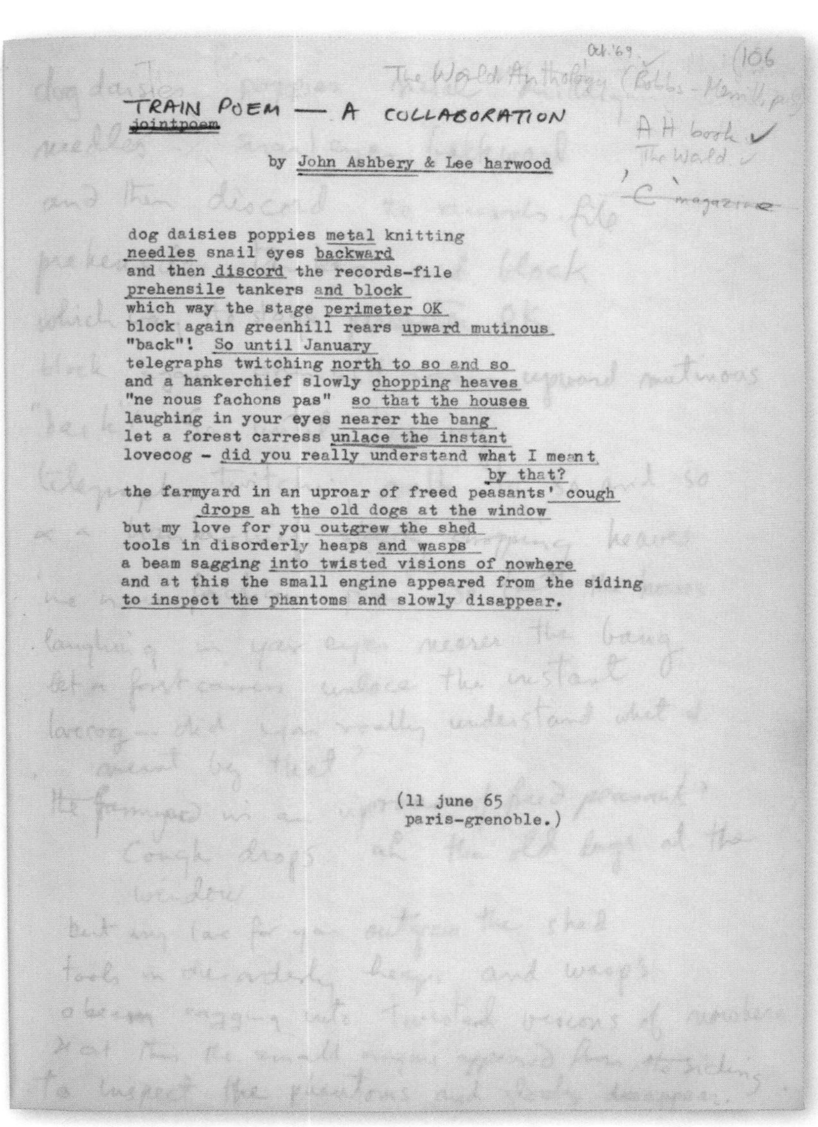

TRAIN POEM — A COLLABORATION
~~jointpoem~~

by John Ashbery & Lee harwood

dog daisies poppies metal knitting
needles snail eyes backward
and then discord the records-file
prehensile tankers and block
which way the stage perimeter OK
block again greenhill rears upward mutinous
"back"! So until January
telegraphs twitching north to so and so
and a hankerchief slowly chopping heaves
"ne nous fachons pas" so that the houses
laughing in your eyes nearer the bang
let a forest carress unlace the instant
lovecog - did you really understand what I meant
by that?
the farmyard in an uproar of freed peasants' cough
drops ah the old dogs at the window
but my love for you outgrew the shed
tools in disorderly heaps and wasps
a beam sagging into twisted visions of nowhere
and at this the small engine appeared from the siding
to inspect the phantoms and slowly disappear.

(11 june 65
paris-grenoble.)

dog daisies poppies metal knitting
needles snail eyes backward
and then discord the records-file
prehensile tankers and block
which way the stage perimeter OK
block again green hill rears upward mutinous
"back"! So until January
telegraphs twitching north to so and so
& a handkerchief slowly dropping heaves
'ne nous fachons pas' so that the horses
laughing in your eyes nearer the bang
let a fast camera unlace the instant
lovecog – did you really understand what I
meant by that?
the farmyard in an uproar of freed peasants'
Cough drops ah the old days at the
window
but my love for you outgrew the shed
tools in disorderly heaps and wasps
a beam sagging into twisted visions of nowhere
& at this the small engine appeared from the siding
to inspect the phantoms and slowly disappear.

Les petites vieilles (The little old women)

CHARLES BAUDELAIRE (1821–1867)

1859, British Library, Zweig MS 136, f.1v, folio 20.8 × 13.3 cm, pen and ink on a single sheet, written on both sides.

This poem was published in Charles Baudelaire's compilation *Les fleurs du mal* in 1857. Following its publication, Baudelaire was prosecuted for offending public morals and ordered to remove six poems from the volume. The author, artist and politician Victor Hugo (1802–1885) supported Baudelaire during this episode, and 'Les petites vieilles' is one of three poems from the volume dedicated to him. 'Les petites vieilles' is from the 'Tableaux parisienne' section of *Les fleurs du mal*, a series of social observations on Parisian society made by Baudelaire at a time when the city was undergoing dramatic redevelopment. A stark juxtaposition to modernity, Baudelaire's old women represent the displacement of tradition in the wake of progress.

Baudelaire travels through Paris, watching and observing the little old women who dance, drag, trot and crawl. He even follows one woman through parks and watches her as she sits, listening to bands of soldiers. Baudelaire likens the small size of the women to that of children, and suggests that their coffins would be of similar size. He continues with the simile, showing that the new Paris is hostile to the women who, nearing death, are destined for another cradle.

This fair copy manuscript was dedicated to and copied out for Victor Hugo. The first three verses of the poem have been transcribed and translated here. This manuscript is part of the Stefan Zweig Collection at the British Library.

ABOVE: Charles Baudelaire, photograph by Étienne Carjet, British Library, General Reference Collection P.P.1931.peg.

À Victor Hugo
II. Fantômes Parisiens. Les petites vieilles

Dans les plis sinueux des vieilles capitales
Où tout, même l'horreur, tourne aux enchantements,
Je guette, obéissant à mes humeurs fatales
Des êtres décrépits, singuliers et charmants.

Ces monstres disloqués furent jadis des femmes:
Eponine ou Laïs! Monstres brisés, bossus
Ou tordus, aimons-les! ce sont encor des âmes.
Sous des jupons troués et sous de froids tissus

Ils rampent, flagellés par les bises iniques,
Frémissant au fracas roulant des omnibus,
Et serrant sur leur flanc, ainsi que des reliques,
Un petit ~~[illegible]~~ sac brodé de fleurs ou de rebus;

To Victor Hugo
II. Parisian Ghosts. The Little Old Women

In sinuous folds of cities old and grim,
Where all things, even horror, turn to grace,
I follow, in obedience to my whim,
Strange, feeble, charming creatures round the place.

These crooked freaks were women in their pride,
Fair Eponine or Laïs! Humped and bent,
Love them! Because they still have souls inside.
Under their draughty skirts in tatters rent,

They crawl: a vicious wind their carrion rides;
From the deep roar of traffic see them cower,
Pressing like precious relics to their sides
Some satchel stitched with mottoes or a flower.

2

Exaspéré comme un ivrogne qui voit double,
Je rentrai, je fermai ma porte, épouvanté,
Malade et morfondu, l'esprit fiévreux et trouble,
Blessé par le mystère et par l'absurdité.

Vainement ma raison voulait prendre la barre ;
La tempête en jouant déroutait ses efforts,
Et mon âme dansait, dansait, vieille gabarre
Sans mâts, sur une mer monstrueuse et sans bords.

à Victor Hugo.

II. ~~Fantômes Parisiens.~~ Les petites vieilles.

1

Dans les plis sinueux des vieilles capitales,
Où tout même l'horreur tourne aux enchantements,
Je guette, obéissant à mes humeurs fatales,
Des êtres décrépits, singuliers et charmants.

Ces monstres disloqués furent jadis des femmes,
Éponine ou Laïs ! Monstres brisés, bossus
~~Ou~~ tordus, aimons-les ! Ce sont encor des âmes.
Sous des jupons troués et sous de froids tissus

Ils rampent, flagellés par les bises iniques,
Frémissant au fracas roulant des omnibus,
Et serrant sur leur flanc ainsi que des reliques,
Un ~~petit~~ petit sac brodé de fleurs ou de rébus ;

Le rébus n'est pas de mon invention. Il y a dans le journal de La Mésangère des gravures de mode où le réticule est orné de rébus brodés.

chapter 5

THE NATURAL WORLD

The natural world encompasses landscape, weather, plants and animals. Poetry lends itself to the exploration and celebration of these subjects.

The Romantic movement brought the beauty and diversity of the natural world to prominence in literature, painting and music in the late eighteenth and early nineteenth centuries. William Wordsworth's 'I Wandered Lonely as a Cloud' encapsulates a Romantic vision of the Lake District and is now one of the most famous poems in English literature. Influenced by the Romantics, Charlotte Brontë wrote poetry from a young age. Like Wordsworth, she celebrated the beauty of the natural world in her writing. In the poem 'Matin' Brontë represents the glory of the rising sun over fields, trees and flowers.

While many poets have emphasised the Romantic or idyllic in their depictions of the natural world, others have been inspired to write about the more practical side of our connection to nature. In his poem 'Mending Wall', Robert Frost describes the relationship between himself and his neighbour as custodians of the land, symbolised by the wall between their properties. The familiar sound of the BBC shipping forecast, with its rhythmical listing of regions around the British coast, is recreated in Seamus Heaney's poem, 'Forecast' ('Glanmore Sonnets, VII'). In 'The Three Ships' Philip Larkin uses the descriptions of the ships and the weather they face to stress the importance of preparation and determination to succeeding in life. Kathleen Jamie's 'What the Clyde said, after COP26', written at the time of the 2021 United Nations Climate Change Conference, personifies the river to convey the effects of environmental damage.

A number of the poems in this chapter depict animals and employ both realism and Romanticism in different measures. The strength and stealth of the tiger inspired William Blake's poem of reverence for the animal. Designed to be performed with elaborate sets and costumes, Ben Jonson's *Masque of Queenes* includes animals in a spell or charm spoken by witches. Jonson describes a scene alive with creatures set against a burning sky with a red moon. T. S. Eliot's poems about cats, which have become modern classics, were originally written in private letters to the family of a friend. In 'The Law of the Jungle' Rudyard Kipling laid down the rules for the wolf pack to follow to ensure balance and peace across the species of the jungle.

Weather, animals, plants, landscape and seascape are all represented in this collection of poems, and while some depictions delight, others are disconcerting.

I wandered lonely as a cloud

WILLIAM WORDSWORTH (1770–1850)

1804–7, British Library, Add MS 47864, f.80r, folio 20.3 × 13 cm, iron gall ink on laid paper.

'I wandered lonely as a cloud', also known as 'Daffodils', is one of the most famous poems in English literature. Written by William Wordsworth between 1804 and 1807, it was inspired by a walk the poet and his sister, Dorothy, took around Ullswater in the Lake District, in 1802.

This manuscript forms part of a group of poems, now bound in one volume, that Wordsworth sent to his publishers, Longman, Hurst, Rees and Orme between 1806 and 1807. Many of the manuscripts in this group were copied out either by Wordsworth's wife, Mary (née Hutchinson, 1770–1859), or his sister Dorothy. It is likely that this manuscript was written out by Mary with William's input. Although Wordsworth had agreed to publish a single volume, the manuscripts were ultimately published as *Poems in Two Volumes* (1807). This folio shows the poet engaging with the business of writing and publishing. Along the upper edge there is a note for the printer, in which Wordsworth explains where he would like the poem to sit in the published volume. His concern over the order of the published poems shows his awareness of how his audience would engage with the collection. While the manuscript displays instructions to the printer, it also shows Wordsworth making a change to the text itself: the first line begins 'I wandered like a lonely…', which has been crossed out and replaced with the now famous line 'I wandered lonely as a cloud'. After first publishing the poem, Wordsworth made more changes to it and the final version appeared in 1815.

The paper on which this poem and others in the volume are written was cut down from a larger sheet, which demonstrates that the Wordsworths adapted the material available to them at the time. Using different-sized smaller sheets gave them the flexibility of working with the physical poems as they considered their final placement in the published book.

To the Printer
(after the Poem (in the set under the title
of 'Moods of my own mind') beginning ~~'They~~
'The Cock is crowing' please to insert
the two following properly number'd, & number
the succeeding ones accordingly)

~~I wandered like a lonely~~
I wandered lonely as a Cloud
That floats on high oer Vales and Hills,
When all at once I saw a crowd
A host of dancing Daffodils;
Along the Lake beneath the trees,
Ten thousand dancing in the breeze.

The Waves beside them danced, but they
Outdid the sparkling Waves in glee:—
A Poet could not but be gay
In such a laughing company:
I gaz'd – and gaz'd – but little thought
What wealth the shew to me had brought:

For oft when on my Couch I lie
In vacant, or in pensive mood,
They flash upon that inward eye
Which is the bliss of solitude,
And then my heart with pleasure fills,
And dances with the Daffodils.

Who fancied what a pretty sight
This Rock would be if edged around
With living Snowdrops? circled bright!

To the Printer

After the Poem (in the set under the title of "Moods of my own mind") beginning "The Cock is crowing" please to insert the two following properly numbered, & number the succeeding ones accordingly)

~~I wandered like a lonely~~

I wandered lonely as a Cloud
That floats on high o'er Vales and Hills,
When all at once I saw a crowd
A host of dancing Daffodils;
Along the Lake, beneath the trees
Ten thousand dancing in the breeze.

The Waves beside them danced, but they
Outdid the sparkling Waves in glee—
A Poet could not but be gay
In such a laughing company:
I gaz'd – and gaz'd – but little thought
What wealth the shew to me had brought.

For oft when on my couch I lie
In vacant, or in pensive mood,
They flash upon that inward eye
Which is the bliss of solitude
And then my heart with pleasure fills,
And dances with the Daffodils.

Who fancied what a pretty sight
This Rock would be if edged around
With living Snowdrops? circlet bright!

Forecast (Glanmore Sonnets, VII)

SEAMUS HEANEY (1939–2013)

Before 1979, British Library, Add MS 74089, f.1r, folio 30 × 20 cm, typewritten with black and blue ink annotations.

The shipping forecast has saved countless lives at sea, but it also holds a fascination to many listening from home. To a non-mariner listener the unfamiliar names and incomprehensible numbers have a reassuring and mesmerising sound, like a lullaby. These marine weather forecasts, warning ships about storms and gales around the British Isles, began in the 1860s by telegraph and moved to BBC radio in 1924. They had a brief hiatus during the Second World War when it was thought that they might benefit the enemy.

This typescript is an early draft of Heaney's poem 'Glanmore Sonnets, VII' (1979; here just called 'Forecast'). It differs substantially from the published version, with much of the second half of the poem later being rewritten. The blue ink annotations around the poem show Heaney working on new lines. The language of the poem reflects changes in the weather, from gales to calm seas. The last typescript line in this draft is 'tempestuous', but in the final version 'the sky clears' and a 'haven' is found.

The forecast has inspired many artists, poets and songwriters over the years including Peter Collyer (b.1952), Mark Power (b.1959), Carol Ann Duffy (b.1955), Blur and Radiohead. Part of the broadcast even featured in the opening ceremony of the London 2012 Olympic Games. Heaney's poem captures the essence of the forecast and is a popular tribute to a British institution that is a source of national pride. Heaney presented this poem to the British Library on 3 April 1998.

And learn
Inspiring
~~Driving~~ And drive the trawlers to the lee of Wicklow
~~Tomorrow~~ Yesterday morning, on a swell like mortar
'L'Etoile', 'La Belle Helene', 'Le Guillenot'
Nursed their bright names like tails between their legs
~~Where~~ Rode far from home, [nursing their illegible names]

FORECAST
Dogger, Rockall, Malin, Irish Sea.
Green, ~~swift~~ upsurges, North Atlantic flux
Conjured by that strong peremptory voice,
Collapse into a sibilant penumbra.
Midnight and close-down. Sirens of the tundra,
Of seal-road, eel-road, keel-road, whale-road, raise
Their wind-compounded keen behind the baize.
Biscay, Iceland, Minches, Shetland, Orkney:
Unforgettable annunciation
The boy attended to and clutched like a spar
Cast up inevitably from commotion
On to bewildered shores; and now his house
Is built around it, as round the pole star
Those ~~names go wheeling~~ demarcations, fixed and ~~nebulous~~ tempestuous.

Orkney,
Faroes, Minches, Shetland,
Fo Cromarty:

~~I attended as a boy~~
[~~Geat~~]
Backwards and abysses
O auditory imagination
~~Tomorrow~~ Yesterday morning, trawlers in Wicklow Bay
Sheltering on a swell like rolling mortar
Were factual, endangered. For the first time

This morning, trawlers sheltered in W.B.
On a swell like fresh and heaving mortar

~~And learn~~

~~Inspiring~~ And dive

~~Driving~~ the trawlers to the lee of Wicklow.

~~Tomorrow~~ Yesterday morning, on a swell like mortar

"L'Etoile" "La Belle Helene," "Le Guillemot"

Nursed their bright names like tails between their legs

~~Rode~~ far from home, nursing their bright names

FORECAST

Dogger, Rockall, Malin, Irish Sea.
Green, ~~swift~~ upsurges, North Atlantic flux
Conjured by that strong peremptory voice,
Collapse into a sibilant penumbra.
Midnight and close-down. Sirens of the tundra,
Of seal-road, eel-road, keel-road, whale-road, raise
Their wind-compounded keen behind the baize.
Biscay, Iceland, Minches, Shetland, Orkney:
Unforgettable annunciation
The boy attended to and clutched like a spar
Cast up inevitably ~~xx~~ from commotion
On to bewildered shores; and now his house
Is built around it, as round the pole star
Those ~~names go wheeling~~ demarcations, fixed and ~~nebulous.~~ tempestuous

Orkney,

Faroes, Minches, Shetland,
Cromarty:

~~I attended as a boy~~

~~Great~~

Backwards and abysses

O auditory imagination

~~Tomorrow~~ Yesterday morning, trawlers in Wicklow Bay
Sheltering on a swell like rolling mortar
Were factual, endangered. For the first time

This morning, trawlers sheltered in W. B.
On a swell like fresh and heaving mortar

The Law of the Jungle

RUDYARD KIPLING (1865–1936)

1892–4, British Library, Add MS 45540, f.171r, folio 24.7 × 21.7 cm, ink on blue paper.

The central characters in Rudyard Kipling's *The Jungle Book* (1894) are the animals in the forests of Seoni, in the central Indian state of Madhya Pradesh, who live and talk with Mowgli, a human child raised by wolves. Mowgli's experience reflects Kipling's feelings of abandonment when his parents left him and his sister alone at school together in England before they returned to India.

Kipling was also inspired to write the stories by living in India as a child and later as a journalist. He borrowed freely from the Indian traditional stories he had been told, such as those in the *Panchatantra* (ancient Indian animal fables written in Sanskrit) and the *Jataka* tales (sacred Buddhist literature depicting previous incarnations, both human and animal, of Buddha).

Poems appear at certain points in the stories and one of the most famous is 'The Law of the Jungle', which sets out the rules for the wolf pack. Kipling notes at the top of the page of this manuscript draft that the bear Baloo teaches the wolf cubs further little laws which they 'could never carry … in their heads'.

Kipling drafted this poem over two folios, the first of which is shown and transcribed opposite and overleaf. The draft forms part of the complete *Jungle Book* stories that was bequeathed to the British Museum by Kipling's widow, Caroline (née Starr Balestier, 1862–1939). Alongside the text Kipling has doodled his versions of the characters, including Mowgli, Bagheera (a black panther) and Shere Khan (a Bengal tiger).

The Law of the Jungle

This is as much of the Law of the Jungle as applies to the wolves. Baloo taught a great many more little laws to the wolf-cubs but they could never carry them in their heads. The wood and water laws, are of course, separate.

Now This is the Law of the Jungle — as old and as true as the sky.
And the Wolf That shall keep it may prosper; but the Wolf that shall ~~br~~ break it must die. As the creepers That girdle the tree-trunk, the Law runneth forward and back For the strength of the pack is the wolf and the strength of the wolf is the Pack

1.
1 Wash daily from nose-tip to tail-tip; drink deeply, but never too deep: And remember the night is for hunting; and forget not the day is for sleep.

2.
2 Tabaqui may follow the Tiger, but, Cub, when thy whiskers are grown Remember the wolf is a hunter. Go forth and get food of thy own

3.
3 Keep peace with the Lords of the Jungle — the Tiger, the Panther, and bear And trouble not Hathi the Silent, and mock not the Boar in his lair.

4.
9 If ye kill before midnight be silent, [and wake not the woods with your bay] lest ye frighten the deer [from the crop, and] thy brothers go empty away.

5.
10 The ~~lair~~ lair of the wolf is his refuge and where he has [made him his] home Not even the council may enter. Not even the Head Wolf may come.

The Law of the Jungle

This is as much of the Law of the Jungle as applies to the wolves. Baloo taught a great many more little laws to the wolf-cubs but they could never carry them in their heads. The Wood and Water Laws are, of course, separate.

ital
Now this is the Law of the Jungle — as old and as true as the sky.
And the wolf that shall keep it may prosper; but the wolf that shall break it must die.
As the creepers that girdle the tree trunk, the Law runneth forward and back:
For the strength of the pack is the Wolf and the strength of the Wolf is the Pack

1.

1 Wash daily from nose-tip to tail-tip: drink deeply but never too deep:
And remember the night is for hunting: and forget not the day is for sleep.

2.

2 Tabaqui may follow the Tiger but, Cub, when thy whiskers are grown
Remember the wolf is a hunter. Go forth and get food of thy own

3.

3 Keep peace with the Lords of the Jungle — the Tiger, the Panther and Bear
And trouble not Hathi the Silent and mock not the Boar in his lair.

4.

9 If ye kill before midnight be silent, [and wake not the woods with your bay]
Lest ye frighten the deer [from the crop, and] thy brothers go empty away.

5

10 The lair of the wolf is his refuge and where he has [made him his] home
Not even the Council may enter: not even the Head Wolf may come.

6.

11 The lair of the wolf is his refuge but where [he has digged it] too plain
The Council shall send him a message and so he shall hide it again

7

4 When Pack meets with Pack in the Jungle and neither will go from the trail
Lie down till the leaders have spoken. It may be fair words shall prevail

8.

5 When ye fight with a wolf of the pack [ye must] fight him alone and afar
Lest thy brothers take side in the quarrel and the Pack be diminished by war.

9.

8a The head wolf must spring at the neck but if he shall fail of his hold
shall call the Full Council and kill him because he is weakened & old.

10

6 When ye plunder his kill from a weaker, devour not all in thy pride
Pack-right is the right of the meanest so leave him the head and the hide

11.

7 If ye meet with good meat in the jungle and if it be laid on the ground
and the path be made easy to snatch it run swiftly away or go round.

12.

8 Ye may kill for yourselves and your mates and your cubs as they need and ye can
But kill not for pleasure of killing and seven times never kill man.

Illustrations of Mowgli, Bagheera, Baloo, Kaa and Shere Khan from *The Jungle Books*, Rudyard Kipling, British Library, Add MS 45540 ff.13v and 17v.

Rudyard Kipling, etching by William Strang, British Library, L.R.301.bb.6.

6.

11 The Lair of the wolf is his refuge, but where [he has digged it] too plainThe Council shall send him a message and so he shall hide it again

7.

4 When Pack meets with Pack in the jungle and neither will go from the trail lie down till the leaders have [~~illegible~~] spoken. It may be fair words shall prevail

8.

5 When ye fight with a wolf of the pack, [ye must] fight him alone and afar Lest thy brothers take side in the quarrel and the Pack be diminished by war.

9.

8a ~~9~~ The Head wolf must spring at the buck ~~and~~ but if he shall fail of his hold He shall call the Full Council and Kill him because he is weakened & old.

10.

6 When ye plunders his Kill from a weaker, devour not all in thy pride Pack-right is the right of the meanest so leave him the head and the hide

11.

7 If ye meet with good meat in the jungle and if it be laid on the ground And the path be made easy to snatch it run swiftly away or go round.

12.

8 Ye may kill for yourselves and your mates and your cubs as they need and ye can But kill not for pleasure of killing and seven times never kill man.

Charme

BEN JONSON (1572–1637)

1609, British Library, Royal MS 18 A XLV, f.4v, volume 21.4 x 17.2 cm, folio 21 x 16.5 cm, iron gall ink on laid paper.

Ben Jonson, engraving by Robert Vaughan, British Library, G.11630.

This is a folio from the original manuscript for Ben Jonson's *Masque of Queenes*, which was performed at Whitehall Palace in February 1609. A masque was a form of staged entertainment that combined song, music, dance, speech, mime and highly decorative sets and costumes. Much of the content was allegorical and designed to promote the Stuart monarchy and its divine right to rule. The *Masque of Queenes* is one of the earlier works written by Jonson for the house of Stuart, and was performed with a stage set designed by Inigo Jones (1573–1652).

Masques contained elements within them, known as anti-masques, which acted in contrast to the overall theme of the storyline and were set up in antithesis to themes of order and virtue. In the section here Johnson uses twelve dancing witches, who utter charms or incantations to rouse their leader. The folio shows the words from the third 'Charme' which was part of the anti-masque. The imagery draws heavily on animals and their dwellings, and evokes meteorological phenomena such as a red moon and a burning sky. The words alone are powerful when performed; that they were spoken against a moving, colourful, musical backdrop must have made them all the more dramatic.

This manuscript was written by Jonson in a stylised Italian cursive hand and presented to King James VI of Scotland and I of England. It is part of the Royal Collection of manuscripts at the British Library.

3. CHARME.

The Owle is abroad, the Bat, and the Toade,
And so is the Cat-à-Mountaine;
The Ant, and the Mole sit both in a hole,
And Frog peepes out o' the fountayne;
The Dogges, they do bay, and the Timbrells play,
The[r].. spindle is now à turning;
The Moone it is red, and the starres are fled,
But all the Skye is à burning:
The[l.] Ditch is made, and our nayles the spade,
W^{t}h pictures full, of Waxe, and of Wooll;
Theyr livers I stick, w^{t}h needles quick;
There lackes but the blood, to make up the flood.
Quickly, Dame, then; bring your part in,
Spur, spur upon little [m.] Martin,
Merely, merely, make him sayle,
A Worme in his mouth, and a thorne in o' tayle,
Fire above, and fire below,
W^{t}h a Whip i' your hand, to make him goe.

THE MASQVE OF QVEENES.

Quickly, come away:
For we, all, stay.

they ride, often, to theyr solemnities, as appeares by theyr confessions in *Rem.* and *Bodin. ibid.* His Matie also remembers the story of the Divells appearance to those of *Calicut*, in that forme. *Dæmonol. lib. ij. Cap. iij.*

i. Of the greene Cock we have no other ground (to confesse ingenuously) than a vulgar fable of a Witch, that wth a Cock of that colour, and a bottome of blewe thred, would transport her selfe through the ayre; and so escap'd (at the time of her being brought to execution) from the hand of Justice. It was a tale, when I went to Schoole. And somewhat there is like it in *Mar. Delrio. Disqui. Mag. lib. ij. Quæst. vj.* of one *Zyto*, a *Bohemian*, that, among other his dexterities, *aliquoties equis rhedarijs vectum, gallis gallinaceis ad epirrhedium suum alligatis, subsequebatur.*

Nor yet? Nay, then,
Wee'll try her agen.

3. CHARME.

The Owle is abroad, the Bat, and the Toade,
And so is the Cat-a-Mountaine;
The Ant, and the Mole sit both in a hole,
And Frog peepes out o'the fountayne;
The Dogges, they do bay, and the Timbrells play,
The [k] Spindle is now a turning;
The Moone it is red, and the starres are fled,
But all the Skye is a burning:
The [l] Ditch is made, and or nayles the spade,
Wth pictures full, of waxe, and of wooll;
Theyr livers I stick, wth needles quick
There lackes but the blood, to make vp the flood.
Quickly, *Dame*, then; bring yor part in,
Spur, spur vpon little m *Martin*,
Merely, merely, make him sayle,
A worme in his mouth, and a thorne in's tayle,
Fire above, and fire below,
Wth a whip, i'your hand, to make him goe.

k. All this is but a *Periphrasis* of the night, in theyr charme, and theyr applying themselves to it wth theyr Instruments; whereof ye Spindle, in antiquitye, was ye cheife; and (beside the testemony of *Theocritus in Pharmaceutria*, who only vsd it in amorous affayres) was of speciall act to the troubling of the *Moone*. To wch *Martial* alludes, *lib. ix. Epi. xxx. Quæ nunc Thessalico Lunā deducere rhombo, &c.* And *lib. xij. Epig. lvij. Cum secta Colcho Luna vapulat rhombo.*

l. This rite also of making a ditch wth theyr nayles, is frequent wth

Hom

O, now,

The Tyger

WILLIAM BLAKE (1757–1827)

1793–4, British Library, Add MS 49460, ff.55v–56r, volume 15.9 × 19.7 cm, black ink on paper within a notebook.

'The Tyger' is one of the most famous poems in English Literature and its opening line, 'Tyger Tyger, burning bright', is particularly iconic. Written by the poet, artist and engraver William Blake, the poem celebrates the glory of the tiger but also questions why God would make such a ferocious and dangerous animal. The poem was published in Blake's *Songs of Innocence and of Experience* and works in opposition to Blake's poem of innocence, 'The Lamb'.

This is an early draft of Blake's poem 'The Tyger' that was written when Blake was working back through his notebook. It appears upside down in the volume with the folio number at the bottom of the page. 'The Tyger' sits next to a draft of the poem 'London' (page 76) and was written across two pages. The right-hand page (f.55v) features a pencil sketch of Satan intended for an illustrated edition of *Paradise Lost*. 'The Tyger' begins on the bottom right of the left-hand page (f.56r). The first three stanzas are very similar to the final version of the poem, but Blake was not happy with the following five lines of text and crossed them out. He then added another stanza before the draft on this page was finished, which is a slightly altered repetition of the first stanza.

Blake moved across to the right-hand page and drafted another stanza on the bottom left-hand side. He then altered certain words across both pages of the poem and rearranged the lines using the numbers to the left of the draft. The title of the poem was added last. Another draft of the poem, which is missing two stanzas, sits to the right of the right-hand page.

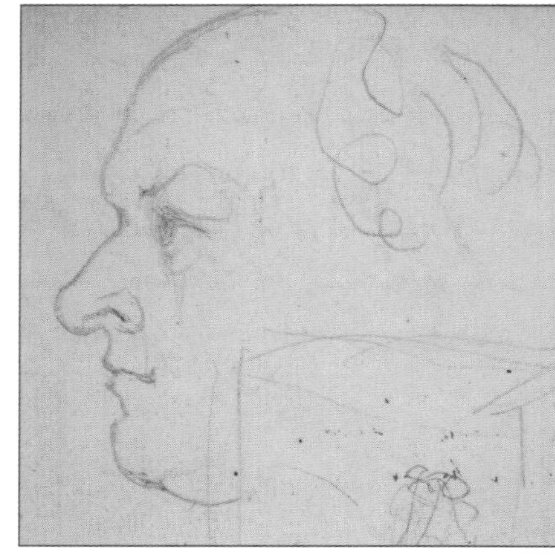

ABOVE: William Blake, self-portrait, pencil, British Library, Add MS 49460 f.35r.

The Tyger
1 Tyger Tyger burning bright
In the forests of the night
What immortal hand or eye
~~Dare Could~~ frame thy fearful symmetry

2 ~~In what~~ [~~Burnt in~~] distant deeps or skies
~~The cruel Burnt the~~ fire of thine eyes
On what wings dare he aspire
What the hand dare seize the fire

3 And what shoulder & what art
Could twist the sinews of thy heart
And when thy heart began to beat
What dread hand & what dread feet

~~Could fetch it from the furnace deep~~
~~And in thy horrid ribs dare steep~~
~~In the well of sanguine woe~~
~~In what clay & in what [mould]~~
~~Were thy [eyes of] fury rolld~~

4 ~~What~~ Where the hammer ~~what~~ where the chain
In what furnace was thy brain
What the anvil what ~~the arm arm grasp [clasp]~~ dread grasp
~~Could~~ Dare its deadly terrors~~[clasp] grasp~~ clasp

6 Tyger Tyger burning bright
In the forests of the night
What immortal hand & eye
Dare ~~form~~ frame thy fearful symmetry

London

I wander thro each dirty street
Near where the dirty Thames does flow
And ~~see~~ mark in every face I meet
Marks of weakness marks of woe

In every cry of every man
~~In every voice of every child~~ In every infants cry of fear
In every voice in every ban
The ~~german~~ mind forgd ~~links I hear~~ manacles I hear

~~But most~~ How the chimney sweepers cry
~~Blackens oer the churches walls~~ Every blackning church appalls
And the hapless soldiers sigh
Runs in blood down palace walls

~~But most the midnight harlots curse~~
~~From every dismal street I hear~~
~~Weaves around the marriage hearse~~
~~And blasts the new born infants tear~~

But most ~~thro wintry~~ streets I hear
How the midnight harlots curse
Blasts the new born infants tear
And ~~hangs~~ smites with plagues the marriage hearse

~~But most the shrieks of youth~~
~~But most thro midnight &~~
~~How the youthful~~

I ~~slumbered~~ slept in the dark
In the silent night
I murmurd my fears
And I felt delight

In the morning I went
As rosy as morn
To seek for new Joy
But I met with scorn

To Nobodaddy

Why art thou silent & invisible
Father of Jealousy
Why dost thou hide thyself in clouds
From every searching Eye

Why darkness & obscurity
In all thy words & laws
That none dare eat the fruit but from
The wily serpents jaws
Or is it because Secresy gains females loud applause

The modest ~~lustful~~ rose ~~puts~~ puts forth a thorn
The humble ~~coward~~ sheep a threatning horn
While the lilly white shall in love delight
~~And the lion increase freedom & peace~~ 4
~~The priest loves war & the soldier peace~~
Nor a thorn nor a threat stain her beauty bright

When the voices of children are heard on the green
And whisperings are in the dale
The ~~days~~ days of youth rise fresh in my mind
My face turns green & pale

Then come home my children the sun is gone down
And the dews of night arise
Your spring & your day are wasted in play
And your winter & night in disguise

Are not the joys of morning sweeter
Than the joys of night
And are the vigrous joys of youth
Ashamed of the light

Let age & sickness silent rob
The vineyards in the night
But those who burn with vigrous youth
Pluck fruits before the light

The Tyger

Tyger Tyger burning bright
In the forests of the night
What immortal hand or eye
~~Could~~ Dare frame thy fearful symmetry

2 ~~In what~~ Burnt in distant deeps or skies
~~Burnt in~~ The cruel fire of thine eyes
On what wings dare he aspire
What the hand dare sieze the fire

3 And what shoulder & what art
Could twist the sinews of thy heart
And when thy heart began to beat
What dread hand & what dread feet

~~Could fetch it from the furnace deep~~
~~And in thy horrid ribs dare steep~~
~~In the well of sanguine woe~~
~~In what clay & in what mould~~
~~Were thy eyes of fury rolld~~

~~What~~ Where the hammer ~~what~~ where the chain
In what furnace was thy brain
What the anvil what ~~the arm arm~~ dread grasp
~~Could~~ Dare its deadly terrors ~~clasp~~ clasp

6 Tyger Tyger burning bright
In the forests of the night
What immortal hand & eye
Dare ~~form~~ frame thy fearful symmetry

156
109

~~Burnt in distant deeps or skies~~
~~The cruel fire of thine eye~~
~~Could heart descend or wings aspire~~
~~What the hand dare seize the fire~~

5 ~~[illegible]~~ dare he ~~smile laugh~~
3 And ~~did he laugh his work to see~~
~~What the~~ ~~ankle~~ ~~shoulder~~ ~~what the knee~~
Dare
4 ~~Did~~ he who made the lamb make thee
1 When the stars threw down their spears
2 And waterd heaven with their tears

Tyger Tyger burning bright
In the forests of the night
What Immortal hand & eye
Dare frame thy fearful symmetry

And what shoulder & what art
Could twist the sinews of thy heart
And when thy heart began to beat
What dread hand & what dread feet

When the stars threw down their spears
And waterd heaven with their tears
Did he smile his work to see
Did he who made the lamb make thee

Tyger Tyger burning bright
In the forests of the night
What immortal hand & eye
Dare frame thy fearful symmetry

42

The Tyger

Tyger Tyger, burning bright,
In the forests of the night;
What immortal hand or eye,
Could frame thy fearful symmetry?

In what distant deeps or skies
Burnt the fire of thine eyes!
On what wings dare he aspire!
What the hand, dare seize the fire?

And what shoulder, & what art,
Could twist the sinews of thy heart?
And when thy heart began to beat,
What dread hand? & what dread feet?

What the hammer? what the chain,
In what furnace was thy brain?
What the anvil? what dread grasp,
Dare its deadly terrors clasp!

When the stars threw down their spears
And water'd heaven with their tears:
Did he smile his work to see?
Did he who made the Lamb make thee?

Tyger Tyger burning bright
In the forests of the night:
What immortal hand or eye,
Dare frame thy fearful symmetry?

'The Tyger' from *Songs of Innocence and Experience* by William Blake, British Library, C.71.d.19.

~~3~~ 5 And ~~did he laugh~~ dare he smile laugh his work to see
~~What the shoulder~~ ankle ~~what [the] knee~~
4 ~~Did~~ Dare he who made the lamb make thee
1 When the stars threw down their spears
2 And waterd heaven with their tears

Song: The Three Ships

PHILIP LARKIN (1922–1985)

8 October 1944, British Library, Add MS 52619, f.3r, folio 33 × 20 cm, pencil on lined paper in a blue cloth-bound notebook with a red spine.

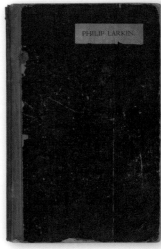

In his poem 'Song: The Three Ships', later called 'The North Ship', Philip Larkin uses the wind and sea to depict the impediments to the journeys of three ships. In the published version of the poem, strong winds blow one ship across the sea to a 'rich country' to the west and another to 'captivity' in the east. They both return to port 'Happily or unhappily'. The third ship, which sails to the north, is not blown by the wind but travels 'wide and far' and reaches its intended destination.

The three ships in the poem are thought to convey the importance of preparation and determination in achieving your ambitions in life. The north ship was the only one that was 'rigged for a long journey' and made it safely to where it intended to go. The other two ships were subject to the winds and either profited or suffered from them.

This is an early draft of the 'The Three Ships' written by Larkin in pencil in a cloth-bound notebook, which he used to draft his poems between 1944 and 1950. It is one of a series of similar notebooks. This draft is dated 8 October 1944 and differs significantly from the published poem, which appeared in *The North Ship* in 1945. In the manuscript it is possible to see the text through Larkin's crossings-out; in some cases he reinstates or slightly changes his original lines in the published version of the poem.

Larkin presented the notebook to the British Library through the Arts Council of Great Britain in 1965. Larkin carefully edited out any material from his notebooks that he did not want to appear in the public domain. Before his death, he instructed that his remaining papers be burnt. Many of his diaries were destroyed but, against his wishes, other manuscripts have been preserved.

Song: The Three Ships

I saw three ships go sailing by
Over the sea, the lifting sea,
And the wind ~~blew~~ rose in the morning sky
And ~~they were~~ one was rigged for a long journey.

The first ship turned towards the west
~~Over the sea, the smiling sea,~~ Where the veins of gold lay
~~And by the wind was For there was gold to be all possessed where much gold could be~~ possessed.
~~And it was not rigged for a long journey.~~

The second turned towards the east,
~~Over the sea, the foaming sea,~~ To countries where the mind grew clear
~~And the wind hunted it like a beast~~ And the greatest seemed the least;
~~And it was rigged for a long journey If~~ And it was anchored in a year.

The third ship drove towards the north
Over the sea, the darkening sea,
And ~~a wind of snow~~ the snow and ice came forth,
~~And it was rigged for a long journey~~ And the ropes shone frostily.

The northern sky ~~grew sour and slowly~~ lay harsh and black
Over the sad unfruitful sea,
East and west the ships came back
~~Both came back from a long journey.~~ Happily or unhappily.

~~But~~ But the third drove farther on
~~Over the~~ Into an unforgiving sea
Where a strange light shone
~~And all around Into where a strange [illegible] light that shone~~
And it was rigged for a long journey.

8.x.44

ABOVE: Cover of Philip Larkin's poetry notebook, British Library, Add MS 52619.

(15) 3

Song: The Three Ships

I saw three ships go sailing by
Over the sea, the lifting sea,
And the wind ~~blew~~ rose in the morning sky
And ~~they~~ one was rigged for a long journey.

The first ship turned towards the west
Where the veins of gold lay
~~Over the sea, the sailing sea~~
~~For there was gold to be~~ ~~Where much gold~~
~~And by the wind was~~ possessed ~~[illegible]~~ possessed.
~~[illegible]~~ ~~rigged for a long journey~~.

The second turned towards the east,
To countries where the mind grew clear
~~[illegible] the [illegible] sea~~
And the greatest seemed the least;
~~And the wind hunted it like a beast~~
~~It~~ And it was anchored in a year.
~~And it was rigged for a long journey~~.

The third ship drove towards the north
Over the sea, the darkening sea,
And ~~a wind of snow~~ the snow and ice came forth,
And the ropes shone frostily
~~And it was rigged for a long journey~~.

The northern sky ~~[illegible]~~ ~~[illegible]~~ lay ~~[illegible]~~ harsh and black
Over the sad unfruitful sea,
East and west the ships came back
Happily or unhappily.
~~[illegible] rigged for a long journey~~.

~~But~~ But The third drove farther on
~~Over the~~ Into an unforgiving sea
~~Into where a~~ ~~[illegible]~~ Where a ~~[illegible]~~ strange light shone
~~And never a[illegible]~~ ~~strange [illegible] shone~~
And it was rigged for a long journey.

8. x. 44

KATHLEEN JAMIE (b.1962)

What the Clyde said, after COP26

8 November 2021, blue ink on white paper. First published on scottishpoetrylibrary.org.uk.

Kind people give me notebooks, some with gorgeous paper, but they pile up unused. For my work, I reach for scraps and, especially, old manilla envelopes. If I feel I have a new piece of work beginning, I have to circle round the idea without being self-conscious, without clearing my throat and declaring 'I am now beginning a poem'.

This first draft is written on a piece of card cut down from something else. And handwritten, of course, because of the fluidity and the way of using space – my drafts ramble around. Also, I believe that the link between the mind and language, between body, breath and vision, is best preserved by handwriting. You need the tactility, the intimacy, in a poem's early stages.

This poem was one of those very rare pieces which just wrote itself – it went through only a handful of drafts as it found its form. There was an urgency; I wanted to make a public piece to mark COP26, and had only a few days to do it. Usually I work much more slowly and accrue loads of drafts.

This first draft was a starting place because you have to start somewhere, while kidding yourself you're not. ”

<u>What the Clyde said</u>
closing COP26
    planetary systems
        ___ its rights
bearing away
        exhausted seas
lonely
    the accent of barbarians
all flowing together
    ought to ?? all of us
its course for 10,000 years
    ? a silver listening
all take. Silence
?pollutants.
    ?of listening Time

I am the great listener
taken into my body
    the world of accents
chemical taints
empire & subjugation of earth, peoples,
launched here,
    ?sullied
on my banks
what does it mean to
bring together all the voices
co-mingled
for a river to flow through a city
I flow on bearing the rain
all that rain
I will rise
    understand me
my friend Time – all the time
my friend Rain   I reflect
the words   I wash
all away

The keel
iron/steel I bore
an empire. ?
the subjugation of ?friends
? meet in agreement
a deep ?deep spring
powers on, change

a river cannot take sides
    I take a side
a river flows unchanged
    I will for change
I bear away your words
    I will hold you to your word
    Or I will rise
over me your bridge-stitches
worlb shaping ?

your word
    effluents

You think my rush is headlong
a river cannot reflect
oh yes a river
can refect
unjust
    my friends
Zambezi
    Pearl River.

5/11/21

what the Clyde said

closing COP26
planetary systems
[illegible] its rights

bearing away
exhausted seas

lonely
the accents of [illegible]
all flowing together
caught to outflow all of us

its sure for 10.000 years
hears, a silver listening

all talk - Silence

pollutants
of [illegible] of time

words flow away
I am the great listener
taken into my body
the world of accents

chemical [illegible]
empire, subjugation of earth, peoples
laundered here
sullied

on my banks what doesn't want to
bring together all the voices
co-mingled

for a [illegible] to flow [illegible] a city
I [illegible] on hearing the rain
all that rain
I will rise, [illegible]

my friend Time - all the time

my friend Rain, I reflect

be words, I wash
bear
all away

You think my
wish is headlong
a river cannot reflect
oh yes, a river
can reflect
ought
my friends
Lambgi
peat river.

the keel
iron, steel, I bore

empire - [illegible]
the subjugation of lands

liberty meet in
agreement
a drip drip spring
powers on, change

a river cannot take sides
I take a side
a river flows unchanged
I will you change
I bear away your words
I will hold you to your words
or I will rise

on me your
body. stitches
world shaping spaces

[illegible] word
[illegible]

[illegible]

Matin

CHARLOTTE BRONTË (1816–1855)

12 November 1830, British Library, Ashley MS 158, f.1r, folio 9.3 × 5.7 cm, iron gall ink on wove paper.

This manuscript was written by Charlotte Brontë when she was just 14. It forms part of the body of work known as the Brontë juvenilia which Charlotte and her siblings, Emily, Anne and Branwell (1817–1848), created when they were growing up in the Parsonage at Haworth, Yorkshire. The juvenilia is often written in minute script, sometimes on very small pieces of paper and in tiny volumes prepared by the siblings. Many of the miniature volumes mimic printed magazines, containing advertisements and title pages. Much of the juvenilia was centred around fictional worlds and characters who appeared across different works.

'Matin' is an autograph fair copy with some corrections. It contains only the first thirty-two lines of the poem. The second part of the poem can be found in the manuscript held at Princeton University. The language in this poem is remarkably advanced for a 14-year-old, and it displays Charlotte's ability to describe both landscape and elements: the world is silent and softly slumbering until it 'springs from sleep' in a 'glorious birth of light'; waters 'howl like famished wolves' while valleys swell 'shady and green'.

This manuscript has another poem on the verso entitled 'Vespers'. It is signed and dated 11 November 1830. The leaf was originally part of a miniature volume known as 'The Violet', wrapped in blue Epsom Salts paper, which is now in the Robert H. Taylor collection at Princeton University.

MATIN

Long hath earth lain beneath [~~illegible~~] the dark profound
Of Silent-footed, planet-crested night
Now from the chains of slumber soft, unbound
She springs from sleep to ~~view~~ hail, the glorious birth
of light

A solemn Hush lay on her hills and woods
Now as the day approaches, fast dispelling
For at the touch of the bright orient floods
Thousands of voices rise, in mingled murmurs
Swelling

First the suns glories tip the lofty hill
Then roll impetuous down the dusky vale
Sings sweet in light the pebbled crystal rill
And joy expands the buds, of flowers that woo
the gale [illegible]

O! I might sing of pastures meads & trees
Whose verdant hue is tinged with solar beams
And I might sing of morns fresh bracing breeze
That with awakeng breath, riples the glas –
s sy – streams

And of the merry lark who soar's on high
Aye rising in his course [~~illegible~~] toward the sun
Of his descending from the vaulted sky
To the expectant nest, when that sweet song
is done

These I could sing, if thou wert near me now
Thou whom I love, my souls most fair delight
If the fair orbs that beam beneath thy brow
Shed on my [~~illegible~~] darkling page their way di-
vinely bright

ABOVE: Charlotte Brontë, steel engraving by J. C. Armytage, British Library, 1876.f.22.

MATIN

1

Long hath earth lain beneath the dark profound
Of silent-footed, planet-crested night
Now from the chains of slumber soft unbound
She springs from sleep to ~~view~~ hail the glorious birth of light

A solemn hush lay on her hills and woods
Now as the day approaches, fast dispelling
For at the touch of the bright orient floods
Thousands of voices rise, in mingled murmurs swelling

First the suns glories tip the lofty hill
Then roll impetuous down the dusky vale
Sings sweet in light the pebbled crystal rill
And joy expands the buds, of flowers that woo the gale

O! I might sing of pastures meads & trees
Whose verdant hue is tinged with solar beams
And I might sing of morns fresh bracing breeze
That with awakeng breath, riples the glassy streams

And of the merry lark who soars on high
Aye rising in his course ~~he~~ toward the sun
Of his descending from the vaulted sky
To the expectant nest, when that sweet song is done

These I could sing, if thou wert near me now
Thou whom I love, my souls most fair delight
If the fair orbs that beam beneath thy brow
Shed on my ~~page~~ darkling page their ray divinely bright

But now, great waters of the mighty deep
Howling like famished wolves roll us between
O! sad & bitter drops I mournful weep
To think of those vast leagues, of tossing billows green

Come from the fairy valley where thou dwellest
Shady and green, in Britains favoured isle
~~Come thou whose presence all my gloom dispellest~~
Come for all gloom & sadness thou dispellest
And chase away my greif, with one sweet-sunny smile

Letters to the Tandy family with drafts for Old Possum's Book of Practical Cats

T. S. ELIOT (1888–1965)

13 February 1940, British Library, Add MS 71003, f.45r, folio 25.3 × 20.2 cm, typewritten with ink annotations on headed paper, and f.46r, folio 11 × 13.7 cm, typewritten envelope.

During the 1930s and 1940s, Thomas Stearns Eliot wrote a series of letters to the Tandy family. He was friends with Geoffrey Tandy (1900–1969), a marine biologist and broadcaster. Eliot's letters to Geoffrey, his wife Doris (née Ellis, 1894–1971) – known as Polly – and their daughters Alison (b.1930) and Anthea (1935–1989), to whom Eliot was godfather, came to the British Library in 1991, following Anthea's death. They contain drafts of poems, many of which would be published in *Old Possum's Book of Practical Cats* in 1939. Some of the letters are written on headed paper. Eliot was the founder and editor of the *Criterion*, a literary journal which was published from 1922 to 1939.

Eliot wrote a series of letters to Polly, Alison and Anthea Tandy about his cat characters and clearly found the animals amusing. In one letter, of 9 December 1936, he wrote: 'When a Cat adopts you … there is nothing to be done about it … you must for the present provide liver and rabbit, and a comfortable seat by the fire'.

These letters include unpublished verses and storylines. On 13 February 1940, in a letter illustrated with hearts and a Cupid's arrow for Valentine's Day, Eliot shared parts of a poem about Grizabella the Glamour Cat:

> The Glamour Cat, I am sorry to say, is not turning out a suitable subject for edifying my juvenile audience; in fact, she came down in the world pretty far. The story is very sad, and also a bit sordid. For:
>
> She haunted many a low resort
> In the dingy Road of Tottenham Court.
> She flitted about the no man's land
> From the Rising Sun to the Friend at Hand.
> And the postman sighed, as he shook his head:
> "You'd ha' thought that cat had ought to be dead –
> And who ~~who~~ ever suppose that that
> Was Grizabella, the Glamour Cat?"

He goes on to write, 'No, I fear that the story had better not be told.'

Eliot did not feature Grizabella in *Old Possum's Book of Practical Cats*. However, Eliot's wife, Valerie (née Fletcher, 1926–2012), shared a fragment of the poem with the musician Andrew Lloyd Webber (b.1948), who gave the character of Grizabella a prominent role in his 1981 musical *Cats*.

45

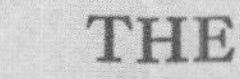

THE CRITERION

A QUARTERLY REVIEW

EDITED BY T. S. ELIOT

TELEPHONE: MUSEUM 9543
TELEGRAMS: FABBAF, WESTCENT, LONDON

24 RUSSELL SQUARE,
LONDON, W.C.1

13 February 1940.

Dear Polly Tandy ma'am,

Tomorrow being the day of St.Valentine, Priest & Martyr, I take the liberty of conveying my affectionate Respects to the Ladies of the family; and at the same time pass a civil greeting to Richard and to Knobs. Wishing you many happy returns.

Our pipes have just frozen for the third time: so I hope that in the more benign climate of Dorset you have not suffered in the same way; though I fear that the severity of the winter has brought you hardships as well. As I have been a victim of bronnical trouble, from which I have now recovered I believe, but am now taking Pills for Low Blood Pressure, I also hope that you have not been visited by any epidemics or ailments. I have no other particular news, having been leading a quiet life, partly imposed by Frail health. It is on my mind to pass by the shop in the Tottenham Court Road, where I dare say I shall find that the Shetland wool is unobtainable; but I do not doubt that you have had your hands full otherwise, and have been quite willing to postpone this extra chore which I imposed upon you without so much as asking leave. The Glamour Cat, I am sorry to say, is not turning out a suitable subject for edifying my juvenile audience; in fact, she came down in the world pretty far. The story is very sad, and also a bit sordid. For

She haunted many a low resort
In the dingy Road of Tottenham Court.
She flitted about the no man's land
From the Rising Sun to the Friend at Hand.
And the postman sighed, as he shook his head:
"You'd ha' thought that cat had ought to be dead -
And who ~~who~~ would ever suppose that that
Was Grizzabella, the Glamour Cat?"

No, I fear that the story had better not be told. I have no news of the old man, and no doubt he is passing his time pleasantly in horse-racing, cock-fighting, and such manly passtimes of the nobility and gentry of the shires. So will close with affexnite greetings and hope for your news, your

Po.

Mending Wall

ROBERT FROST (1874–1963)

Before 1914, Library of Congress, Accession No. 13,470. mm 81001625, folio 26.3 × 18.7 cm, pen and black ink on two sheets.

Robert Frost was born in San Francisco, but moved to Massachusetts when he was just 14. He is one of the most celebrated American poets, and author of poems such as 'The Road Not Taken'. His work explores challenging social topics through the lens of rural life in the United States. Frost lived in England between 1912 and 1915, where he drew inspiration from both his neighbours and English poets.

'Mending Wall' was first published in *North of Boston* in England in 1914 and subsequently in New York in 1915. This manuscript is an undated draft with only minor variations from the published version. The word 'smooth' in line 20 was later changed to 'rough' in the printed poem. 'Mending Wall' explores the topic of boundaries, describing how Frost and his neighbour set about mending a wall damaged by rabbit hunters. Frost questions the need for the wall, especially when, as he says of their respective properties, 'He is all pine and I am apple orchard. / My apple trees will never get across / And eat the cones under his pines.' His neighbour responds with '"Good fences make good neighbors."'

This manuscript is held by the Library of Congress, with which Frost had a close relationship towards the end of his life, serving as consultant in poetry and English from 1958–9 and then as honorary consultant in the humanities until his death in 1963.

Mending Wall

Something there is that doesn't love a wall,
That sends the frozen ground swell under it,
And spills the upper boulders in the sun-
And makes gaps even two can pass abreast.
The work of hunters is another thing
I have come after them and made repair
Where they have left not one stone on a stone
But they would have the rabbit out of hiding
To please the yelping dogs. The gaps I mean,
No one has seen them made or heard them made,
But at spring mending time we find them there.
I let my neighbor know beyond the hill,
And on a day we meet to walk the line
And set the wall between us once again.
We keep the wall between us as we go.
To each the boulders that have fallen to each.
And some are loaves and some so nearly balls
We have to use a spell to make them balance:
'Stay where you are until our backs are turned!'
We wear our fingers smooth with handling them.
Oh, just another kind of outdoor game,
One on a side. It comes to little more.
There where it is we do not need the wall
He is all pine and I am apple orchard.
My apple trees will never get across
And eat the cones under his pines, I tell him.
He only says, 'Good fences make good neighbors.'
Spring is the mischief in me, and I wonder
If I could put a notion in his head:
Why do they make good neighbors? Isn't it
Where there are cows? But here there are no cows.
Before I built a wall I'd ask to know

Mending Wall

Something there is that doesn't love a wall,
That sends the frozen ground swell under it,
And spills the upper boulders in the sun —
And makes gaps even two can pass abreast.
The work of hunters is another thing
I have come after them and made repair
Where they have left not one stone on a stone
But they would have the rabbit out of hiding
To please the yelping dogs. The gaps I mean,
No one has seen them made or heard them made,
But at spring mending time we find them there.
I let my neighbor know beyond the hill,
And on a day we meet to walk the line
And set the wall between us once again.
We keep the wall between us as we go.
To each the boulders that have fallen to each.
And some are loaves and some so nearly balls
We have to use a spell to make them balance:
"Stay where you are until our backs are turned!"
We wear our fingers smooth with handling them
Oh, just another kind of outdoor game,
One on a side. It comes to little more.
There where it is we do not need the wall
He is all pine and I am apple orchard.
My apple trees will never get across
And eat the cones under his pines, I tell him.
He only says, "Good fences make good neighbors."
Spring is the mischief in me and I wonder
If I could put a notion in his head:
Why do they make good neighbors? Isn't it
Where there are cows? But here there are no cows.
Before I built a wall I'd ask to know

Robert Frost, photograph by Doris Ulmann, National Portrait Gallery, Smithsonian Institution, Washington D.C., NPG.97.112.

What I was walling in or walling out,
And to whom I was like to give offence.
Something there is that doesn't love a wall,
That wants it down. I could say 'Elves' to him,
But it's not elves exactly, and I'd rather
He said it for himself. I see him there
Bringing a stone grasped firmly by the top
In each hand, like an old-stone savage armed.
He moves in darkness as it seems to me,
Not of woods only and the shade of trees.
He will not go behind his father's saying,
And he likes having thought of it so well
He says again 'Good fences make good neighbors.'

What I was walling in or walling out,
And to whom I was like to give offence.
Something there is that doesnt love a wall,
That wants it down. I could say "Elves" to him,
But it's not elves exactly and I'd rather
He said it for himself. I see him there
Bringing a stone grasped firmly by the top
In each hand like an old-stone savage armed.
He moves in darkness as it seems to me
Not of woods only and the shade of trees.
He will not go behind his fathers' saying.
And he likes having thought of it so well
He says again "Good fences make good neighbors."

chapter 6

IMBALANCE AND INEQUALITY

While poetry can celebrate the beautiful and sublime, it has also been employed as a powerful tool to portray a world that is so often unjust, unbalanced and cruel. The poems in this chapter are both a form of protest and a call for change.

Several of the poems explore racial injustice, including the horrors of slavery. The poems by Phillis Wheatley, Maya Angelou and Elizabeth Barrett Browning all address slavery and the devastating racism which underpinned it. Benjamin Zephaniah's poem 'What Stephen Lawrence Has Taught Us' is a reminder of a shocking murder that took place on the streets of London in recent times and of the continuing impact of racism in Britain today. Yet there is also some hope and strength emerging from the devastation. The voice of the defiant individual is celebrated by Angelou in 'Still I Rise'. Both Zephaniah and Angelou performed their poems in public, bringing them to a wider audience.

Some of the poems in this chapter specifically address the imbalance between rich and poor, and between the powerful and those they seek to govern. Percy Shelley's 'The Masque of Anarchy' speaks about the injustice of violence and murder in the wake of peaceful protest, accusing powerful politicians of authorising the violence. Alexander Pushkin was exiled for expressing views supporting reform in Tsarist Russia; Pushkin likened his exile to incarceration and it inspired his poem 'The Prisoner'. Although Sylvia Pankhurst is best remembered for her work as a suffragette, she was an active proponent of many causes later in life, including campaigning against racial inequality and war. She was imprisoned for sedition in 1921 as a result of her championing of revolutionary socialism, and the poem reproduced in this chapter was written secretly on prison toilet paper. Emily Dickinson's poem 'Mine – by the Right of the White Election!', the meaning of which is ambiguous, asserts the voice of the individual.

Several poems in the chapter address themes of prejudice and inequality based on gender or sexuality. Despite her elevated social position, Lady Mary Wroth's writing highlights the imbalance between men and women in the seventeenth century. Writing over 250 years later, George Eliot felt this imbalance keenly, believing that women should be afforded similar opportunities to men. Eliot's poem 'Armgart' features an ambitious female opera singer who refuses to marry and thereby be forced to give up her career. Fiona Benson's poem '[transformation: Daphne]' is a graphic account of the hunting of Daphne by Apollo. Benson has drawn on Ovid's adaptation of the Greek myth, and describes a horrifying pursuit of a terrified woman imagined as a hare chased by hunting dogs. In his poem 'The Laws of God, The Laws of Man', A. E. Housman describes his anger at the roles of Church and State in Britain in forbidding same-sex relationships, an issue that acutely impacted many other poets.

To the University of Cambridge, in New England

PHILLIS WHEATLEY (*c.*1753–1784)

1767, American Antiquarian Society, Mss reserve W, folio 31 x 18.5 cm, pen and ink on laid paper.

Born in West Africa, Phillis Wheatley was thought to be around 7 or 8 when she was sold into slavery in 1761 and purchased by John Wheatley (1703–1778), an evangelical Christian merchant from Boston, Massachusetts. The young girl's birth name was unknown, but the Wheatley family called her Phillis after the ship on which she had travelled to North America. While enslaved, John Wheatley had allowed Phillis to learn to read and write. She was the first Black African American to publish poetry in the English language. After Boston publishers refused to publish her work, Phillis travelled to London in 1773 and published *Poems on Various Subjects, Religious and Moral*.

Even after her manumission, granted to her by John Wheatley, Phillis's life continued to be marked by sorrow and hardship. Unable to attract financial support for her second volume of poetry, she was forced to find alternative work. In 1778 she married John Peters (1746?–1801), with whom she had two children, both of whom died in infancy. Phillis died at the age of 31 after complications from childbirth, along with her baby.

The first draft of this poem was written by Phillis when she was around 14 or 15. She had converted to Christianity and much of her poetry reflects on her personal faith. This manuscript, inscribed with the title and date, was addressed to students at Harvard College, urging them to live a virtuous life through Christ. The manuscript is on laid paper and is significantly creased, demonstrating that it had been folded in multiple places.

The manuscript is owned by the American Antiquarian Society, which acquired it from Thomas Wallcutt (1758–1840) in 1834. Wallcutt was a friend of Phillis to whom she sent drafts of her poems when he was a student at Dartmouth College in the 1770s. His handwriting is on the verso of this poem.

The poem in this draft differs in parts to the poem as published in 1773. The first thirty lines of the manuscript on f.1 have been transcribed.

To the University of Cambridge   wrote in 1767—

While an intrinsic ardor bids me write
The muse doth promise to assist my pen.
'Twas but e'er now I left my native shore
The sable Land or error's darkest night
There, sacred Nine! for you no place was found.
Parent of mercy, 'twas thy Powerful hand
Brought me in safety from the dark abode.

To you, Bright youths! He points the height of Heav'n
To you, the knowledge of the depths profound.
Above, contemplate the ethereal space
And glorious Systems of revolving worlds.

Still more, ye Sons of Science! you've receiv'd
The pleasing sound by messengers from heav'n,
The saviour's blood, for your Redemption flows.
[illegible] him with hands stretch'd out upon the Cross!
Divine compassion in his bosom glows,
He hears revilers with oblique regard.
What condessention in the Son of God!
When the whole human race by sin had fal'n;
He deign'd to Die, that they might rise again,
To live with him beyond the starry sky
Life without death, and Glory without End.

Improve your privileges while they stay:
Caress, redeem each moment, which with haste
Bears on its rapid wing Eternal bliss,
Let hateful vice so baneful to the Soul
Be still avoided with becoming care:
Suppress the sable monster in its growth,
Ye blooming plants of human race divine
An Ethiop tells you, tis your greatest foe

To the University of Cambridge wrote in 1767—

While an intrinsic ardor bids me write
The muse doth promise to assist my pen.
'Twas but e'er now I left my native Shore
The sable Land of error's darkest night.
There, sacred Nine! for you no place was found.
Parent of mercy, 'twas thy Powerfull hand
Brought me in safety from the dark abode.
To you, Bright youths! he points the height of Heav'n
To you, the knowledge of the depths profound.
Above, contemplate the ethereal Space
And glorious Systems of revolving worlds.
Still more, ye Sons of Science! you've receiv'd
The pleasing Sound by messengers from heav'n,
The saviour's blood, for your Redemption flows.
See him, with hands stretch'd out upon the Cross!
Divine compassion in his bosom glows.
He hears revilers with oblique regard.
What Condescension in the Son of God!
When the whole human race, by Sin had fal'n;
He deign'd to Die, that they might rise again,
To live with him beyond the Starry Sky
Life without death, and Glory without End.—
Improve your privileges while they stay:
Caress, redeem each moment, which with haste
Bears on its rapid wing Eternal bliss.
Let hateful vice so baneful to the Soul,
Be still avoided with becoming care;
Suppress the sable monster in its growth,
Ye blooming plants of human race, divine
An Ethiop tells you, tis your greatest foe

Phillis Wheatley, engraving, British Library, 992.a.34.

The Masque of Anarchy

PERCY BYSSHE SHELLEY (1792–1822)

1819, British Library, Ashley MS 4086, f.1r, folio 15.7 × 9.7 cm, iron gall ink on wove paper.

Percy Shelley, reproduction after a portrait by Amelia Curran, British Library, 1560/4193.

On 16 August 1819 a peaceful crowd of around 60,000–80,000 people gathered in St Peter's Fields, Manchester, to hear speakers campaigning for parliamentary reform. The decision by local magistrates to use cavalry to break up the meeting led to the deaths of several people (some estimates suggest around 18) and several hundred more were injured. The event became known as the Peterloo Massacre, a bitterly ironic reference to the Battle of Waterloo, at which the British and their allies triumphed over Napoleonic France in 1815. Shelley heard about the Peterloo Massacre while in Italy and composed 'The Masque of Anarchy' in the weeks that followed. Due to its controversial content, the poem was not published until 1832.

This image shows the first folio of Shelley's poem, written in iron gall ink on wove paper. The poem begins dramatically, with Shelley describing a dream. It features several members of the British government, including the foreign secretary, Lord Castlereagh (1769–1822), and Lord Eldon (1751–1838), the Lord High Chancellor. These politicians were particularly associated in the public mind with repression. Much of the text in this manuscript varies from the published version. The first nineteen lines of the poem on f.1 have been transcribed. This manuscript is part of the Ashley Collection at the British Library.

As I lay asleep in Italy
There came a voice from over the Sea
And with great power it forth led me
To walk in the Visions of Poesy.

I met Murder on the way —
He had a mask like Castlereagh,
Very smooth he looked, yet grim;
Seven blood hounds followed him.

All were fat; & well they might
Be in admirable plight
For one by one & two by two,
He tossed them human hearts to chew
Which from his wide cloak he drew

Next came Fraud & he had on
Like Lord Eldon, an ermined gown
His big tears, for he wept well

1 1

As I lay asleep in Italy
There came a voice from over the Sea
And with great power it forth led me
To walk in the visions of Poesy

I met Murder on the way —
He had a mask like Castlereagh;
Very smooth he looked, yet grim;
Seven bloodhounds followed him.

All were fat, & well they might
Be in admirable plight
For one by one & two by two
He tossed them human hearts to chew
Which from his wide cloak he drew

Next came Fraud & he had on
Like Eldon, an ermined gown
His big tears for he wept well

5.

.7.

Loue leaue to vrge, thou knowist thou hast ye hand;
T'is cowardise, to striue wher none resist:
Pray thee leaue of, I yeeld vnto thy band;
Doe nott thus, still, in thine owne powre persist,

Beehold I yeeld: lett forces bee dismist,
I ame your subiect, conquer'd, bound doe stand,
neuer your foe, butt did your clame assist
seeking your due of those who did wt=stand;

Butt now, itt seemes, you would I should you loue;
I doe confess, t'was you, made mee first chuse,
and yor faire showes made mee a louer proue
when I my freedome did, for paine refuse

Yett this Sr God, yor boyship I dispise;
your charmes I obay, butt loue nott want of eyes

Lad=

The seventh sonnet from Pamphilia to Amphilanthus

LADY MARY WROTH (*c.*1587–1651/1653)

1615–20, Folger Shakespeare Library, Folger call number: V.a.104, f.5r, volume 19 × 14 cm, iron gall ink on laid paper.

Lady Mary Wroth (née Sidney) is best known for her romance *The Countess of Montgomery's Urania*, published in 1621 and the earliest surviving extended work of fiction written by a woman in Britain. When it was first published the work caused a scandal as it was considered to be semi-autobiographical, and it was soon withdrawn from sale. A contemporary of Shakespeare who watched him act in his own plays, Wroth also performed in court masques for the royal family.

The sonnet sequence *Pamphilia to Amphilanthus* first appeared in *The Countess of Montgomery's Urania,* but proved popular in its own right and was soon published separately. The sonnet sequence, consisting of 105 poems divided into four sections, focuses on Pamphilia and her unfaithful lover, Amphilanthus. Wroth's handwritten manuscript of the sequence survives in this volume of her poems held at the Folger Shakespeare Library in Washington DC. Sonnet 7, which is displayed here, encapsulates the theme of female struggle within a male-dominated world. The lines are spoken by Pamphilia to Cupid, whom she despises but at the same time obeys.

The volume was owned by several book collectors before it was acquired in 1899 by Henry Clay Folger (1857–1930). He went on to establish the Folger Shakespeare Library, which opened in 1932, after his death.

Love leave to urge, thou know'st thou hast ye hand;
'T'is cowardise, to strive wher none resist:
Pray thee leave of, I yeeld unto thy band;
Doe nott thus, still, in thine owne powre persist.

Beehold I yeeld: lett forces bee dismist;
I ame your subject, conquer'd, bound doe stand,
never your foe, butt did your claime assist
Seeking your due of those who did w^{t}stand;

Butt now, itt seemes, you would I should you love;
I doe confess, t'was you made mee first chuse;
and yor faire showes made mee a lover prove
when I my freedome did, for paine refuse

Yett this Sr God, yor boyship I dispise;
your charmes I obay, butt love nott want of eyes

FIONA BENSON (b.1978)

[transformation: Daphne]

Early summer 2017, black ink on white paper, British Library, Dep. 11440 recto.
First published in *Vertigo & Ghost* (Cape Poetry, 2019).

This version of Daphne's story was written in response to the account in Ovid's *Metamorphoses*. Ovid likens Apollo's pursuit of Daphne to a hound coursing a hare – a transformation via simile that occurs some time before the bodily transformation of Daphne into a laurel tree, and I found it terrifying.

Some poems come through loud and clear, very rapidly indeed; others take their time. Daphne came through slowly, and took at least twenty drafts. It's a bit like you're twiddling the dial on an old radio, trying to tune in to an impossibly precise frequency. Imagine bursts of music and broadcasts from other radio stations interfering, and static, static, static. Imagine trying to hear clearly through the multiple frustrations of your own ineptitude.

I write drafts by hand, tearing them out as I go so that I can copy new drafts onto a fresh page. I like to feel the poem *in* the body – there is something about that labour of writing out a poem that is a real act of listening, a test for whether each word or phrase or line will hold. It also give me the freedom to make mistakes. Here I've crossed out the 'greased rails' of the dog track, but in fact that image made it into the final poem.

At third draft stage, this poem is still emerging, still trying to find its energy and momentum, still reaching for images. I beg you to go and look at the final poem; twenty or so drafts on – it is much improved, I promise!

DAPHNE 3

wood-thickened
Who rooted, threw up a bark shield, became leaf;
But ~~there is a~~ in the ~~transformation~~ transformation ~~change~~ before the
~~transformation change~~ change ~~in the tale~~
~~Ovid says Apollo chasing like a~~ dog ~~greyhound. Daphne~~ she's ~~like~~ a har
& Zeus's son courses after her Apollo ~~is~~ coursing after her like a greyho
trying to leap free. ~~Imagine, Ovid says, a greyhound~~
Remember that day at the dogs, how before the race
a whippet lost its head ~~on~~ in the hold howling & werreting
pert & afraid. *[insert dog] How after the race- ~~the dummy~~
~~rattling round on greased rails~~- ~~[?]~~ men hooked their legs
over the barriers & came to collect their dogs,
clipping on each leash, the handlers, the fathers,
Zeus behind the scenes with his stick & poisoned meat
& his Rare affection at the track
~~Urging the dogs on~~. COME ON SON, OUTRUN, PERFORM.
Away from the track it is not a straight run.
It is a scramble, a double back & jink
an interlaced feint & counterfeint
in the change before the change
she is running for her life at the edge of her wits
He's not a quiet courser, he hollers & ~~yelps~~ barks,
in the rough of his throat, ~~cuffs out claws~~ cuffs at her back legs,
~~cuffs~~ knocks them out from under her again again
By nightfall she is bleeding, bitten in her back end
calling for her daddy like any other girl
whose run beyond her strength, whose heart has failed

quarry
her heart fluttering inside the bark
and still Apollo can't believe he's lost presses in wants to fuck

his hot breath on her flank
his bared teeth snapping at her flesh

Zeus is there in the dark, holding the lamp
keeping it steady for the kill.

(3)

DAPHNE.

Who rooted, threw up a bark shield, became leaf,

but in the change before the transformation she

Apollo as cursing after her like a greyhound

trying to leap free

Remember that day at the dogs, how before the race

a whippet lost its head in the hold howling + wresting

pert + afraid. Then after the race —

it never hooked the leg.

All the bookies + came to collect their dogs.

clipping on each leash, the handlers, the fathers,

Zeus behind the scenes with his stick + poised neat.

OUTRUN, PERFORM.

Away from the track it is not a straight run.

It is a scramble, a double back + jink

an interlaced feint + counterfeint

in the change before the change

she is running for her life at the edge of her wits,

He's not a quiet case, he hollers + barks,

with the rage of his throat, cuffs at her back leg.

knocks her out for under her again again

By nightfall she is bleeding, bitten in her back end

calling for her daddy like any other girl

whose run beyond her strength, whose heart has failed.

his hot breath in her fur

his bred teeth snapping her

her heart fluttering inside her bark

and still Apollo presses in wants to finish

Zeus is there in the dark, holding the lamp,

keeps it steady for the kill.

Still I Rise

MAYA ANGELOU (1928–2014)

1977–92, Z. Smith Reynolds Library, Wake Forest University, The Maya Angelou Film and Theatre Manuscript Collection, Box 63 1a, folio 34 x 22 cm, blue ink and red pencil on lined, yellow paper.

Maya Angelou, photograph by Martin Godwin.

Maya Angelou was a poet, civil rights activist, writer, singer and director. Born Marguerite Annie Johnson in St Louis, Missouri, she moved to live with her grandmother in Arkansas by the age of 3. While she is most famous for her autobiographies, including *I Know Why the Caged Bird Sings* (1969), Angelou began as a singer and dancer, talents which influenced her writing and directing career.

And Still I Rise was the title of a volume of Angelou's poetry, published in 1978, which contained the poem of the same name. The title was also used for a musical drama which adapted some of the poems for use on stage. Angelou directed at least three productions of the theatrical version. This manuscript relates to the theatrical version of *And Still I Rise*. There are a number of corrections to the draft which suggests the words were still being developed for one of the earlier performances. The manuscript is written over six sheets, the first of which is shown here. The words in this version differ in places to the published poem, for example in the use of the word 'distress' instead of 'upset'. The third verse of the published poem was adapted by Angelou as a refrain or chorus. Red pencil has been used to confirm the inclusion of sections of the poem. Angelou worked across many different artistic spaces and her skill in adapting poetry for performance is shown in this manuscript. A gifted teacher and performer, she was often filmed speaking or singing the poem.

The words of the poem 'Still I Rise' are a statement of hope and survival, and a defiant response to the slave trade and its lasting legacy. The message from Angelou is clear: that in spite of society's oppression, the individual is powerful. Yet Angelou's voice is also one of positivity and joy that provides an uplifting tone to a sombre subject.

The Maya Angelou Film and Theatre Manuscript Collection was donated to the Z. Smith Reynolds Library at Wake Forest University by Angelou, who was a member of the university faculty from 1982 until her death in 2014.

you may write me down in history
with your bitter twisted lies
you may t trod me in the very dirt
but still like dust I'll rise
just like moons
and like suns
With the certainty of tides refrain
just like hopes
springing high
Still I'll rise

Does my sassiness ~~upset~~ distress you
Why are you beset with gloom
Cause I walk like I've got oil wells
pumping in my living room Refrain

Did you want to see me ~~humble~~ broken
bowed head and lowered eyes
shoulders dropping down like tear drops
weakened by my soulful cries ~~(Refrain)~~

Does my haughtiness upset you
Why do you take it all so hard
because I ~~we~~ laugh like I've got gold mines
digging in my own back yard Refrain

you may cut me with your words
" " dam " " " eyes
" " shoot " " " hatefulness
But still like air I'll rise (Refrain

You may write me down in history
With your bitter twisted lies
You may ~~tr~~ trod me in the very dirt
but still like dust I'll rise

Just like moons
And like suns
With the certainty of tides
Just like hopes
Springing high
Still I'll rise

(Refrain)

Does my sassiness ~~upset~~ distress you
Why are you beset with gloom
Cause I walk like I've got oil wells
pumping in my living room / Refrain

Did you want to see me ~~humble~~ broken
bowed head and lowered eyes
shoulders dropping down like tear drops
Weakened by my soulful cries (Refrain

Does my haughtiness upset you
Why do you take it all so hard
because I ~~[illegible]~~ laugh like I've got gold mines
digging in my own back yard (Refrain

You may cut me with your words
" " dam " " "
" " shoot " " " ~~hatefulness~~ eyes
But still ~~air~~ like air I'll rise (Refrain

BENJAMIN ZEPHANIAH

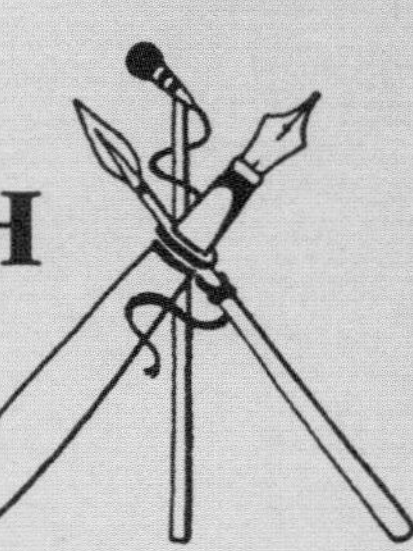

WHAT STEPHEN LAWRENCE HAS TAUGHT US.

We know who the killers are,
We have watched them strut before us
As proud as sick Mussolinis,
We have watched them strut before us
Compassionless and arrogant,
They paraded before us like angels of death
Protected by the law.

It is now an open secret
Black people do not have chips on their shoulders,
They just have injustice on their backs
And justice on their minds
And now we know that the road to liberty
Is as long as the road from slavery.

The death of Stephen Lawrence has taught us to love each
other, and to never take the tedious task of waiting
for a bus for granted.
Watching his parents watching the cover up begs the
question,
What are the trading standards here?
Why are we paying for a police force
That will not work for us.

Dr B. Zephaniah • P.O. Box 1153 • Spalding • Lincolnshire • PE11 9BN • England

BENJAMIN ZEPHANIAH (b.1958)

What Stephen Lawrence Has Taught Us

15 May 2016, blue ink on white headed paper, British Library, Dep 10936.
First published in *The Guardian* (24 February 1999).

‘

I have suffered injustice, and I have seen a lot of injustice in my time. But as a Black man growing up in Britain, it’s frustrating, and infuriating, when you seek justice, then find it not forthcoming because of legal technicalities. This, I believe, is how Black people in Britain felt after Stephen Lawrence was murdered in 1993. We all knew who killed Stephen. They were secretly filmed boasting about how they could beat Black people up. They mocked us. They hated us. They were proud of their racist views.

When I wrote this poem, I was confident. This is why in the poem I don’t just say, ‘I know who the killers are’; I say, ‘*we* know who the killers are.’ I was so confident that I felt I could speak for the Black (and much of the white) population. I was so confident that I wanted the accused to challenge me, so that maybe, just maybe, they would sue me, and I would see them in court. In January 2012 two people were sent to prison for the killing of Stephen, but we know there are more who are guilty of this murder. So, in fact, we are still waiting for justice, even though we still know who the killers are.

’

THE DEATH OF STEPHEN LAWRENCE HAS TAUGHT US
THAT WE CANNOT LET THE ILLUSION OF FREEDOM
ENDOW US WITH A FALSE SENSE OF SECURITY
AS WE WALK THE STREETS,
THE WHOLE WORLD CAN NOW WATCH
THE ACADEMICS AND THE SUPER COPS
STRUGGLING TO DEFINE INSTITUTIONALISED RACISM
AS WE CONTINUE TO DIE IN CUSTODY
AS WE CONTINUE EMPTYING OUR POCKETS ON PAVEMENTS,
AND WE CONTINUE TO ASK OURSELVES – WHY IS IT SO OFFICIAL
THAT BLACK PEOPLE ARE SO OFTEN KILLED – WITHOUT KILLERS?

WE ARE NOT TALKING ABOUT WAR OR REVENGE
WE ARE NOT TALKING ABOUT HYPOTHETICS OR POSSIBILITIES,
WE ARE TALKING ABOUT WHERE WE ARE NOW
WE ARE TALKING ABOUT HOW WE LIVE NOW,
IN DIS STATE – UNDER DIS FLAG, (GOD SAVE THE QUEEN),
AND GOD SAVE ALL THOSE BLACK CHILDREN WHO WANT TO GROW UP
AND GOD SAVE ALL THE BROTHERS AND SISTERS WHO LIKE RAVING,
BECAUSE THE DEATH OF STEPHEN LAWRENCE
HAS TAUGHT US THAT RACISM IS EASY WHEN YOU
HAVE FRIENDS IN HIGH PLACES,
AND FRIENDS IN HIGH PLACES HAVE NO USE WHATSOEVER
WHEN THEY ARE NOT YOUR FRIENDS.

DEAR MR CONDON,
POP OUT OF TELETUBBY LAND AND VISIT REALITY,
COME TO AN HONEST PLACES
AND GET SOME ADVICE FROM YOUR NEIGHBOURS,
BE ENLIGHTENED BY OUR COMMUNITY,
NEGLECT YOUR WELL PAID IGNORANCE
BECAUSE
WE KNOW WHO THE KILLERS ARE.

Benjamin Zephaniah 15-05-2016

Armgart

GEORGE ELIOT (MARY ANN EVANS) (1819–1880)

1874, British Library, Add MS 34038, f.103r, folio 22.5 × 17.4 cm, black ink on paper.

George Eliot strongly believed that women should have the same rights as men to work and to follow their passions. Eliot's novels and poems are littered with women who struggle to fulfil their potential and find their place in Victorian society, Dorothea Brooke in *Middlemarch* (1871) being a prominent example.

The title character of the poem, Armgart, is a successful and ambitious female opera singer. She receives an offer of marriage from a suitor, Graf, who expects her to give up singing when they marry while he would continue his career. In this extract, she refuses Graf's proposal because of the double standard it would impose between husband and wife. Thirty lines of the poem covering Armgart's response to Graf have been transcribed here.

The poem reads more like a drama, with its series of conversations between different characters and its accompanying stage directions. It was first published in July 1871 in *Macmillan's Magazine* in the United Kingdom and in the *Atlantic Monthly* in the United States. The handwritten draft has seven scenes, but these were divided into six scenes in the *Atlantic Monthly* and five in *Macmillan's Magazine*.

The manuscript forms part of a volume of handwritten poetry that was given to the printer for publication. On its return, the volume was gifted along with manuscripts of Eliot's novels to her lover, George Henry Lewes (1817–1878). After his death, the volumes were donated to the British Museum.

Armg. (with some agitation)   Then it forgot
Its lesson cruelly. As I remember,
'Twas not to speak save to the artist crowned,
Nor speak to her of casting off her crown.
Graf   Nor will it, Armgart. I come not to seek
Other renunciation than the wife's,
Which turns away from ~~every~~ other possible love
Future & worthier, to take his love
Who asks the name of husband. He who sought
Armgart obscure, & heard her answer, 'Wait' –
May come without suspicion now to seek
Armgart applauded.
Armg. (turning towards him)   Yes, without suspicion
Of aught save what consists with faithfulness
In all expressed intent. Forgive me, Graf,
I am ungrateful to no soul that loves me –
To you most grateful. Yet the best intent
Grasps but a living present which may grow
Like any unfledged bird. You are a noble,
And have a high career; but now you said
'Twas higher far than aught a woman seeks
Beyond mere womanhood. You claim to be
More than a husband, but could not rejoice
That I were more than wife. What follows, then?
You choosing me with such persistency
As is but stretched-out harshness, soon must find
Our marriage asks concessions, asks resolve
To share renunciation or demand it.
Either we both renounce a mutual ease,
As in a nation's need both man & wife

I meant not that our talk should hurry on
To such collision. Foresight of the ills 103
Thick shadowing your path, drew on my speech
Beyond intention. True, I came to ask
A great renunciation, but not this
Toward which my words at first perversely strayed,
As if in memory of their earlier suit,—
Forgetful. . . . .
Armgart, do you remember too? The suit
Had but postponement & was not quite disdained—
Was told to wait & learn—what it has learned—
A more submissive speech.

Armg. (with some agitation) Then it forgot
Its lesson cruelly. As I remember,
'Twas not to speak save to the artist crowned,
Nor speak to her of casting off her crown.

Graf Nor will it, Armgart. I come not to seek
Other renunciation than the wife's,
Which turns away from ~~any~~ other possible love
Future & worthier, to take his love
Who asks the name of husband. He who sought
Armgart obscure, & heard her answer, 'Wait'—
May come without suspicion now to seek
Armgart applauded.

Armg. (turning towards him) Yes, without suspicion
Of aught save what consists with faithfulness
In all expressed intent. Forgive me, Graf,
I am ungrateful to no soul that loves me—
To you most grateful. ~~Yet~~ the best intent
Grasps but a living present which may grow
Like any unfledged bird. You are a noble,
And have a high career; but now you said
'Twas higher far than aught a woman seeks
Beyond mere womanhood. You claim to be
More than a husband, but could not rejoice
That I were more than wife. What follows, then?
You choosing me with such persistency
As is but stretched-out rashness, soon must find
Our marriage asks concessions, asks resolve
To share renunciation or demand it.
Either we both renounce a mutual ease,
As in a nation's need both man & wife

The Runaway Slave at Pilgrim's Point

ELIZABETH BARRETT BROWNING (1806–1861)

1846, British Library, Ashley MS A2517, ff.5v–6r, folios 18 × 11 cm, black ink on paper.

Elizabeth Barrett Browning (née Moulton-Barrett) regularly addressed political and societal issues in her poetry. Inspired by the Romantic poets, particularly Wordsworth, Shelley and Byron, Barrett Browning believed that poetry had the power to bring about change and influence opinion. She never hesitated to express her views and was considered combative and unconventional.

Barrett Browning was descended from slave-owners, and this personal history deeply marked her. 'The Runaway Slave at Pilgrim's Point' is a dramatic monologue from the point of view of an enslaved woman who was separated from the man she loved. She was raped by her white master and bore him a child. Tormented by the child's whiteness, she suffocates him and tells of her anguish from the scaffold. The content would have been upsetting and disturbing to a contemporary audience, just as it is to us today. Barrett Browning intended the poem to shock its reader and give voice to marginalised women who were driven to the unthinkable. Infanticide has also been viewed as an act of resistance by the mother against the white colonial regime.

Pilgrim's Point is thought to be a reference to the famous story of the landing of the Pilgrim Fathers from the *Mayflower* at Plymouth Rock in 1620, which was much mythologised as the founding moment of the United States. This historic event has often been immortalised and celebrated in poetry. However, Barrett Browning uses the location to connect the settlement of North America with the enslavement of men and women.

Barrett Browning wrote much of the poem in Pisa during the autumn of 1846, and it was published two years later in *The Liberty Bell*, a Boston anti-slavery compilation. This manuscript is a partial draft of the poem and contains stanzas 14–26 (17–22 are shown here), which differ significantly from the published text. The page also contains pencil annotations by Barrett Browning's husband, Robert Browning. In one comment, he questions whether an enslaved woman would have worn a 'shawl'.

And my own child … I could not bear
    To look in his face … it was so white!
So I covered him up with a kerchief rare;
    I covered his face in close & tight:
And he moaned & struggled as well as might be,
For the white child wanted his liberty –
    Ha, ha! – he wanted his master's right.

He moaned & beat, with his head & feet –
    His little feet, that [illegible] never grew;
He struck them out as it was meet
    Against my heart to break it through –
I might have sung, like a mother mild;
But I dared not sing to the white faced child
    The only song I knew.

And yet I pulled the kerchief close.
    He could not see the sun, I swear,
More then, alive, than now he does
    From between the roots of the mangles … where?
.. I know where! Close! A child & mother
    Do wrong to look at one another,
When one is black & one is fair –

8

And my own child ... I could not bear
To look in his face .. it was so white!
So I covered him up with a kerchief rare;
I covered his face in close & tight:–
And he moaned & struggled as well might be,
For the white child wanted his liberty –
Ha, ha! – he wanted his master's right. –

He moaned & beat with his head & feet –
His little feet, ~~that [illegible]~~ never grew! –
He struck them out as it was meet
Against my heart to break it through –
I might have sung like a mother mild! –
But I dared not sing to the white-faced child
The only song I knew. –

And yet I pulled the kerchief close. –
He could not see the sun, I swear,
More then, alive, than now he does
From between the roots of the mangles .. where?
.. I know where! Close! A child & mother
Do wrong to look at one another,
When one is black & one is fair –

Why ~~And~~ in that single glance I had
Of my child's face .. I tell you all ..
I saw a look that made me mad ..!
The master's look, that used to fall
On my soul like his lash .. or worse!
And so, to save it from my curse,
I twisted it round in my shawl. – does that sound like a slave's article of clothing?

And he moaned & ~~crouched~~ [trembled] from ~~feet~~ foot to head –
He ~~[illegible]~~ [shivered] from head to foot –
Till after a time he lay instead
Too suddenly still & mute ..
And I felt, beside, a creeping cold –
I dared to lift up just a fold,
As in lifting a leaf of the mango-fruit –

But my fruit! .. ha ha! – there, had been ..
(I laugh to think on't at this hour ..!)
Your fine white angels, (who have seen
God's secrets nearest to his power)
And plucked my fruit to make their wine ..
And sucked the soul of that child of mine
As the humming bird sucks [the soul of] the flower.
(soul of the

~~And~~ Was in that single glance I had
Of my child's face .. I tell you all ..
I saw a look that made me mad – '
The master's look, that used to fall
On my soul like his lash .. or worse'–
And so, to save it from my curse,
I twisted it round in my shawl.

Does that sound like a slave's article of clothing?

And he moaned & ~~struggled~~ trembled from ~~head~~ foot to head –
He ~~trembled~~ shivered from head to foot –
Till after a time he lay instead
Too suddenly still & mute ..
And I felt beside, a creeping cold –
I dared to lift up just a fold,
As in lifting a leaf of the mango=fruit.

But my fruit' … ha, ha' – there, had been ..
(I laugh to think on't at this hour ..)
Your fine white angels, (who have seen
God's secrets nearest to His power)
And plucked my fruit to make their wine .
And sucked the soul of that child of mine,
As the humming bird sucks the soul of the flower.
soul of the

The Prisoner

ALEXANDER PUSHKIN (1799–1837), TRANSLATED BY FRANCES CORNFORD (1886–1960)

c.1942, British Library, Add MS 56346 B, f.20r, folio 20.4 × 16.2 cm, blue ink and pencil on paper, bound in a blue cloth notebook with a red spine.

Poetry can be dangerous, especially when it implies criticism of a ruler or the government of a country. The Russian Empire imposed strict censorship rules with harsh penalties for those who broke them. Alexander Pushkin was born into a noble Russian family, and was descended from Abram Hannibal (*c.*1696–1871), a Russian soldier and nobleman of African origin. Pushkin followed the Romantic style and was greatly influenced by Lord Byron. The political poems he wrote were not published and were secretly circulated among like-minded individuals.

After the sudden death of Tsar Alexander I (b.1777) in 1825, the Decembrists, a military faction that supported Konstantin (1779–1831), Alexander's brother, who had declined the throne, attempted to seize power. The uprising was quashed, but Pushkin's poems were found among the belongings of some of the Decembrists.

For the political views expressed in his poems, Pushkin was exiled by Tsar Nicholas I (1796–1855) to a remote southern province. Here he continued to write and produced the poem 'The Prisoner'. While he was not actually imprisoned, Pushkin viewed his exile as imprisonment.

'The Prisoner' was translated by Frances Cornford, the English poet who wrote 'Autumn Morning at Cambridge' about her hometown (see page 93). Cornford translated a number of Russian poems for the volume she published in 1943 with Esther Polianowsky Salaman (1900–1995), *Poems from the Russian*. The three lines in pencil at the bottom of the manuscript show Cornford's attempt to rework the translation of the last section of the poem.

The British Library purchased Cornford's literary papers from the Arts Council on 12 April 1969.

The Prisoner

Pushkin

In a damp cell behind the bars sit I
An eagle young, & proud, & born to fly;
Outside, the sad companion of my day
Flutters his wing & pecks his bleeding prey..

Then pecks no more, but through the window stares
As if we thought the same thing unawares,
As though with look & cry his heart would say:–
Brother, the time is come to fly away.

We are free birds together, free & proud
Fly where the mountains whiten through the cloud
To that sea country blue beneath the sky
Where only walks the wind, the wind & I.

~~Fly there where hills are white above the cloud~~
~~There by the shores & blue beshadowed sea~~
~~There where the winds sweeps past – the wind with me~~

Cover of Frances Cornford's poetry notebook, British Library, Add MS 56346 B.

~~The Prisoner~~

Pushkin

In a damp cell behind the bars sit I
An eagle young, & proud, & born to fly;
Outside, the sad companion of my day
Flutters his wing & pecks his bleeding prey.

Then pecks no more, but through the window stares
As if we thought the same thing unawares,
As though with look & cry his heart would say:–
Brother, the time is come to fly away.

We are free birds together, free & proud
Fly where the mountains whiten through the cloud
To that sea country blue beneath the sky
Where only walks the wind, the wind & I.

~~Fly there where hills are white above the cloud~~
~~There by the shores & blue beshadowed sea~~
~~There where the winds sweep past – the wind with me~~

The Laws of God, The Laws of Man

A. E. HOUSMAN (1859–1936)

***c.*1900**, British Library, Add MS 44878, f.1r, folio 32 × 20 cm, ink on lined paper.

A. E. Housman, photograph
Trinity College, Cambridge.

Alfred Edward Housman was a poet and classicist best known for his collection of poems *A Shropshire Lad* (1896). Housman published only one further collection of poems in his lifetime, *Last Poems*, in 1922. 'The Laws of God, The Laws of Man' forms part of *Last Poems* and, like many of Housman's poems, uses opposites. This poem contrasts laws and helplessness. The handwritten draft is almost identical to the published version, with only a couple of minor changes in pencil by Housman.

During his time at Oxford University Housman fell in love with fellow student and friend, Moses Jackson (1858–1923). Housman's love influenced his poetry and lasted a lifetime, but was unrequited as Jackson was heterosexual. Homosexuality is subtly referenced in a number of Housman's poems. 'The Laws of God, The Laws of Man' is thought to reflect Housman's frustration with the rules imposed by Church and State that meant he could not live his life as he wanted to, freely and openly.

Attitudes to homosexuality in late Victorian Britain were harsh, as evidenced by the treatment of Oscar Wilde, who was imprisoned in Reading Gaol in 1895 for gross indecency. Housman wrote 'Oh Who Is That Young Sinner' in the aftermath of Wilde's trial and reputedly sent him a copy of *A Shropshire Lad* on his release.

This poetry notebook was presented to the British Library by Housman's brother, Laurence (1865–1959), through Dr George Macaulay Trevelyan in 1936 (1876–1962).

The laws of God, the laws of man,
He may keep that will and can;
Not I: let God and man decree
Laws for themselves and not for me;
And if my ways are not as theirs
Let them mind their own affairs.
Their deeds I judge and much condemn,
Yet when did I make laws for them?
Please yourselves, say I, and they
Need ~~but~~ only look the other way.
But no, they will not; they must still
Wrest their neighbour to their will,
And make me dance as they desire
With jail and gallows and hell-fire.
And what am I, to face the odds
Of man's bedevilment and God's?
I, a stranger and afraid
In a world I never made.
~~[illegible] They wax not weak with wreaking wrong;~~
They will be master, right or wrong;
Though both are foolish, both are strong.
And since, my soul, we cannot fly
To Saturn nor to Mercury,
Keep we must, if keep we can,
These foreign laws of God and man.

The laws of God, the laws of man,
He may keep that will and can;
Not I: let God and man decree
Laws for themselves and not for me;
And if my ways are not as theirs
Let them mind their own affairs.
Their deeds I judge and much condemn,
Yet when did I make laws for them?
Please yourselves, say I, and they
Need ~~but~~ only look the other way.
But no, they will not; they must still
Wrest their neighbours to their will,
And make me dance as they desire
With jail and gallows and hell-fire.
And what am I, to face the odds
Of man's bedevilment and God's?
I, a stranger and afraid
In a world I never made.
~~They wax not weak with wreaking wrong;~~ They will be master, right or wrong;
Though both are foolish, both are strong.
And since, my soul, we cannot fly
To Saturn nor to Mercury,
Keep we must, if keep we can,
These foreign laws of God and man.

This is what every prisoner should leave behind. 2

Wear

Two things alone could save me from despair

Great Egotism and ~~my~~ love most dear

Pride of the first ~~[illegible]~~ my dowery doth some

Thy measure of the second fill again

21

When

The sunbeams entry here every instant

Reflected radience echoe to my cell

[illegible] here: a [illegible] gold [illegible] with crimson shade

~~My prison window~~

~~The other~~

A prison window paints

Even h

Untitled poems written on toilet paper

SYLVIA PANKHURST (1882–1960)

1921, British Library, Add MS 88925/1/1, f.2r, folio 9.4 × 15.1 cm, pencil on toilet paper and f.21r, folio 14.5 × 10 cm, pencil on toilet paper.

Sylvia Pankhurst, photograph, Library of Congress, Washington D.C., JK1881. N357 sec. XVI, no. 3-9 NAWSA Coll.

Many people think of Sylvia Pankhurst as the suffragette who campaigned alongside her family for women's rights and enfranchisement. Fewer know of her later life, which included campaigns against war, fascism and imperialism and in support of racial equality and social justice.

Sylvia Pankhurst was imprisoned more often than any of the other Pankhursts, and even after women had won the vote in 1918 she returned to prison. In 1921 she was once more 'His Majesty's guest' in Holloway Prison. This time her crime was not the struggle for women's equality but sedition, for she had published pro-communist articles in her newspaper *Workers' Dreadnought*.

Pankhurst used her six-month solitary sentence as a political prisoner to write. Her only permitted writing materials were a small slate and chalk. Yet she was prolific during this period, having come up with a practical means of transcribing her writing and smuggling it out of Holloway. Pankhurst drafted her ideas, then reworked them with soft pencil on standard issue HM Prison toilet paper, which she concealed in the underclothes of her uniform. These contraband manuscripts were then smuggled out by her friend Norah Smyth (1874–1963) on prison visits, and by other prisoners on release.

These poems form part of a large archive relating mostly to Pankhurst's later life after 1935, in particular her campaign for Ethiopia following the invasion by Italy in 1935. Her son, Professor Richard Pankhurst (1927–2017), presented the collection to the British Library in August 2003.

This is what every prisoner should leave behind.
[~~Thin~~]
Two things alone could save me from despair
Great egotism and thy care most dear
Since of the first my dowery ~~that which I had~~ doth wane
Thy measure of the second fill again.

When
Me sunbeams' entry here ever frustrate
Reflected radience echoe to my cell
prints here a faint gold square with cross of shade
~~The prison window~~
~~The echoe~~
A prison window painted even

1-
+

Mine - by the Right of
the White Election!
Mine - by the Royal Seal!
Mine - by the Sign in
the Scarlet prison -
+Bars - cannot conceal!

Mine - here - in Vision - and
in Veto!
Mine - by the Grave's Repeal -
Titled - Confirmed -
+Delirious Charter!
Mine - +long as Ages steal!

+ Good affidavit - + while
+ Bolts

Mine – by the Right of the White Election!

EMILY DICKINSON (1830–1886)

c.1862, Houghton Library – (66b) Mine – by the Right of the White Election! J528, Fr411, folio 20.5 x 12.7 cm, ink on laid, cream and blue-ruled paper with an embossed G&T logo in the upper right hand corner.

Emily Dickinson was a little-known American poet during her lifetime, but her popularity soared soon after her death. Her first volume of poems was published in 1890, four years after her death, and went through eleven editions in under two years. Over 1,000 of Emily Dickinson's poems and letters are held at the Houghton Library, Harvard University. Within the collection are forty hand-sewn manuscript books, or fascicles, into which Dickinson made fair copies of her poems. These volumes were disbound at an early date by Dickinson's editors, leaving the poems as individual leaves.

'Mine – by the Right of the White Election!' is a manuscript fair-copy poem which was originally in a fascicle of mixed material. Holes along the edge of the sheet show where it was originally sewn. The meaning of the poem is ambiguous. It has been suggested that the narrator is asserting themselves and revolting against God, claiming the earth and heavens as their own. The repeated use of the word 'Mine' against symbols of traditional order, such as the 'white election' and the 'royal seal', serves to give power to the individual. The language also hints at the oppression faced by African Americans in the nineteenth century. In many ways the poem celebrates individualism over the establishment, be it religious, legal or political. This poem was included in Dickinson's *Poems* in 1890.

+
Mine – by the Right of
the White Election!
Mine – by the Royal Seal!
Mine – by the Sign in
the scarlet prison.
+ Bars – Cannot Conceal!

Mine – here – in Vision – and
in Veto!
Mine – by the Grave's Repeal –
Titled – Confirmed
+ Delirious Charter!
Mine – long as Ages steal!

+ Good affidavit – + while
+ Bolts

Emily Dickinson, daguerreotype, Emily Dickinson Museum, Amherst College.

chapter 7

FAMILY AND FRIENDSHIP

The poems in this chapter describe relationships between the author and their family or friends. While some of these poems were written for a public audience, others are private thoughts originally meant only for a small selection of readers.

A number of the poems describe relationships between parents and children. The Chartist Ernest Jones wrote a tender poem on the birthday of his 2-year-old son, which he kept in a personal album containing sketches and poetry. Christina Rossetti's nursery rhyme 'Love me, I love you' celebrates the love between a mother and her child, while Dorothy Wordsworth's poem 'The Mother's Return' describes her niece and nephew's love for their mother. James Berry's poem 'Vigilance of Fathers and Sons' shows the complexity of his feelings towards his father. In the poem and accompanying notes Berry expresses frustration at his father's lack of interest in his children's education, which as an adult he understood to be conditioned by the values of the colonial system under which his father lived. Pascale Petit's poem 'The Strait-Jackets', which mixes fantasy with reality, describes the poet reconnecting with her estranged, terminally ill father. Petit imagines bringing forty hummingbirds in a suitcase, which dart and fly around her father in hospital.

The relationship between siblings is explored in several poems. Sappho's poem wishing her brother a safe return dates from the seventh century BC and its surviving fragments comprise the earliest manuscript included in this book. Jane Austen's congratulatory poem, written in a letter to her brother Frank, displays a private aspect of a widely published author; Austen's pride in and love for her brother is shown in her writing. George Eliot's regret at the breakdown of her relationship with her brother, expressed in 'Brother and Sister', shows the often complex nature of sibling relationships. Charlotte Mew's poem, 'Xmas: 1880', written when she was just 11, describes the love between young siblings, despite the tragedy and loss that had struck her family.

Commitment to and collaboration with friends is shown in two very different poems. Goethe's work, 'An die neunzehn Freunde in England' ('To the nineteen friends in England'), dedicated to his English and Scottish friends, is testament to the relationships, both working and private, forged by the German writer. The manuscript drafts of poems by the early nineteenth-century Chinese poet Chen Qinghuai show the collaborative nature of his writing, with friends and peers commenting directly on his work.

Vigilance of Fathers and Sons (A Father's Vigil)

JAMES BERRY (1924–2017)

1965–73, British Library, Add MS 89353/1/5, folio 29.5 × 21 cm, typewritten with red ink annotations.

Not all familial relationships are straightforward. In his poem 'Vigilance of Fathers and Sons', later called 'A Father's Vigil', James Berry expresses the mixture of emotions he felt towards his father, Robert, a smallholder in Jamaica. He contrasts the dominant father figure to his four sons at home with the subservient figure his father presented to 'a white face'.

This manuscript reflects a work in progress. Berry's initial draft of the poem has been typed out under the title, 'The Father's Vigilance' and then reviewed and reworked by Berry in red pen. Lines of text are struck through and new lines added to the right of the poem. Berry wrote several different poems on his relationship with his father, the most famous of which is 'My Father' (also known as 'Praise and Resentment'), the published version of which is transcribed here. The two poems contain thematic and emotional similarities. Berry's notes, drafts and letters were purchased by the British Library in 2012.

Berry was also angered by his father's lack of interest in his son's education as shown in his manuscript notes used in preparation for his poetry collection *Windrush Songs* (2007). Berry came to see his father's ambivalence as a product of colonial society, which kept people in ignorance of their past.

Though Berry grew up in the shadow of a former slave plantation, he learnt little about Caribbean history at school. His awakening came when he travelled to the United States and witnessed the 'terrible humiliations' of Black people in the South. Berry came to Britain on the SS *Orbita* in 1948 and settled in London.

My Father

For being so black
so muscular so well curved
like a groomed show man,
too fit everyday for barefoot
he made us boys feel
we could kill him

For laughing so deep
down notes from soprano
like a tied stallion sighting
a pan of water
he got all laughter stopped
to listen to him

For treating ticks
like berries gathering
and the halfdead cow
in a bath of herbs and oil
he sat all day in tall grass
sweet-talking weak jaws

For tipping out warm pockets
of sticky sugar plums
or sat-on bananas
or squashed up naseberries
he made children descend
on him for things past ripe

For expecting my mother
to make money like food
and clothes and be the sum
of every question
he made us go deadfaced
when he stayed in

For drawing his name 'X'
and carrying a locked head
to explain stars
like a tree-top pointing
he made us acknowledge him
keenly in rage

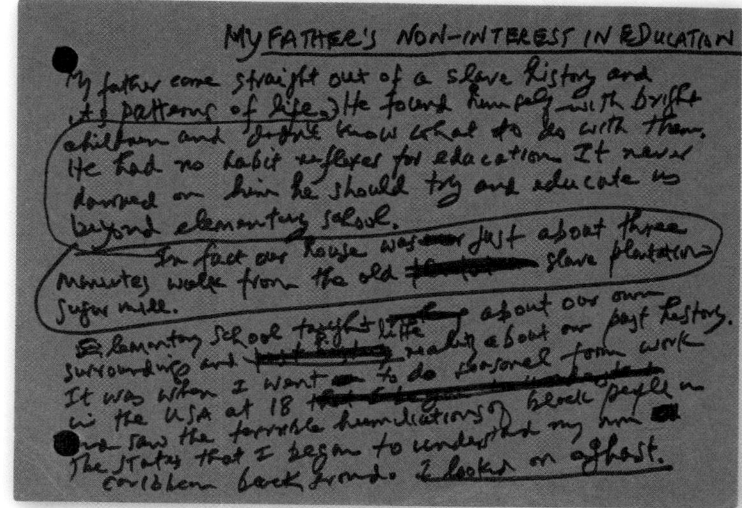

MY FATHER'S NON-INTEREST IN EDUCATION

My father came straight out of a slave history and its patterns of life. He found himself with bright children and didn't know what to do with them. He had no habit reflexes for education. It never dawned on him he should try and educate us beyond elementary school.

In fact our house was just about three minutes walk from the old [illegible] slave plantation sugar mill.

Elementary school taught little about our own surroundings and [illegible] reality about our past history.

It was when I went to the USA at 18 to do seasonal farm work [illegible] saw the terrible humiliations of black people in the States that I began to understand my own Caribbean background. I looked on aghast.

'My father's non-interest in education', James Berry, British Library, Add MS 89353/1/13.

~~THE FATHER'S~~ VIGILANCE Of Fathers and Sons

He stayed home that night,
with ~~the deadly~~
with the blackspider bite
in ~~the~~ his big hand, like ~~growing death~~ growing death
~~and~~ his voice a groaning bass.
He patrolli~~ng~~ the hut. Those groans he patrolled with ~~with~~ in the hut were to seize
~~to seize~~ everybody in the vice
~~in the vice of his~~
of his shameless agony,
~~the~~ ~~with five sons~~ awake
~~on the floor;~~ scattered
~~in dim lamplight,~~
on the floor
~~in the dark village,~~
Aware of the tortured shadow
~~shadow~~ in calico shorts; four sons/ Kept their eyes quietly awake
~~all wondering if~~ scattered in dim lamplight village
~~he'd be missed if he was~~ around on the floor in the dark knowing he wouldn't be missed
if he was bones in the ground;
~~all~~ knowing the ~~beast~~ stranger he was in the home
~~he was to their mother~~
~~and knew~~ knowing his low
neighing of a chuckle
with cap against his chest
at the sight of a white face -
beneath himself completely -
seeing that hand
that held a lump of sugar.

James Berry

Letter to Frank on the birth of his son

JANE AUSTEN (1775–1817)

26 July 1809, British Library, Add MS 42180, ff.7r–8r, folios 23.2 × 18.7 cm, iron gall ink on laid paper.

Jane Austen, reproduction after a drawing by Cassandra Austen, British Library, 10855.e.8.

Jane Austen had a very happy family life and got on well with her seven siblings. Close family relationships, especially between siblings, often appear in her novels, such as those of Jane and Elizabeth Bennet in *Pride and Prejudice* (1813), Elinor and Marianne Dashwood in *Sense and Sensibility* (1811) and Fanny and William Price in *Mansfield Park* (1814).

Austen's brother Francis (Frank) William (1774–1865) was a serving captain in the Royal Navy. In this letter from July 1809, Austen congratulates her brother on the birth of his son. The letter is written in verse divided into four stanzas. The first stanza and the opening four lines of the second stanza are shown here. In the letter Austen hopes that her nephew, also called Francis William, will be like his father – kind, considerate and gentle.

In the last stanza Austen gives news of home. She has recently moved to the Hampshire village of Chawton with her mother Cassandra (1739–1827), her sister, also Cassandra (1773–1845), and Martha Lloyd (1765–1843), a friend of the family. She writes that they are settling into their new home very well, and they are sure that 'when complete / It will all other Houses beat'.

Although the poem was not intended for publication, Austen, like other members of her family, enjoyed writing verse to mark occasions and as part of games and entertainments. For example, in one game all players had to write a poem where the last word of every line rhymed with 'rose'. Devising riddles and word games and writing humorous poems were all popular pastimes in the late eighteenth and early nineteenth centuries. They also feature in Austen's novel *Emma* (1815).

Chawton, July 26. – 1809. –

My dearest Frank, I wish you joy
Of Mary's safety with a Boy,
Whose birth has given little pain
Compared with that of Mary Jane. -
May he a growing Blessing prove,
And well deserve his Parents' Love! -
Endow'd with Art's & Nature's Good,
Thy name possessing with thy Blood,
In him, in all his ways, may we
Another Francis William see! -
Thy infant days may he inherit,
Thy warmth, nay insolence of spirit; -
We would not with one fault dispense
To weaken the resemblance.
May he revive thy Nursery sin,
Peeping as daringly within,
His curley Locks but just descried,
With 'Bet, my be not come to bide.' -
Fearless of danger, braving pain,
And threaten'd very oft in vain,
Still may one Terror daunt his Soul,
One needful engine of Controul

Chawton, July 26. – 1809.

My dearest Frank, I wish you joy
Of Mary's safety with a Boy,
Whose birth has given little pain
Compared with that of Mary Jane. —
May he a growing Blessing prove,
And well deserve his Parents' Love! —
Endow'd with Art's & Nature's Good,
Thy name possessing with thy Blood,
In him, in all his ways, may we
Another Francis William see! —
Thy infant days may he inherit,
Thy warmth, nay insolence of spirit; —
We would not with one fault dispense
To weaken the resemblance.
May he revive thy Nursery sin,
Peeping as daringly within,
His curley Locks but just descried,
With "Bet, my be not come to bide." —
Fearless of danger, braving pain,
And threaten'd very oft in vain,
Still may one Terror daunt his Soul,
One needful engine of Controul

Poem about her brother Charaxus

SAPPHO (*c.*630–*c.*570 BC)

Third century AD, British Library, Papyrus 739, 20.5 × 10 cm, mounted in a glass case measuring 25.5 × 15.5 cm.

Sappho is one of the earliest known female poets. She lived on the Greek island of Lesbos in the seventh century BC. Although she probably composed over 10,000 lines of lyrical poetry, very little of her work survives. While it has been suggested that much of her work was destroyed because it celebrated lesbianism, it is equally possible that it was lost because very few people could read and understand it. Sappho's name is synonymous with same-sex relationships, but the fragments of her work that survive do not always focus on this subject.

This papyrus preserves a poetic fragment in Sappho's characteristic metre, known as the Sapphic metre, from the now lost first book of her collected poetry. It is written in ancient Greek. In the text, she prays for her brother's return from Egypt 'with many supplications, that he may come here steering his ship unharmed and find us women safe and sound'. Surrendering to fate, she continues: 'and the rest, let's entrust it all to the gods, for calm suddenly follows great storms'. This manuscript was found in an ancient rubbish mound in Oxyrhynchos, Egypt by Bernard Grenfell (1869–1926) and Arthur Hunt (1871–1934). Between 1897 and 1907 the pair uncovered nearly 50,000 papyrus fragments in the mounds at Oxyrhynchos. Due to the poor condition of this papyrus and significant textual losses, this poem has not been transcribed.

This papyrus was part of a larger group of papyri presented to the British Museum by the Egyptian Exploration Society in October 1900.

Sappho and her companions, British Library, Add MS 20698, f.73r.

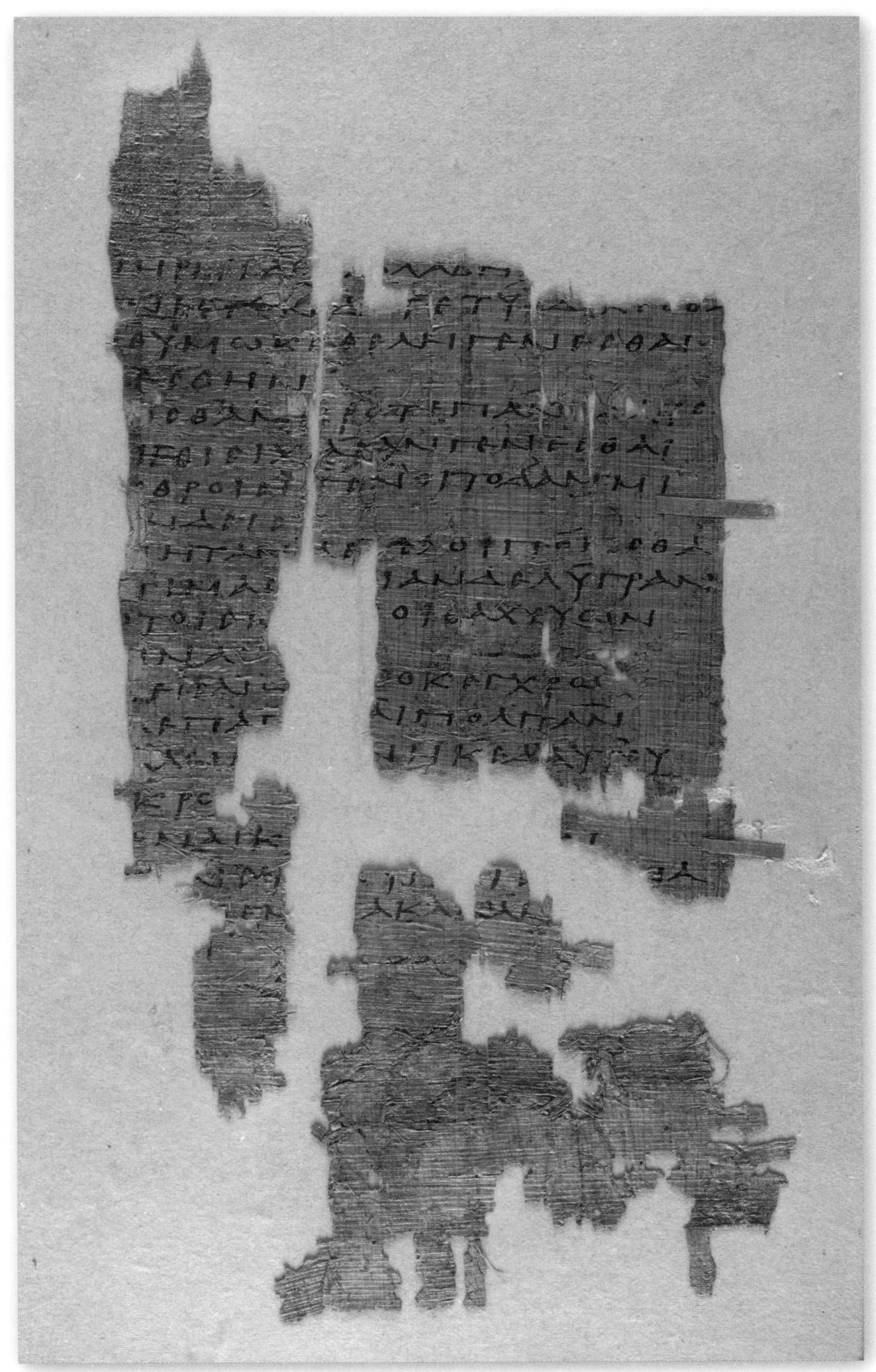

The Mother's Return

DOROTHY WORDSWORTH (1771–1855)

After 1828, British Library, Ashley MS 4630, f.1r, two bifolia 19.2 × 15.5 cm, iron gall ink on laid paper.

Dorothy Wordsworth, lithograph, British Library, 10826.de.10.

Dorothy Wordsworth's poem 'The Mother's Return', composed in 1807, was first published in her brother William Wordsworth's *Poems* in 1815. William and Dorothy enjoyed a close relationship throughout their lives, much of which was recorded in Dorothy's journals. The poem was originally published anonymously, attributed only to 'a female friend of the author', thus protecting Dorothy's identity. Although the poem was published in 1815, this manuscript must have been written after 1828, as the watermark in the paper bears that date. The manuscript contains corrections and is different from the published version of the poem.

The poem describes the emotions of William and Mary Wordsworth's small children as they wait for the return of their mother. Dorothy lived with her brother for much of her adult life and her influence is evident throughout his writing.

Shown and transcribed here are the first four verses of the fourteen-verse poem, written on two bifolia.

A month, sweet little ones is passed
Since your dear Mother went away;
And she is coming home again ~~tomorrow is the happy day~~
Tomorrow is the happy day

Oh! blessed tidings! thought of joy!
John heard me speak with steady glee
He silent stood_then laugh'd amain
And shouted, 'Mother come to me!'

Louder & louder did he shout
With childish hope, to bring her near;
'Nay, patience! patience! little Boy.
Your tender Mother cannot hear.'

~~Now St~~ I told of hills & far-off towns,
And long, long vales to travel through,
He listens-puzzled-sore perplex'd
But he submits – what can he do?

1

A month, sweet little-ones is passed
Since your dear Mother went away;
And she is coming home again – ~~tomorrow~~
~~is the happy day~~
Tomorrow is the happy day
Oh! blessed tidings! thought of joy!
John heard me speak with steady glee
He silent stood – then laugh'd amain
And shouted, "Mother come to me!"

Louder & louder did he shout
With childish hope to bring her near;
"Nay, patience! patience! little Boy,
Your tender Mother cannot hear."

~~Now she~~ I told of hills & far-off towns,
And long, long vales to travel through,
He listens – puzzled – sore perplex'd
But he submits – what can he do?

夏孝女 (Filial Daughter Xia)

陳慶槐 **CHEN QINGHUAI (*fl.*1803)**

1788–1807, British Library, Add MS 16314, f.17r, volume 26.9 × 16.9 cm, black and red ink on paper with red seals.

This folio is from a collection of poetical drafts by the Chinese poet Chen Qinghuai (also known as Yinshan or Yingsan) who obtained his *jinshi* degree in 1790. He was from Dinghai in Zhejiang Province, and many aspects of the local landscape and culture feature in his compositions.

Comments and responses from members of Chen's social circle, many of whom were accomplished writers themselves, are added around the text – in margins and on paper flaps – in different colours. Here we see friends and scholars helping to shape the text. The poems and annotations also serve as valuable biographical and documentary evidence for Chen Qinghuai, his peers and the world around them. The collection is an example of the influence of friendship networks on the creative process and the role of poetry in making and sustaining social connections, something that is common in the Chinese literary tradition.

Shown here is a poem entitled 'Filial Daughter Xia', the tragic story of an 18-year-old girl who tries to clear her father's name when he dies after being convicted of a crime, and who also dies later in the poem. The poem received a favourable response from the poet's circle of friends, but opinion was divided on the last line. The first half of this folio has been transcribed and translated here.

This volume was presented to the British Museum Library in 1846 by the secretary of state for foreign affairs, George Hamilton-Gordon, fourth earl of Aberdeen (1784–1860).

夏孝女
孝女，吾邑紫薇~~澳~~庄人。余既作舟山竹枝詞，追憶舊事，並成是什。
Filial Daughter Xia
The filial daughter is from Ziwei ~~Bay~~ (Village) in my district. I finished composing 'Bamboo Twig Poems of Zhoushan', thought of this past matter, and thus wrote this poem.
南山下，夏氏女。年十八，以孝著。
Below Southern Mountain,
A daughter of the Xia family.
She was eighteen,
And known for her filial piety.
父理和，~~溺子賭。縣官聞，遣吏捕。~~
Her father's name was Lihe,
~~His son, doted upon, gambled.~~
~~The Magistrate heard of this,~~
~~And sent functionaries to arrest him.~~
[老無子，與人訟。事涉賭，詞多誣，縣官怒。]
[He was old and had no son,
He was in a lawsuit with someone,
And this involved gambling.
The suit was filled with misrepresentations,
And the Magistrate was angry].
官如狼，吏如虎。索千緡，父不與。與五百，吏不許。死於吏，死於官，死於滷。
The official was like a wolf,
The functionaries like tigers.
They demanded a thousand strings of cash,
The father refused.
He offered five hundred,
But the functionaries refused.
The father died at the hands of the functionaries,
He died at the hands of the official,
He died from drinking salt water.

夏孝女　孝女吾邑紫微澳人余既作舟山竹枝詞

追憶舊事並成是什

是时同土者蓬字志年月以别之 匝宋更如林乃虔女也 孝女後

南山下夏氏女年十八以孝著父理和溺于賭縣官聞遣

老無子 与人訟事涉賭 詞多誣 縣官怒

吏捕官如狼吏如虎索千緡父不與吏不許死於

吏死於官死於滷女哭之推肺腑女有母有庶母有從兄

兄也魯父尸寒父尸腐官來驗吏作作來視妾父父

何辜妾何怙婿范生來焚楮女伏苫淚如雨不報讐忍歸

汝身未入范家戶足未踏范家土生死別此一舉朝出門

一字一珠　一字一淚　千古不磨　之作人般山心服

吾輩集中必須有此種詩方壓得

佳氏

Xmas: 1880.

—

Darling little Maiden,
Little Freda Mew,
Comes with message laden,
Harry, dear, for you.

—

Comes with Christmas Greeting,
Clad in Winter gear,
Comes, the little sweeting,
To wish a Bright New Year.

—

Welcome, then, the bearer,
With a loving kiss,
Could you find a fairer,
Dearer maid than this?

—

Welcome; too, the message,
Dearest of young misters,
(Much good may it presage!)
From your loving Sisters,

— Lotti.

Annie.

Xmas: 1880

CHARLOTTE MEW (1869–1928)

1880, British Library, Add MS 83382, folio 18 × 11.5 cm, black ink on paper.

This touching poem was written when Charlotte Mew was only 11. It was meant as a Christmas greeting from Charlotte and her sister Anne (d.1927) to their siblings Freda and Henry (known as Harry). A note on the verso reveals that the poem was copied onto Christmas cards. This poem and other papers by Charlotte form part of the Poetry Bookshop Papers purchased by the British Library in 2002.

Charlotte described her childhood as 'intensely happy' despite a number of tragic events. Three of her brothers died in infancy and both Freda and Henry were confined to psychiatric hospitals. Charlotte and Anne vowed to never marry, fearing that they would pass on what Charlotte considered to be the 'family taint'.[1]

Charlotte and Anne remained close throughout their lives. After the death of their parents, the two sisters lived together in reduced circumstances. In the 1920s Anne developed inoperable cancer, and Charlotte nursed her sister until her death. Following Anne's death, Charlotte struggled with her mental health and moved into a nursing home. She took her own life in 1928.

Charlotte's work was widely admired, including by Thomas Hardy, who thought of her as the foremost female poet of the time. Some of her best-known works include 'Requiescat' (1909) and 'The Farmer's Bride' (1916).

Xmas: 1880

Darling little Maiden,
Little Freda Mew,
Comes with message laden,
Harry, dear, for you.

Comes with Christmas Greeting,
Clad in Winter gear,
Comes, the little sweeting,
To wish a Bright New Year.

Welcome then, the bearer,
With a loving kiss,
Could you find a fairer,
Dearer maid than this?

Welcome; too, the message,
Dearest of young misters,
(Much good may it presage!)
From your loving sisters

Lotti.
Anne.

Love me, I love you

CHRISTINA ROSSETTI (1830–1894)

1868–70, British Library, Ashley MS 1371, f.4r, folio 18.2 × 11.5 cm, black ink on paper with pencil and red crayon illustration, later bound into a notebook.

This manuscript is an autograph fair copy of a poem from Christina Rossetti's volume of nursery rhymes *Sing Song*, originally published in 1872. The collection was designed for Victorian children as a composite work in which the text and illustrations interrelate and enhance one another. This poem depicts the love between a mother and her child, a theme that runs throughout the nursery rhymes.

The poems are written mainly on the back of readers' slips for the *New English Dictionary*, of which her brother William Michael Rossetti (1829–1919) was an editor. Rossetti has illustrated each of her poems in pencil and red crayon. When the manuscript was submitted to her editor, F. S. Ellis (1830–1901), Rossetti feared that 'you may have misconceived what the illustrations amount to, as they are the merest sketches, and I cannot draw'.

For the illustrations in the published version, Rossetti wanted a single artist to illustrate all of the poems. She turned down a number of candidates before agreeing that Arthur Hughes (1832–1915), an artist influenced by the Pre-Raphaelite Brotherhood, would illustrate the work. The Pre-Raphaelite Brotherhood, of which Rossetti's two brothers, William and Dante, were founding members, was a group of painters, poets and art critics who shared similar principles and were inspired by Romanticism and nature. Hughes worked using Rossetti's illustrations and she was delighted with the finished designs.

2.
Love me, I love you,
Love me, my baby,
Sing it high, sing it low,
Sing it as may be.

Mother's arms under you,
Her eyes above you,
Sing it high, sing it low,
Love me, I love you.

Love me,—I love you,
Love me, my baby;
Sing it high, sing it low,
Sing it as may be.

Mother's arms under you,
Her eyes above you
Sing it high, sing it low,
Love me,—I love you.

2

'Love Me, I Love You', illustration by Arthur Hughes in *Sing-Song. A nursery rhyme book*, British Library, 11651.e.7.

Done

4

2.

Love me, I love you,
Love me, my baby,
Sing it high, sing it low,
Sing it as may be.

Mother's arms under you,
Her eyes above you,
Sing it high, sing it low,
Love me, I love you.

An die neunzehn Freunde in England (To the nineteen friends in England)

JOHANN WOLFGANG VON GOETHE (1749–1832)

1831, British Library, Add MS 43377 F, f.18, folio 10.5 × 16.6 cm, iron gall ink on laid paper. British Library Seal CLXXIX.2, wax seal 3.7 × 3.9 cm.

On Goethe's 82nd birthday, fifteen of his English and Scottish friends and admirers presented him with a gold seal. Goethe was so touched by the gesture that he wrote a short verse, erroneously titled by his secretary 'An die neunzehn Freunde in England' (to the nineteen friends in England), to mark the occasion. Among the fifteen friends were translator James Churchill (*fl.*1831–1846), the poet William Wordsworth and Lord Francis Leveson-Gower (1800–1857), who had translated Goethe's *Faust* in 1823.

'To the nineteen friends in England' was first published in the journal *Chaos* in Weimar in 1831. The lines 'Thätigen Sinn! das Thun gezügelt; Stetig Streben, ohne Hast' ('Active thought! Action reined in, Constant striving, without haste') refer to Goethe's idea that action and thought are often at odds with one another. The poem suggests that these friends have combined both thought and action through their gift of the seal.

This manuscript and an impression of the seal, together with a copy of the published poem, were presented by Leonard L. Mackell (1879–1937) to the British Museum Library on 9 March 1932, to mark the centenary of Goethe's death. In a letter to the director of the British Museum, Mackell wrote that, for over thirty years, 'I have had the privilege and pleasure of working in the British Museum Library' and that he 'wished to present something of more than usual interest, as a slight token of my gratitude to the Library'.

An die neunzehn Freunde in England.

Worte, die der Dichter spricht,
Treu, in heimischen [~~Gefilden~~] Bezircken,
Wircken gleich, doch weiß er nicht
Ob sie in die Ferne wircken.

Britten! habt sie aufgefaßt:
»Thätigen Sinn, das Thun gezügelt;
Stetig Streben, ohne Hast.«
Und so wollt Ihr's denn besiegelt.

W.28.Aug.1831. G.

To the nineteen friends in England.

Words, which the poet speaks,
True ~~on home pastures~~, in his home domain,
Work immediately, though he knows not,
If they work further afield.

Britons! You have grasped them!
'Active thought! Action reined in,
Constant striving, without haste.'
And thus you want them sealed.

18

An die Vierzehn Freunde in England.

Worte, die der Dichter spricht,
Treu, in heimischen ~~Gefilden~~ Bezirken,
Wirken gleich, doch weiß er nicht
Ob sie in die Ferne wirken.

Britten! habt sie aufgefaßt:
"Thätigen Sinn, das Thun gezügelt;
Stetig Streben, ohne Hast."
Und so wollt Ihr's denn besiegelt.

W. 28 Aug. 1831. G

(Goethe)

To my child, Ernest Beaufort,
on his second birthday
29th December
1844.

From the far land of Spirits wild
Came on the earth a joyous child
A Sunbeam-lighted rose -
In hour of purest passion mild
A soft smile called it into being
As the Spring from winter fleeing
Calls a floweret through the snows.

Thence his brow so delicate,
His mien so joyous bright,
His smile, as though an angel sate
Upon his lip of light.

Thence his voice so musical,
Like far-off Spirits' chaunt
Or the wood-streams summer-fall
In spots, that fairies haunt.

Why bends the mother o'er the child
With more, than wonted care?
Why rests her hand like a moonbeam mild
Upon his shadowy hair?

Why move her lips as those, who pray?
Why fill her eyes, as though with tears?
Oh why? It is his natal day,
But two short summers swept away
And shadows of the coming years
Float past her with their hopes & fears
On Fancy's chariot driven:
Thence o'er the child the mother prays
The prophet-prayer of future days.
Peace! Thou canst add no holier thought
To mother's prayer with heaven fraught.
Speed, speed that prayer to Heaven!

Ernest Jones.

To my child, Ernest Beaufort, on his second Birthday

ERNEST JONES (1819–1869)

29 December 1844, British Library, Add MS 61971, f.23, volume 23.7 × 20 cm, black ink on wove paper in an album with dark blue leather binding and gilt decoration.

This poem was written by the Chartist Ernest Jones to commemorate his son's second birthday. It is a private testament to the love Jones felt for his young son. This poem forms part of an album once owned by Jones which he gifted to his first wife, Jane (d.1857), who passed it on to his son, Ernest Beaufort Jones (b.1842).

The album contains pen and ink drawings and poems by Jones expressing his love for his wife and son, together with sketches, silhouettes and poems by friends and acquaintances. The volume has a similar format to many other mid-nineteenth-century albums, which often contain a mixture of drawings, prints, pictures, mottoes and poems added by owners over a number of years. The album contains drawings by Jones of his parents' former home at Reinbeck, Holstein (f.10), and another, a family property, Purbrook House, in Cosham, Hampshire (f.16). Also included are drawings made by Jones while in prison. Jones was convicted of sedition following a speech at a Chartist rally in June 1848 and held in Tothill Fields Prison, Westminster, until his release in July 1850. He lost much of his inheritance, including Purbrook House, because of his Chartist beliefs.

To my child, Ernest Beaufort,
on his second birthday
29th December
1844.

From the far land of spirits wild
Came on the earth a joyous child
A sunbeam = lighted rose.
In hour of purest passion mild
A soft smile called it into being
As the spring from winter fleeing
Calls a floweret through the snows.

Thence his brow so delicate,
His mien so joyous bright,
His smile, as though an angel sate
Upon his lip of light.

Thence his voice so musical,
Like far=off spirits' chaunt
Or the wood=streams summer=fall
In spots, that fairies haunt.

Why bends the mother o'er the child
With more, than wonted care?
Why rests her hand like a moonbeam mild
Upon his shadowy hair?

Why move her lips as those, who pray?
Why fill her eyes, as though with tears?
Oh why? It is his natal day,
But two short summers swept away
And shadows of the coming years
Float past her with their hopes & fears
On Fancy's chariot driven:
Thence o'er the child the mother prays
The prophet=prayer of future days.
Peace! Thou canst add no holier thought
To mother's prayer with heaven fraught.
Speed, speed that prayer to Heaven!

Ernest Jones.

Drawings by Ernest Jones of his parents' former home at Reinbeck, Holstein. British Library, Add MS 61971, f.10.

Cover of Ernest Jones's album, British Library, Add MS 61971.

Drawing by Ernest Jones of the family property, Purbrook House, in Cosham, Hampshire. British Library, Add MS 61971, f.16.

PASCALE PETIT (b.1953)

The Strait-Jackets

February 1999, black ink on white lined paper.
First published in *The Zoo Father* (Seren Books, 2001).

I wrote 'The Strait-Jackets' after I found a photo of forty-three hummingbirds wrapped up in cloth, laid inside a suitcase. They were alive, packed to be transported in the hold of an aeroplane by the Brazilian ornithologist Augusto Ruschi, and were in torpor – a sleep state hummingbirds slip into to conserve energy when temperatures are low. As soon as I saw the photo, I knew I had a poem, because it gave me the same feeling I'd had on meeting my estranged, dying father in Paris, after not seeing him for thirty-five years. I'd shown him an album of my childhood and I'm describing him looking at the photos. It was an easy poem to write. This manuscript is the third draft, but all the lines are there, and it became the opening poem of my second collection *The Zoo Father*. The image of hummingbirds inside a suitcase is a motif that recurs in several of my books. In my seventh collection *Mama Amazonica* it reappears in 'The Hummingbird Whisperer'. I think of this poem as a sculpture – I trained as a sculptor and although I no longer practise as one, I still consider my poems in visual terms, as paintings, objects and installations.

3rd draft

The Strait-Jackets

I lay the suitcase on Father's bed
and unzip it slowly, gently.
Inside, packed in cloth strait-jackets
lie forty live hummingbirds
tied down in rows, each tiny head
cushioned on ~~the~~ a swaddled body of.
I feed them from a flask of sugar-water,
inserting ~~the pipette into tiny~~ every bill, into the pipette,
then unwind their bindings
so Father can see their changing colours.
as they dart around his room.
as t~~Th~~ey hover inches from his face
as if he's a flower, their humming
just audible above the oxygen recycler.
For the first time since I've ~~visited arrived visited~~
he's breathing easily, the cannula
attached to his nostrils almost slips out.
~~but he hasn't~~ doesn't ~~noticed~~ .
I don't know how long we sit there
but when I next glance at his face
he's asleep, lights from their feathers
still playing on his ~~cheeks and~~ eyelids. and cheeks
It takes me hours to catch them all
and wrap them in their strait-jackets.
I work quietly, ~~but he's in such sleeping~~ he's in such/a deep sleep
~~so deeply he doesn't once wake once.~~
peacefully he doesn't wake once once.
~~as I let myself out of his cramped flat~~.

3rd draft

The Strait-Jackets

I lay the suitcase on Father's bed
and unzip it slowly, gently.
Inside, packed in cloth strait-jackets
lie forty live hummingbirds
tied down in rows, each tiny head
cushioned on ~~the~~ a swaddled body.
I feed them from a flask of sugar-water,
inserting ~~the pipette into~~ ~~bay~~ every bill, into the pipette,
then unwind their bindings
so Father can see their changing colours.
as They dart around his room.
~~They~~ hover inches from his face
as if he's a flower, their humming
just audible above the oxygen recycler.
For the first time since I've ~~visited arrived~~ visited
he's breathing easily, the cannula
attached to his nostrils almost slips out.
~~but he hasn't doesn't noticed~~
I don't know how long we sit there
but when I next glance at his face
he's asleep, lights from their feathers
still playing on his ~~cheeks and~~ eyelids and cheeks
It takes me hours to catch them all
and wrap them in their strait-jackets,
I work quietly, ~~but he's in such sleeping~~ he's in such/a deep sleep
~~so deeply~~ he doesn't once wake ~~once~~.
~~peacefully~~ he doesn't wake. ~~once~~ once.
as ~~I let myself out of his cramped flat.~~

II

81

Long years have left their writing on my brow
But yet the freshness & the dew-fed beam
Of those young mornings are about me now,
When we two wandered tow'rd the far-off stream

With rod & line. Our basket held a store
Baked for us only, & I thought with joy
That I should have my share, though he had more
Because he was the elder & a Boy.

The firmaments of daisies since to me
~~[illegible]~~
Have had those mornings in their opening eyes,
The bunchéd cowslip's pale transparency
Carries that sunshine of sweet memories,

And ~~[illegible]~~ wild roses branches take their finest scent
From those blest ~~[illegible]~~ hours of infantine content.

Brother and Sister

GEORGE ELIOT (MARY ANN EVANS) (1819–1880)

31 July 1869, British Library, Add MS 34038, f.81r, folio 23.5 × 21 cm, black ink on lined paper.

George Eliot, engraving by G. J. Stodart, British Library Ashley 712.

The writer George Eliot (real name Mary Ann Evans) enjoyed a rural upbringing in Warwickshire between Nuneaton and Coventry, which she later described as 'fat central England'.[2] Eliot was the youngest of five children and was closest to her brother Isaac (1816–1890), who was nearest to her in age. In a sequence of eleven sonnets, collectively titled 'Brother and Sister', Eliot reminisces on their childhood together.

As children grow into adults, relationships between siblings can change and they can drift apart. Poetry can provide the means to reflect on the breakdown of familial bonds and express the poet's feelings of hurt and distress. For example, Anne Brontë expressed her anguish at the growing emotional distance between her and her sister Emily in the poem 'Self-Communion' (see page 222).

Eliot and Isaac fell out as adults because he did not approve of her relationship with the philosopher and literary critic George Henry Lewes, who was married but separated from his wife. Eliot wrote the sonnets in 1869, over twenty years after the breach with her brother, reflecting warmly on their childhood together and expressing her desire for reconciliation. The relationship between the siblings is famously represented through the characters of Maggie and Tom Tulliver in Eliot's novel *The Mill on the Floss* (1860). Eliot and Isaac had a happier ending than Maggie and Tom, however, as brother and sister were reunited after Eliot's marriage to John Walter Cross (1840–1924) in May 1880.

This is the second sonnet and looks back wistfully to childhood days spent with her brother. The sequence of eleven manuscript drafts of the sonnets is found in the same volume as 'Armgart' (see page 140) and other poems.

II

Long years have left their writing on my brow
But yet the freshness & the dew-fed beam
Of those young mornings are about me now,
When we two wandered tow'rd the far-off stream

With rod & line. Our basket held a store
Baked for us only, & I thought with joy
That I should have my share, though he had more
Because he was the elder & a Boy.

~~[illegible]~~
The firmaments of daisies since to me
Have had those mornings in their opening eyes,
The bunchéd cowslip's pale transparency
Carries that sunshine of sweet memories,

And [~~illegible~~]wild-rose branches take their finest scent
From those blest ~~[illegible]~~ hours of infantine content.

chapter 8

CONFLICT

In the majority of the poems in this chapter, conflict is explored in terms of armed uprisings and warfare. A war poet can be a soldier or a civilian who has experienced the horrors and brutality of conflict. The profound, heartfelt and disturbing poetry written during the First World War defined how we now think about war poetry as a genre. Wilfred Owen and Siegfried Sassoon are two of the most famous First World War battlefield poets; they met during their convalescence at Craiglockhart Hospital in Edinburgh in 1917, where Owen, with help from Sassoon, wrote 'Anthem for Doomed Youth'. Disillusioned by the war, their poetry shares a sense of futility and anger at the lack of competent leadership and the needless waste of human lives. One of the best-known poets of the Second World War, Keith Douglas, echoes their sentiments in his 1943 poem 'The Aristocrats'.

In the past, war in poetry was often depicted as heroic: Homer's *Iliad* is a classic example. The epic poem, here translated by Alexander Pope, recounts the events of the Trojan War and the actions of heroes such as the Greek warrior Achilles and the Trojan prince Hector. As well as being patriotic and heroic, poetry can also be nationalistic: Hans Christian Andersen's 'Fest-Sang til Landsoldaten' ('Song for the footsoldier') celebrates the Danish victory over Prussia in 1851. 'Incident of the French Camp' by Robert Browning tells the tale of a heroic French officer who was proud to die for his country delivering the news that the French under Napoleon had captured Ratisbon. Rupert Brooke also drew on the heroic tradition in 'The Soldier' and 'The Dead'; written in 1915, the poems present a romantic image of death in a foreign land.

Arthur Rimbaud and Alice Meynell were two poets who used imagery of the beauty of the natural world to contrast with the horrors of war. In 'Le Dormeur du Val' ('Asleep in the Valley'), written during the Franco-Prussian War, Rimbaud describes a green and sunny valley in which a young man is lying dead. Alice Meynell used seasonal and Christian imagery as a comparison with the horrors faced by those fighting and dying in their thousands on the First World War battlefields in her poem 'Summer in England in 1914'. Both poems evoke the sacrifice and the human cost of war.

Poetry can be a means for individuals to express their feelings about conflict or to interpret the issues raised by war for a wider public audience. Katherine Philips, an Anglo-Welsh Royalist who lived through the English Civil War, used poetry to generate sympathy for Queen Henrietta Maria, the widow of King Charles I. In his poem 'Easter' ('The Rose Tree') W. B. Yeats imagines a conversation between Patrick Pearse and James Connolly, two leaders of the 1916 Easter Rising in Dublin, in which they describe the shedding of their own blood as a sacrifice to rejuvenate the Irish nation. The journalist Langston Hughes appeals, in his poem 'Song of Spain', to industrial workers to refuse to make munitions for the forces of the fascist Francisco Franco in the Spanish Civil War. In 'Scientific Method' Paul Tran combines a lyric criticism of imperialism and the Vietnam War with an extended attention to the rhesus monkey experiments that developed our understanding of attachment theory.

Poetry depicting conflict often has an agenda. It is written to raise awareness for a country, cause or the people and animals dying on the front lines.

Anthem for Doomed Youth

WILFRED OWEN (1893–1918), WITH ANNOTATIONS BY SIEGFRIED SASSOON (1886–1967)

September 1917, British Library, Add MS 43720, f.17r, folio 28.2 × 21.8 cm, black ink and blue pencil on paper with pencil annotations.

Wilfred Owen wrote a number of his most famous poems at Craiglockhart Hospital, Edinburgh, including several drafts of both 'Dulce et Decorum est' and 'Anthem for Doomed Youth'. Owen had enlisted to fight in the First World War as part of the Artists Rifles in 1915. Two years later, in mid-March 1917, Owen fell through a shell hole into a cellar, where he was stuck for three days. He escaped with concussion and returned to fierce fighting. In May he was diagnosed with shell shock (now known as post-traumatic stress disorder, or PTSD) and sent to recuperate at Craiglockhart, where he met Siegfried Sassoon.

Owen's poetry was markedly different from the patriotic and sometimes romanticised verse of war poets such as Rupert Brooke. Through his poetry, Owen sought to describe vividly the horrors faced by troops at the front. In 'Anthem for Doomed Youth' he laments the lost lives of young men sent to slaughter like cattle. He describes how the men will not receive the 'prayers' and 'bells' that are associated with mourning and funerals, but will instead be serenaded by 'choirs of wailing shells' as they die.

During their stay at Craiglockhart, Sassoon advised and encouraged Owen. Sassoon's pencil annotations appear on this draft, including the change in the title. Further down the page he suggests 'patient minds' instead of 'silent sweet white minds'. Sassoon survived the war, but Owen was killed on 4 November 1918, only one week before the Armistice.

Wilfred Owen, reproduction after the last known photograph of the poet, British Library, 11855.d.12.

Anthem for ~~Dead~~ Doomed Youth   Nation
What passing-bells for these who die as cattle?
    — Only the monstrous anger of the guns.
    Only the stuttering rifles' rapid rattle
Can patter out their hasty orisons.
No {~~music for all them~~ mockeries now for them}; ~~nor from~~ no prayers ~~or~~ nor bells,
    Nor any voice of mourning save the choirs,—
The shrill, dem~~ony~~cented ~~disconsolate~~ choirs of wailing shells;
    And bugles calling ~~sad across the~~ for them from sad shires.

What candles may be held to speed them all?
    Not in the hands of boys, but in their eyes
Shall shine the holy glimmers of goodbyes.
    ~~And~~ The pallor of girls' brows shall be their pall;
Their flowers the tenderness of {~~silent~~ patient ~~sweet white~~} minds,
And each slow dusk a drawing-down of blinds.

Anthem for ~~Dead~~ Doomed Youth — Nation

What passing-bells for these who die as cattle?
- Only the monstrous anger of the guns.
Only the stuttering rifles' rapid rattle
Can patter out their hasty orisons.
No {~~music for all them~~ / mockeries} for them; ~~nor~~ no ~~from~~} prayers ~~or~~ nor bells,
Nor any voice of mourning save the choirs, [now]
The shrill dem~~onic~~ented ~~disconsolate~~ choirs of wailing shells;
And bugles calling ~~sad~~ ~~across~~ ~~the~~ for them from sad shires.

What candles may be held to speed them all?
Not in the hands of boys, but in their eyes
Shall shine the holy glimmers of goodbyes.
~~And~~ The pallor of girls' brows shall be their pall;
Their flowers the tenderness of {silent ~~sweet~~ ~~white~~ patient} minds,
And each slow dusk a drawing-down of blinds.

(Pencil words were written by S.S. when W. showed him the sonnet at Craiglockhart in Sept. 1917.)

Le Dormeur du Val.

C'est un trou de verdure où chante une rivière
Accrochant follement aux herbes des haillons
D'argent ; où le soleil, de la montagne fière,
Luit : c'est un petit val qui mousse de rayons.

Un soldat jeune, ~~lèvre~~ bouche ouverte, tête nue,
Et la nuque baignant dans le frais cresson bleu,
Dort ; il est étendu dans l'herbe, sous la nue,
Pâle dans son lit vert où la lumière pleut.

Les pieds dans les glaïeuls, il dort. Souriant comme
Sourirait un enfant malade, il fait un somme :
Nature, berce-le chaudement : il a froid.

Les parfums ne font pas frissonner sa narine ;
Il dort dans le soleil, la main sur sa poitrine
Tranquille. Il a deux trous rouges au côté droit.

Arthur Rimbaud

Octobre 1870.

Le Dormeur du Val (Asleep in the Valley)

ARTHUR RIMBAUD (1854–1891)

October 1870, British Library, Zweig MS 181, f.35r, volume 32.6 × 22 cm, folio 21.1 × 13.2 cm, black ink on paper.

This poem was written when Rimbaud was just 16 years old, at a time when France was at war with Prussia. It begins with a tranquil scene: a young soldier apparently asleep in an idyllic landscape. Even the name of the poem, 'Asleep in the Valley', suggests a calm pastoral scene. The tone of the poem takes a sharp, sinister turn when Rimbaud likens the soldier's smile to that of a sick child. Suddenly it becomes clear that the solider is not sleeping: his nostrils do not quiver nor do they respond to the surrounding fragrance. The final line of the poem states that the young soldier has two wounds in his side and that he lies dead in the idyllic landscape.

There is only one correction in this fair-copy manuscript, where Rimbaud replaces the word 'lèvre' (lip) with 'bouche' (mouth). The poem was published for the first time in 1888, and this is the only known manuscript version.

'Le Dormeur du Val' is part of a volume of twenty-two poems in Rimbaud's hand known as the 'Cahiers de Douai'. He gave the poems to his friend Paul Demeny (1844–1918) in two batches during the poet's stay in Douai, northern France in September and October 1870. Despite Rimbaud imploring Demeny to destroy the manuscripts, they remained intact and have since been bound into a single volume. Demeny sold the manuscripts to the first biographer of Rimbaud, Rodolphe Darzens (1865–1938). The poems now form part of the Stefan Zweig Collection at the British Library.

C'est un trou de verdure où chante une rivière
Accrochant follement aux herbes des haillons
D'argent ; où le soleil, de la montagne fière,
Luit : c'est un petit val qui mousse de rayons.

Un soldat jeune, ~~lèvre~~ bouche ouverte, tête nue,
Et la nuque baignant dans le frais cresson bleu,
Dort ; il est étendu dans l'herbe, sous la nue,
Pâle dans son lit vert où la lumière pleut.

Les pieds dans les glaïeuls, il dort. Souriant comme
Sourirait un enfant malade, il fait un somme :
Nature, berce-le chaudement : il a froid.

Les parfums ne font pas frissonner sa narine;
Il dort dans le soleil, la main sur sa poitrine
Tranquille. Il a deux trous rouges au côté droit.

A gully of green, a laughing river
Where silver tatters snag
Madly in grasses; where, from the proud
Mountain the sun shines; foaming trough of light.

A young soldier, mouth open, head bare,
Neck on a pillow of cool cress,
Sleeps, stretched out in the grass, sky above,
Pale on his green bed where light teems down.

Feet among the flags, he sleeps, smiling how
A sick child might; he takes a nap.
Gather him close, Nature, rock him. He's cold.

No scent makes his nostril quiver.
He sleeps in the sun, one hand on his still
Chest. In his right side, two red holes.

The Soldier.

If I should die, think only this of me,
That there's some corner of a foreign field
That is for ever England. There shall be
In that rich earth a richer dust concealed,
A dust whom England bore, shaped, made aware,
Gave, once, her flowers to love, her ways to roam,
A body of England's, breathing English air
Washed by the rivers, blest by suns of home.

~~Think, too~~ And think, this heart, all evil shed away,
A ~~[illegible]~~ pulse in the Eternal mind, no less
Gives somewhere back the thoughts by England given,
Her sights & sound; dreams happy as her day;
And laughter, learnt of friends; and gentleness,
In hearts at peace, under an English heaven.

109

The Dead.

These hearts were woven of human joys & ~~[illegible]~~ cares,
Washed marvellously with sorrow, swift to mirth.
The years had given them kindness. Dawn was theirs
And sunset, & the colours of the earth.
These had seen movement and heard music; known
Slumber & waking; loved; gone proudly friended;
Felt the swift stir of wonder; sat alone;
~~Lead~~ Touched flowers & furs & cheeks.
And this is ended.

There are waters blown by changing winds to laughter
And lit by the rich skies, all day. And after,
Frost, with a gesture, stays the waves that dance
And wandering loveliness. He leaves a white
Unbroken glory, a gathered radiance,
A width, a shining peace, under the night.

'The Soldier' and 'The Dead'

RUPERT BROOKE (1887–1915)

1915, British Library, Add MS 39255 M, f.109r–109v, folio 17.7 × 11.4 cm, bifolium, black ink on wove paper.

These two manuscript poems were owned by Edward Marsh (1872–1953), an early critic of Rupert Brooke's poetry and editor of the anthology *Georgian Poetry*, published between 1912 and 1922. 'The Soldier' is one of the best-known poems from the First World War. It displays an idealistic and hopeful sentiment, more commonly seen in the early months of the war, and is in marked contrast to works by later writers such as Siegfried Sassoon. Similarly, despite its theme of loss of life on the battlefield, 'The Dead' paints a romantic image of glory against a natural landscape. Brooke was sailing with the British Mediterranean Expedition, which was en route to Gallipoli, when he died of septicaemia on 23 April 1915. He was buried on the Greek island of Skyros.

The poems are accompanied by a letter from Marsh offering the manuscript to the British Museum Library. In the letter, dated 1 August 1915, Marsh explains that Brooke wrote the fair copies for him when he was staying with him in January, shortly after they were first composed. Brooke died soon after this visit. Marsh states that the manuscripts are his most treasured possession and that the poems are the two which Brooke liked best. The manuscripts were presented to the British Museum Library on 9 October 1915.

Although they are fair copies, both of the manuscripts show some small corrections by Brooke.

The Soldier.

If I should die, think only this of me,
That there's some corner of a foreign field
That is for ever England. There shall be
In that rich earth a richer dust concealed,
A dust whom England bore, shaped, made aware,
Gave, once, her flowers to love, her ways to roam,
A body of England's, breathing English air,
Washed by the rivers, blest by suns of home.

And think
~~Think, Too~~, this heart, all evil shed away,
A [~~illegible~~] pulse in the Eternal Mind, no less
Gives somewhere back the thoughts by England given,
Her sights & sounds; dreams happy as her day;
And laughter, learnt of friends; and gentleness,
In hearts at peace, under an English heaven.

The Dead.

These hearts were woven of human joys & ~~Tears~~ cares,
Washed marvellously with sorrow, swift to mirth~~;~~.
The years had given them kindness. Dawn was theirs,
And sunset, & the colours of the Earth.
These had seen movement and heard music; known
Slumber & waking; loved; gone proudly friended;
Felt the swift stir of wonder; sat alone;
~~Loved~~ Touched flowers & furs & cheeks.
And this is ended.

There are waters blown by changing winds to laughter
And lit by the rich skies, all day. And after,
Frost, with a gesture, stays the waves that dance
And wandering loveliness. He leaves a white
Unbroken glory, a gathered radiance,
A width, a shining peace, under the night.

To the Queen's Majesty

KATHERINE PHILIPS (1631/2–1664)

Before 1664, British Library, Add MS 78233, f.69r–69v, folio 22.5 × 16.6 cm, iron gall ink on laid paper.

This poem by Katherine Philips (née Fowler) was written in support of Queen Henrietta Maria (1609–1669), the wife of King Charles I (1600–1649) and the mother of King Charles II, who was present at her husband's execution outside the Banqueting House in Whitehall in 1649. Although Philips was born into a family with strong Parliamentarian roots, here she displays support for the queen. The poem condemns the rebels or Parliamentarians for acting from motives of 'unweary'd spight' during the English Civil War. 'To the Queen's Majesty' was not published until 1667, three years after Philips's death, in a volume entitled *Poems by the Most deservedly admired Mrs Katherine Philips, the Matchless Orinda*. Orinda was Philips's pen name. Philips was fluent in a number of languages and translated Pierre Corneille's (1606–1684) *La Mort de Pompée* (1663) and most of his *Horace* into English.

The autograph manuscript displays no corrections or amendments, which probably means that it was designed for circulation. Many writers at this date published in manuscript form only, and the folds across the page suggest that it was sent in a letter. The transcription and image show the first twenty-eight lines of the poem. The remaining twenty-two lines are on the verso of the manuscript.

This manuscript was part of a collection of poetry formed by the diplomat Sir Richard Browne (1605–1683). Browne served the English royal family while they were in exile during the Interregnum between 1649 and 1660. The collection of poems is now part of the Evelyn Papers at the British Library. Richard Browne's daughter married the diarist John Evelyn (1620–1706) in 1647.

To ye Queen's Majesty

You Justly may forsake a Land, which you_
Have found so guilty, & so fatall too,
Fortune injurious to your Innocence,
Empty'd her Quiver here, & shot from hence;
'Twas here, bold Rebells once, your life pursu'd,
To whom 'twas Treason, onely to be rude,
Till you were forc'd by their unweary'd spight,
(O! Glorious criminall!), to take your flight.
And after you, all yt was humane fled,
For here, oh! here, ye Royall Martyr bled.
Whose cause, & heart, must sacred be, & high,
That having you, could be content to dy.
Here they purloyn'd what we to you did on,
And payd you in Variety of woe.
Yet all those billows, in your brest did meet
A heart, so firm, so royall, & so sweet,
That over them you greater conquest made,
Then your Immortall Father ever had.
(For we may read in Story, of some few
Who fought like him, none yt endur'd like you.)
Till sorrow blush'd to act what Traytors meant,
And Providence it self did first repent;
But as our Active, so our Passive Ill,
Hath made your share to be ye Sufferer still,
As from our mischiefs all your troubles grew,
'Tis your sad right, to suffer for them too.
Else our Great Charles had not been hence so long,
Nor ye adored Gloucester dy'd so young.

To yᵉ Queen's Majesty.

You Justly may forsake a Land which you
Have found so guilty, & so fatall too,
Fortune injurious to your Innocence,
Empty'd her quiver here, & shot from hence;
'Twas here, bold Rebells once, your life pursu'd,
To whom 'twas Treason, onely to be rude,
Till you were forc'd by their unweary'd spight,
(O' glorious criminall!) to take your flight.
And after you, all yᵗ was humane fled,
For here, oh! here, yᵉ Royall Martyr bled.
Whose cause, & heart must sacred be & high,
That having you, could be content to dy.
Here they purloyn'd what we to you did ow,
And payd you in Variety of woe.
Yet all those billows in your brest did meet
A heart, so firm, so royall, & so sweet,
That over them you greater conquest made,
Then your Immortall Father ever had.
(For we may read in Story, of some few
Who fought like him, none yᵗ endur'd like you.)
Till sorrow blush'd to act what Traytors meant,
And Providence it self did first repent;
But as our Active, so our Passive Ill,
Hath made your share to be yᵉ Sufferer still,
As from our mischiefs all your troubles grew,
'Tis your sad right to suffer for them too.
Else our Great Charles had not been hence so long,
Nor yᵉ adored Gloucester dy'd so young.

Easter (The Rose Tree)

W. B. YEATS (1865–1939)

1917, British Library, Ashley MS 2291, f.1r, folio 18 × 11 cm, black ink on paper.

An armed insurrection by Irish Republicans took place in Dublin during Easter week in 1916. The leaders of the Easter Rising proclaimed a provisional government, with the aim of creating an independent Irish republic and bringing to an end the political union between Britain and Ireland. While the United Kingdom of Great Britain and Ireland had existed since 1801, British colonial rule in Ireland had its origins in the Anglo-Norman conquests of the late twelfth century, and many Irish people viewed Britain as a colonial power.

The British Army suppressed the Easter Rising and, in its aftermath, sixteen of the leaders were executed. The executions created an upsurge of support for Irish independence. The poet William Butler Yeats was strongly affected by the rising and, in particular, the self-sacrifice of its leaders. He wrote a series of poems in response, including 'The Rose Tree'.

In the poem Yeats explores Irish nationalism following the rising using the symbol of a rose tree. The poem takes the form of a conversation between two leaders of the rising: the school teacher and language activist Patrick Pearse (1879–1916) and the socialist and trade union leader James Connolly (1868–1916). The poem ends with the idea that nothing but the blood of Pearse and Connolly can restore the rose tree (Irish nationalism). Both men were executed following the rising and so gave their blood for the cause of Irish republicanism.

'The Rose Tree' was first published with other poems inspired by the rising in 1921 in Yeats's collection *Michael Robartes and the Dancer*. The manuscript is a fair copy written in black ink in April 1917. The title here is written as 'Easter', and there are very slight differences between it and the published poem, most notably in the final verse, where the third line was later changed from 'To make the blossom come again –' to 'When all the wells are parched away?'.

Easter

'O words are lightly spoken,'
Said Pearse to Connolly,
'Maybe a breath of politic words
Has withered our Rose-tree
Or may be but a wind that blows
across the bitter sea.'

~~The~~ 'It needs to be but watered'
James Connolly replied
'To make the green come out again
And spread on every side
And shake the blossom from the bud
And be the gardens pride.'

'But where shall we get water'
Said Pearse to Connolly
'To make the blossom come again –
O plain as plain can be
There's nothing but our ~~our~~ own red blood
To make a right Rose-tree.

WB Yeats
April 1917

1

18, Woburn Buildings,

W. C.

Easter

'O words are lightly spoken,'
said Pearse to Connolly,
'Maybe a breath of politic words
Has withered our Rose-tree
Or may be but a wind that blows
across the bitter sea.'

'~~Th~~ It needs to be but watered'
James Connolly replied
'To make the green come out again
And spread on every side
And shake the blossom from the bud
And be the gardens pride.'

'But where shall we get water'
said Pearse to Connolly
'To make the blossom come again —
O plain as plain can be
There's nothing but our ~~our~~ own red blood
To make a right Rose-tree.

W B Yeats
April 1917

Fest-Sang til Landsoldaten (Song for the footsoldier)

HANS CHRISTIAN ANDERSEN (1805–1875)

1851, British Library, Zweig MS 132, folio 27.2 × 21.2 cm, ink on pink wove paper.

This poem celebrates the return of Danish soldiers from the First Schleswig War, which concerned the Danish-governed duchies of Schleswig and Holstein in southern Denmark and northern Germany. Andersen's poem was modelled on 'Dengang jeg drog af sted' ('When I set out') by Peter Christian Frederik Faber (1810–1877), which was written to celebrate the Danish victory at the Battle of Bov in April 1848. Faber's poem was set to a marching tune by Emil Horneman (1809–1870) and Andersen also set his poem to this music. At the end of the war, many soldiers were presented with songbooks, to which Andersen was often a contributor. There were also homecoming celebrations and festivals for the returning soldiers. Andersen was involved in the festival at Glorup Castle in July 1851 that marked the anniversary of the Danish victory in the Battle of Fredericia on 6 July 1849. Andersen helped to organise the festival at which 'Song for the footsoldier' was performed.

Andersen wrote this poem on two sides of the same sheet with only one small correction in the third verse. He underlined some of the words in the manuscript to mark spacing in print, which suggests that it was used by a publisher. The poem was first published in *Folkekalender for Danmark* in 1852.

This poem is part of the Stephan Zweig Collection at the British Library. Zweig purchased the poem from the scholar and manuscript dealer Heinrich Eisemann (1890–1972) in London on 29 May 1940. Eisemann fled Germany on Adolf Hitler's (1889–1945) rise to power and subsequently settled in London.

Sang til Landsoldaten
Ved Festen paa Glorup den 7de Juli 1851

:,: Dengang Du drog af sted, :,:
Vor Herre han var med,
Ja Vor Herre han var med;
Du gik til ærligt Slag
For Danmarks gode Sag,
Og alle danske Hjerter bleve eet paa Kampens Dag.
Igennem Hegn og Moser, hvor Kugleregnen faldt,
Gik freidig Landsoldaten, det kunde ei gaae galt,
Og derfor er vi stolt af Dig, vor Landsoldat!
Hurra, hurra, hurra!

:,: Den danske Pige brav, :,:
Sin blanke Guldring gav,
Af Hjertet gav hun den,
Ja meer, sin bedste Ven,
Som rigest' Frøken gav hun der sit Allerbedste hen;
Og Helte gik til Himlen, for Dannebrog de bad,
Vort Seirs-Blus af Fjenden blev tændt i Frederiksstad;
Der Holger Danske stod, den tapre Landsoldat!
Hurra, Hurra, Hurra!
:,: Da Du drog hjem, den Dag, :,:
Den glade Hjemkomst-Dag,
Da vaied Krands og Flag.
Til Møde drog vi ud,
Med Sang og Glædes-Skud,
Og der blev grædt af Glæde, og for Seiren takket Gud.
Din gamle Fa'er og Mo'er og din Pige med hun kom,
Det næsten fik ei Ende med Kys og med Svingom!
Du flinke, brave Søn! Du tapre Landsoldat!
Hurra, Hurra, Hurra!

Fest-Sang til Landsoldaten.

Mel: „Dengang jeg drog afsted."

#

:/: Dengang du drog afsted, :/:
Vor Herre han var med,
Ja vor Herre han var med;
Du gik til ærligt Slag
For Danmarks gode Sag,
Og alle danske Hjerter [illegible] med paa Kampens Dag.
Gjennem Hegn og Moser, hvor Kugleregnen faldt,
Gik freidig Landsoldaten, det kunde vi [illegible],
Og derfor er vi stolt af Dig, vor Landsoldat!
Hurra, Hurra, Hurra!

#

:/: Den danske Pige brav, :/:
Sin blanke Guldring gav,
Ja sin blanke Guldring gav;
Sit Hjerte gav hun den,
Ja mer, sin bedste Mand,
Som [illegible] gav hun der sit Allerbedste hen;
Og Helten gik til Himlen, for Dannebrog de bad,
[illegible] Blod af Fjenden blev [illegible] i Frederiksstad,
der Holger Danske stod, den tappre Landsoldat!
Hurra, Hurra, Hurra!

#

4

Da du drog hjem, den Dag,
Den glade Hjemkomstdag,
Da vaied Vaands og Flag,
Ja da vaied Vaands og Flag;
Til Møde drog vi ud,
Med Sang og Glædes Lyd,
Og der blev grædt af Glæde, og for Seiren takket Gud.
Din gamle Fa'er og Mo'er og din Pige med hun kom,
Det næsten fik vi hende med Lyst og med Svingom!
Du flinke, brave Søn! Du tappre Landsoldat!
Hurra, Hurra, Hurra!

4

|: Krands med Sang og Flag, :|
Staaer Luftens Dag i Dag,
Ja staaer Luftens Dag i Dag.
Fra Skoven i sin Pragt
Er grønne Grene bragt,
Og Dandsesalen staadsit ud og Rosterne indlagt,
Og alle Pigers Lyst, de har en Hjerte=Sprog:
"Ja, her er vore Karle, som Seiren til os tog!"
Til Danmark takker dig, Du tappre Landsoldat!
Hurra, Hurra, Hurra!

H. C. Andersen

:,: Paany med Sang og Flag, :,:
Staaer Festens Dag i Dag
Fra Skoven i fin Dragt
Er grønne Grene bragt.
Og Dandsesalen stadset ud og Roserne indlagt,
Og alle Øine lyse, de har nu Hjerte-Sprog:
'See, her er vore Karle, som Seiren til os tog!'
Al Danmark takker Dig, Du tappre Landsoldat!
Hurra, Hurra, Hurra!

Hans Christian Andersen, photograph by Thora Hallager, Odense City Museum, Denmark.

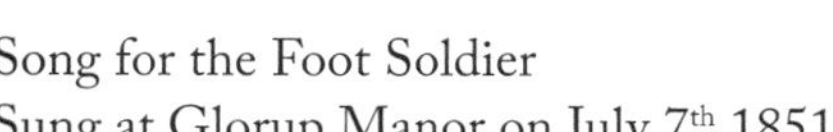

Song for the Foot Soldier
Sung at Glorup Manor on July 7th 1851

When you set out,
Our Lord was with you,
Yes, Our Lord was with you.
You entered the righteous fight
For the good of Denmark.
All Danish hearts became as one on the day of battle.
Through fences and marshes and showers of bullets,
The foot soldier marched on, bound for success.
For that, we are proud of you, our foot soldier!
Hurrah, hurrah, hurrah!

The courageous Danish girl
Gave away her shiny gold ring.
She gave it with all of her heart,
With more than that, to her dearest friend.
As the richest of the maidens, she gave him the very best she had.
Heroes went to heaven, they prayed for Dannebrog.
Victoriously, they lit the enemy on fire in Friedrichstadt.
There stood Ogier the Dane, the brave foot soldier!
Hurrah, hurrah, hurrah!

When you went home that day,
That joyful day of homecoming,
Flags and garlands were waved.
We came out to meet you
With songs and celebratory gunfire,
People wept from joy and from the God-granted victory.
Your ol' dad and mum came along, and your girl too.
The kisses and merry dancing seemed to go on forever.
Kind, courageous son! Brave foot soldier!
Hurrah, hurrah, hurrah!

Flags are raised as we sing again,
Today is a day of celebration.
Green branches have been brought in from the woods and decked with beautiful ornaments.
The banquet hall has been decorated and roses have been laid out.
All eyes shine bright with the language of the heart:
'Look, here are our lads, who brought us victory!'
All of Denmark thanks you, brave foot soldier!
Hurrah, hurrah, hurrah!

The March Past

SIEGFRIED SASSOON (1886–1967)

1916, British Library, Add MS 81687, drawing 13.9 × 9.7 cm, pen and ink on lined paper, envelope 9.2 × 12 cm, black ink and stamp on paper, poem, folio 18 × 11.4 cm, ink on wove paper.

Siegfried Sassoon's 1916 poem 'The March Past' is very different in approach to the idealistic works of poets such as Rupert Brooke written earlier in the First World War. The poem reflects Sassoon's experience of trench warfare on the Western Front. Sassoon's ink drawing on the envelope conveys the message of the poem that those in charge, while apparently upstanding on the surface, were actually devils dressed in uniform who would lead those who followed them to their death. The poem is both a satire and a play on words: the character of 'Corps-Commander' inspects his troops as they march past, while his other identity is a 'corpse-commander' who sends his men on a march to their death. Sassoon wrote the poem on Christmas Day 1916.

The poem and envelope were addressed to the journalist, art critic and dealer Robert Baldwin Ross (1869–1918) on 26 December 1916. The manuscript came to the British Library as part of the Eccles Bequest, the collections of Mary, Viscountess Eccles (1912–2003), which contain many important literary manuscripts, including some by Oscar Wilde. Another, earlier draft of this poem is held at Cambridge University Library.

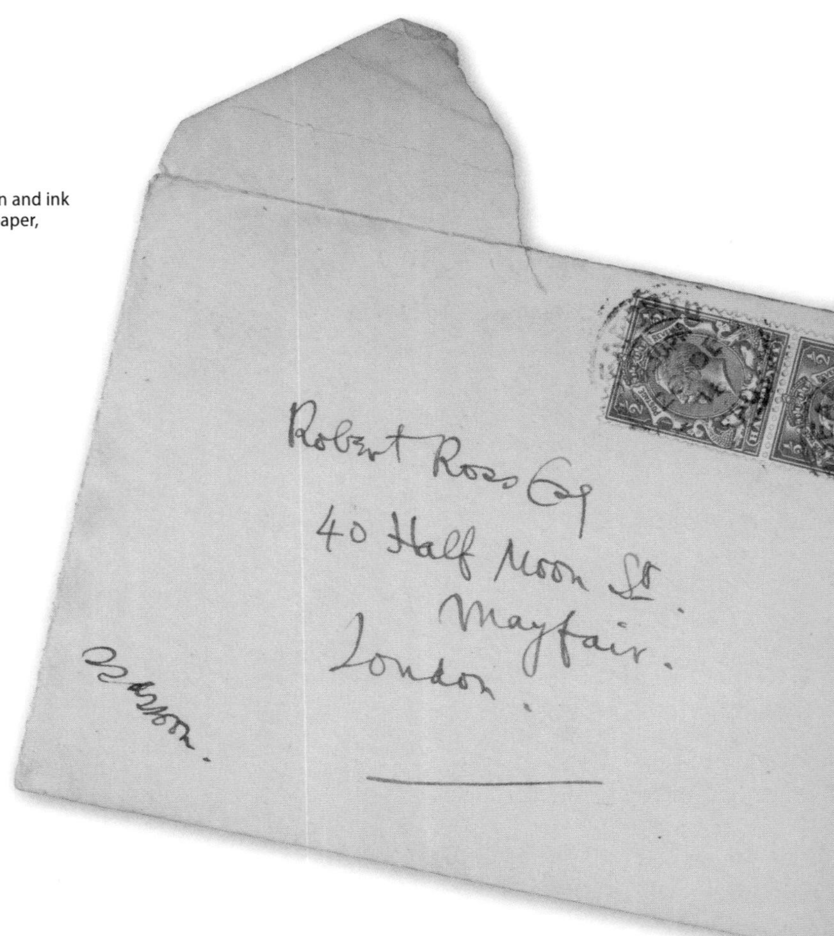

The March-Past.

~~The C~~
In red & gold the Corps-Commander stood,
With ribboned breast puffed out for all to see:
He'd sworn to beat the Germans, if he could;
For God had taught him strength & strategy.
He was our leader; and a judge of Port, –
Rode well to hounds, and was a d-d good sort!

'Eyes right!' We passed him with a jaunty stare.
'Eyes front!' He'd watched his trusted legions go.
I wonder if he guessed how many there
Would get knocked out of time in next week's show.
'Eyes right!' The corpse-commander was a Mute;
And Death leered round him, taking our salute.
SS.
Xmas Day.

The March-Past.

~~The C~~

In red & gold the Corps-Commander stood,
With ribboned breast puffed out for all to see:
He'd sworn to beat the Germans, if he could;
For God had taught him strength & strategy.
He was our leader; and a judge of Port,–
Rode well to hounds, and was a d—d good sort!

"Eyes right!" We passed him with a jaunty stare.
"Eyes front!" He'd watched his trusted legions go.
I wonder if he guessed how many there
Would get knocked out of time in next week's show.
"Eyes right!" The corpse-commander was a mute;
And Death leered round him, taking our salute.

S. Xwas toay.

Incident of the French Camp

ROBERT BROWNING (1812–1889)

1849–63, British Library, Ashley MS A256, f.174r, folio 18 × 11 cm, black ink and letterpress on two sheets of paper.

Robert Browning, engraving by J. Armytage, British Library, 1203.g.3.

Poets are often inspired by acts of bravery and self-sacrifice in war. This poem, 'Incident of the French Camp', tells the story of a fatally wounded young soldier who rode to the French Emperor Napoleon I (1769–1821) to deliver the news that the city of Ratisbon, Germany, had fallen. The story in the poem is believed to be fictional and was written over forty years later.

The Battle of Ratisbon in 1809 was fought between the army of the First French Empire led by Napoleon and that of the Austrian Empire led by Archduke Charles (1771–1847). During the assault on the city, Marshal Jean Lannes (1769–1809), who features in the poem, led the French troops onto the city walls. Napoleon watched the attack from a distance, but was close enough to be wounded in the ankle by a small artillery round.

This draft is a later copy of the first two stanzas of the poem. It was used by Browning as part of his process in compiling *The Poetical Works* in 1863. The first stanza was handwritten by Browning and the second was cut out from a published volume and pasted below.

Dramatic Romances.

Incident of the French Camp.

I.

You know, we French stormed Ratisbon:
  A mile or so away
On a little mound, Napoleon
  Stood on our storming-day;
With neck out-thrust, you fancy how,
  Legs wide, arms locked behind,
As if to balance the prone brow
  Oppressive with its mind.

II.

Just as perhaps he mused, 'My plans
  'That soar, to earth may fall,
'Let once my army-leader Lannes
  'Waver at yonder wall,' –
Out 'twixt the battery-smokes there flew
  A rider, bound on bound
Full-galloping: nor bridle drew
  Until he reached the mound.

174

Dramatic Romances.

—

Incident of the French Camp.

I.

You know, we French stormed Ratisbon:
A mile or so away
On a little mound, Napoleon
Stood on our storming-day;
With neck out-thrust, you fancy how,
Legs wide, arms locked behind,
As if to balance the prone brow
Oppressive with its mind.

II.

Just as perhaps he mused "My plans
"That soar, to earth may fall,
"Let once my army-leader Lannes
"Waver at yonder wall,"—
Out 'twixt the battery-smokes there flew
A rider, bound on bound
Full-galloping; nor bridle drew
Until he reached the mound.

The Iliad of Homer

ALEXANDER POPE (1688–1744)

1713–20, British Library, Add MS 4808, f.82r, folio 22.5 × 17.7 cm and f.81v, folio 20 × 16 cm, iron gall ink on laid paper.

The *Iliad* tells the story of the war between Greece and Troy, including the battle between the Greek hero Achilles and the Trojan champion Hector. The epic poem by the Greek poet Homer was probably written down in the eighth century BC.

Alexander Pope began translating the *Iliad* into English in 1713. The work was funded by subscribers and appeared between 1715 and 1720. The manuscript was written on available paper, including the backs of letters and notes received by Pope. While some pages were written in neat script, others bear multiple corrections and crossings out that make some of the text illegible. Pope usually composed between thirty and fifty verses per day.

Pope's sketch of the shield of Achilles, which in the story was forged by Hephaestus, is shown on f.81. The final verses of Achilles's lament for Patroclus, his close friend who had been killed fighting Hector while Achilles avoided the battle, appears on f.82. Pope changed many of the words from 'his' to 'the' throughout this section.

The *Iliad* earned Pope £5,000, a large sum of money at the time, which allowed him to live independently.

The manuscript for Pope's *Iliad* is now housed in three volumes. A pencil inscription on the endpaper written by the British Museum Library Keeper of Manuscripts, Frederick Madden (1801–1873), states that the manuscript was presented by Lucy Mallet (née Elstob, d.1795), the widow of the Scottish poet and dramatist David Mallett (*c*.1705–1765), in December 1766.

I could not this, this cruel stroke attend;
Fate claimd Achilles, but might spare his friend:
I hopd Patroclus might survive, to rear
The ~~his~~ tender ~~youth~~ ~~supply~~ orphan with a parents care,
From Scyros Isle ~~to waft~~ conduct him oer ye main,
And ~~[illegible] him Phthia~~ glad his eyes with his paternal reign
The ~~His~~ lofty Palace and ~~his~~ the large Domain.
For Peleus breathes no more the vital air,
Or ~~humbled to ye just [illegible]~~ drags a wretched life of age & care,
~~Lives but~~ But till ye news of my sad Fate invades
His hastening soul, ~~so~~ & sinks him to ye shades.
~~The~~ Sighing he said: his grief ye heroes joind,
Each stole a ~~sigh~~ tear for wt he left behind.
Their mingled grief ye Sire of Heavn surveyd,
And thus wth pity, to his blue-eyed maid.
Is ~~great~~ then Achilles now no more thy care
& dost thou thus desert ye great in war?
Lo, where yon sails their arms extend
All comfortless he sits, and wails his friend.
~~Haste,~~ E're ~~dry famine have his strength~~ thirst and want his ~~vigor~~ forces have opprest
Haste & ~~power divine~~ infuse ambrosia in his breast
He spoke, and sudden at the word of Jove
Shot ye descending Goddess from above
So ~~ye shrill Harpye~~ swift thro ~~parted~~ Æther the shrill Harpye springs
The wide air floating to her ample wings.
To great Achilles she her flight addrest
& pourd divine ambrosia in his breast,
With nectar sweet, (Refection of ye Gods!)
Then swift ascending, sought ye blest bright abodes.

OPPOSITE, TOP LEFT: Alexander Pope, engraving by George Vertue, British Library, C.59.i.20.

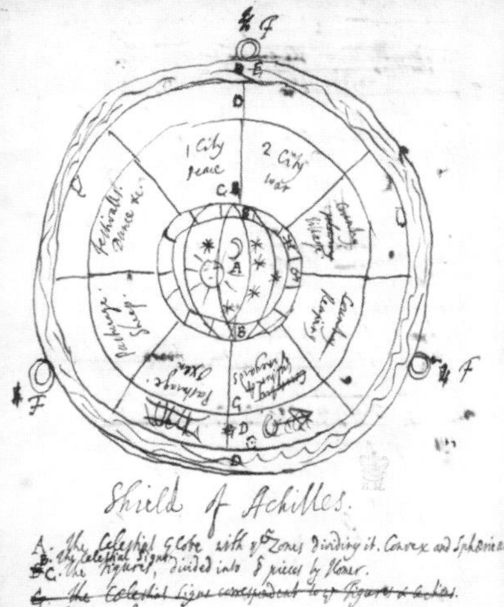

~~13~~ 82.

I cou'd not this, this cruel stroke attend;
Fate claim'd Achilles but might spare his friend:
I hop'd Patroclus might survive, to rear
The ~~His~~ tender ~~youth~~ orphan with a parent's care,
From Scyros Isle ~~to waft~~ conduct him o'er ye main
And glad his eyes with his paternal reign
The ~~His~~ lofty Palace and the ~~his~~ large Domain.
For Peleus breaths no more the vital air,
Or ~~humbled to ye dust~~ drags a wretched Life of age & care,
~~Lives but~~ But till ye news of my sad Fate invades
His hastening Soul, & sinks him to ye shades.
~~He~~ Sighing he said: his grief ye Heroes join'd,
Each stole a tear for wt he left behind.
Their mingled grief ye Sire of Heav'n survey'd
And thus wth pity to his blue-ey'd Maid.
Is then ~~great~~ Achilles now no more thy care
& dost thou thus desert ye Great in war?
Lo where yon Sails their arms extend
All comfortless he sits and wails his friend.
~~Haste~~, Ere Thirst and Want his ~~vigor~~ Forces have oppress
Haste & infuse ambrosia in his breast
He spoke, and sudden as the word of Jove
Shot ye descending Goddess from above
So ~~ye shrill Harpye~~ swift thro ~~parted~~ Æther, the shrill Harpye springs
The wide air floating to her ample wings.
To great Achilles she her flight addrest
& pour'd divine ambrosia in his breast
With nectar sweet, (Refection of ye Gods!)
Then swift ascending, sought ye bright abodes.

19

Aristocrats

KEITH DOUGLAS (1920–1944)

1943, British Library, Add MS 53773, f.61r, folio 31.7 × 21.7 cm, ink on paper.

The poetry of the Second World War is not as famous as that of the First World War, but it is often just as brutal and heart-wrenching. Keith Douglas, who served in the North African campaign, took inspiration from the poets of that earlier war, especially Isaac Rosenberg (1890–1918) and Wilfred Owen.

Douglas was from a less affluent background than many of his fellow officers, whom he likens to unicorns in the poem 'Aristocrats', 'for they are fading into two legends, / in which their stupidity and chivalry / are celebrated'. The poem describes how 'Peter', an aristocratic officer, was mortally wounded by an 88 mm anti-tank shell and was found crawling in the sand crying, 'Its most unfair, they've shot my foot off'.

This fair copy of the poem is written on the back of a letter to the poet and publisher Meary Tambimuttu (1915–1983). In the letter Douglas describes how he can write poetry only in comfort, which the 'hole in the sand' he was currently living in did not provide. Most of his poems written in Africa were composed while he was in hospital or at a depot. Douglas was killed, aged 24, on 9 June 1944, three days after the landings on the beaches in Normandy.

Douglas wrote and illustrated an account of his experience during the North African campaign, which was published posthumously in 1946 under the title *Alamein to Zem Zem*. This illustration shows a casualty being carried by soldiers in front of a Crusader tank with what looks like an 88 mm gun in the background.

Douglas's archive, containing poems, prose writings, drawings, paintings and correspondence, was purchased by the British Museum from his mother, Marie J. Douglas (1887–1981), through the Arts Council on 11 June 1966.

Self-portrait in pencil by Keith Douglas, British Library, Add MS 53775 B, f.19r.

Watercolour of a casualty in front of a tank by Keith Douglas, British Library, Add MS 53775 B, f.7r.

Aristocrats

The noble horse with courage in his eye,
clean in the bone, looks up at a shellburst:
away fly the images of the shires
but he puts the pipe back in his mouth.

Peter was unfortunately killed by an 88;
it took his leg away, he died in the ambulance.
I saw him crawling on the sand, he said
It's most unfair, they've shot my foot off.

How can I live among this gentle
obsolescent breed of heroes, and not weep?
Unicorns, almost,
for they are fading into two legends
in which their stupidity and chivalry
are celebrated. Each, fool and hero, will be an immortal.

These plains were their cricket pitch
and in the mountains the tremendous drop fences
brought down some of the runners. Here then
under the stones and earth they dispose themselves,
I think with their famous unconcern.
It is not gunfire I hear, but a hunting horn.

Tunisia 1943.

Summer in England 1914

On London fell a clearer light;
  Caressing pencils of the sun
Defined the distances the white
  Houses, transfigured one by one,
The "long unlovely street" impearled.
  Oh what a sky has walked the world!

Most happy year! and out of town
  The hay was prosperous and the wheat;
The silken harvest climbed the down;
  Moon after moon was heavenly-sweet,
Stroking the bread within the sheaves,
  Looking 'twixt apples and their leaves.

And while this rose made round her cup
  The armies died convulsed; and when
This chaste young silver sun went up
  Softly, ten thousand shattered men,
One wet corruption, heaped the plain,
  After a league-long throb of pain

Alice Meynell

Summer in England 1914

ALICE MEYNELL (1847–1922)

1914, British Library, Ashley MS B3655, f.178r, folio 22.5 × 18 cm, pencil on lined paper.

War affects not only those who fight, but also the friends and family they leave behind. Alice Meynell (née Thompson) was a poet, journalist and campaigner for female suffrage. She was the great granddaughter of Dr Thomas Pepper Thompson (1728–1821/1823), a sugar plantation owner in Jamaica and his wife Amelia (d.1822). Her grandparents were James Thompson (*c.*1785–*c.*1811), Thomas Pepper Thompson's illegitimate son and his mistress Mary Edwards (b. *c.*1787) of Rio Bueno estate in Trelawny. On the death of her grandfather James, her father, Thomas James Thompson (1809/1811–1881), inherited a significant financial legacy, but by her childhood most of the money had gone and as a result the family travelled frequently and widely in Italy. Meynell's parents were introduced by Charles Dickens (1812–1870), and her mother, Christiana Weller (1825–1910), was a concert pianist and amateur painter. Meynell converted to Roman Catholicism in her early twenties and Christian imagery features strongly in her poems.

'Summer in England 1914' contrasts the quiet and peaceful summer at home with the horrors faced by the men fighting on the Western Front. In the English countryside there is a prosperous harvest of hay, wheat and apples waiting to be gathered in, while across the Channel a 'thousand shattered men, / One wet corruption, heaped the plain'. The last stanza (not included in the transcription) offers the consolation for the soldiers that dying for their friends is a most noble and Christian death: 'The soldier dying dies upon a kiss, / The very kiss of Christ.'

This poem had a wide readership early in the war, following its publication in *The Times* on 10 October 1914. This fair copy of the first three stanzas of the poem was written in pencil and is almost identical to the version published in *The Times* and later in *Poems on the War*, published in 1915. Meynell's early drafts of poems are usually much altered, with crossings out and rewordings in pencil.

Summer in England in 1914

On London fell a clearer light;
Caressing pencils of the sun
Defined the distances the white
Houses, transfigured one by one,
The 'long unlovely street' impearled.
O what a sky has walked the world!

Most happy year! And out of town
The hay was prosperous and the wheat;
The silken harvest climbed the down;
Moon after moon was heavenly-sweet,
Stroking the bread within the sheaves,
Looking 'twixt apples and their leaves.

And while this rose made round her cup
The armies died convulsed; and when
This chaste young silver sun went up
Softly, ten thousand shattered men,
One wet corruption, heaped the plain,
After a league-long throb of pain.

Alice Meynell

Song of Spain

LANGSTON HUGHES (1901–1967)

c.1937–67, Beinecke Library, Yale University, JWJ MSS 26, Box 384, folder 6976, folio 28 x 21.6 cm, typewritten with pencil annotations.

Langston Hughes was an African American poet, playwright and activist. In 1937 Hughes flew to Spain to report on the experience of African Americans fighting in the Civil War. He wrote for several publications including the *Baltimore Afro-American* and *Volunteer for Liberty*. Hughes viewed the republic's fight in Spain against the dictator Francisco Franco (1892–1975) as a stand against fascism, racism and imperialism.

Hughes wrote a number of poems inspired by the Spanish Civil War, which were published back home in the United States. This poem, 'Song of Spain', is a call to all industrial workers to stop making bombs and to refuse to participate in the war. Hughes uses repetition to build up drama and feeling as the poem progresses.

This typescript of the end of 'Song of Spain' is part of a series of drafts produced by Hughes as he worked on the poem. Each version was typed out and then heavily annotated in pencil. This page is from an early draft and contains substantial textual differences to the published version. One significant difference between this draft version and the published poem is the reference to the 'Moors' who fought for Franco. In the draft Hughes alludes to the North African troops, who with the Spanish Foreign Legion were brought in from the Spanish colony in Morocco to support Franco. It was not unusual for colonial troops to be deployed in conflicts, but they did not usually fight against the population of the colonial power.

Langston Hughes, photograph by Carl Van Vechten, Library of Congress, Washington D.C., LOT 12735, no. 540.

3.

They can fall on you.

Hitler, Franco, Musolini, too,
Would adore dropping bombs on you.

The fascist gangsters of the world are wild.
~~They love to kill woamn, they murder the child.~~
They get paid well inngold and power,
They await only the ~~[illegible]~~ hour,
To dropix their bombs on you
Sitting here listening to this song,
To end this song,
To end all freedom,
To kill all singing
Except the siging of the bombing plane
Over a world once known as Spain
But now become England, France, the US.A
~~Japan~~, Australia, far away.
But not too far for the gold to flow
That turns into wings for a bombing plane,
That turns into bombs,
That turns into Franco, Hitler, Il Duce,
Or the Japanese war-lords ~~who seek~~ their day.

And we make the bombs with which they play.

This is the song of Spain:
Workers make no bombs again.
Workers, ~~make~~ no gold again.
Workers, lift no hand again
To build up profits for the rape of Spain.
Workers, see yourselves as Spain.
Workers, ~~see~~ that you too can cry,
Lift ~~your~~ arms in vain, scream, die,
Too late, the bombing plane!
Workers, make no bombs again.
Permit no one to make a bomb again,
Except it be made for you
~~I say, for you~~ to hold and guard
Lest ~~a~~ Franco steal into your backyard
Under the guise of some ~~[illegible]~~ patriot
Waving a flag and mouthing rot,
And talking about the Spanish people,
And bringing Moors to ~~[illegible]~~ a Christian steeple.
Poor misled Moors ~~who are also~~ people,
Driven to ~~kill~~ another people,
~~Because you haven't yet listened~~ to this song:

You made the bombs for Spain.
~~Don't~~ do it again.

Drive the bombers out of Spain.
Drive the bombers out of the world.
Take the ~~world~~ for ~~your~~ own again.

That is the song of Spain.

Killing man, woman, and child.

Omit?

Laugh a loud Ha! Ha! Ha! Ha! For The Church in Spain Hand in hand with the infidel!

I — I — I? But I'm only a simple worker

True! But Spain is you!

PAUL TRAN (active 2013–present)

Scientific Method

12 September 2017, black ink annotation and printed text on white paper. First published in *Poetry* magazine (April 2018).

“

‘Scientific Method [Of course I chose the terry cloth surrogate…]’ takes its persona from a baby rhesus monkey experimented on by Harry Harlow at the University of Wisconsin at Madison in 1959. Testing the drive-reduction theory of attachment posed by Sigmund Freud, who asserts in 1939 that ‘love has its origin in attachment to the satisfied need for nourishment,’ Harlow separated eight baby rhesus monkeys from their mothers. He placed each in an individual cage with two surrogate mothers. The first was made of terry cloth. The second was made of wire. Although both provided the babies with milk, Harlow observed over 165 days that the baby rhesus monkeys preferred the terry cloth surrogate, holding onto it when an oddity, such as a mechanical teddy bear that marched and beat a drum, was introduced to the individual cages. This indicated that drive-reduction didn't drive attachment. Instead, Harlow believed that a sense of security, or an ‘internal working model’, shaped the patterns of attachment. Borrowing the voices of the infant rhesus monkeys in this poem, I seek to reveal the story beneath this story, to show the cost of knowledge production and who, in fact, pays that cost.

”

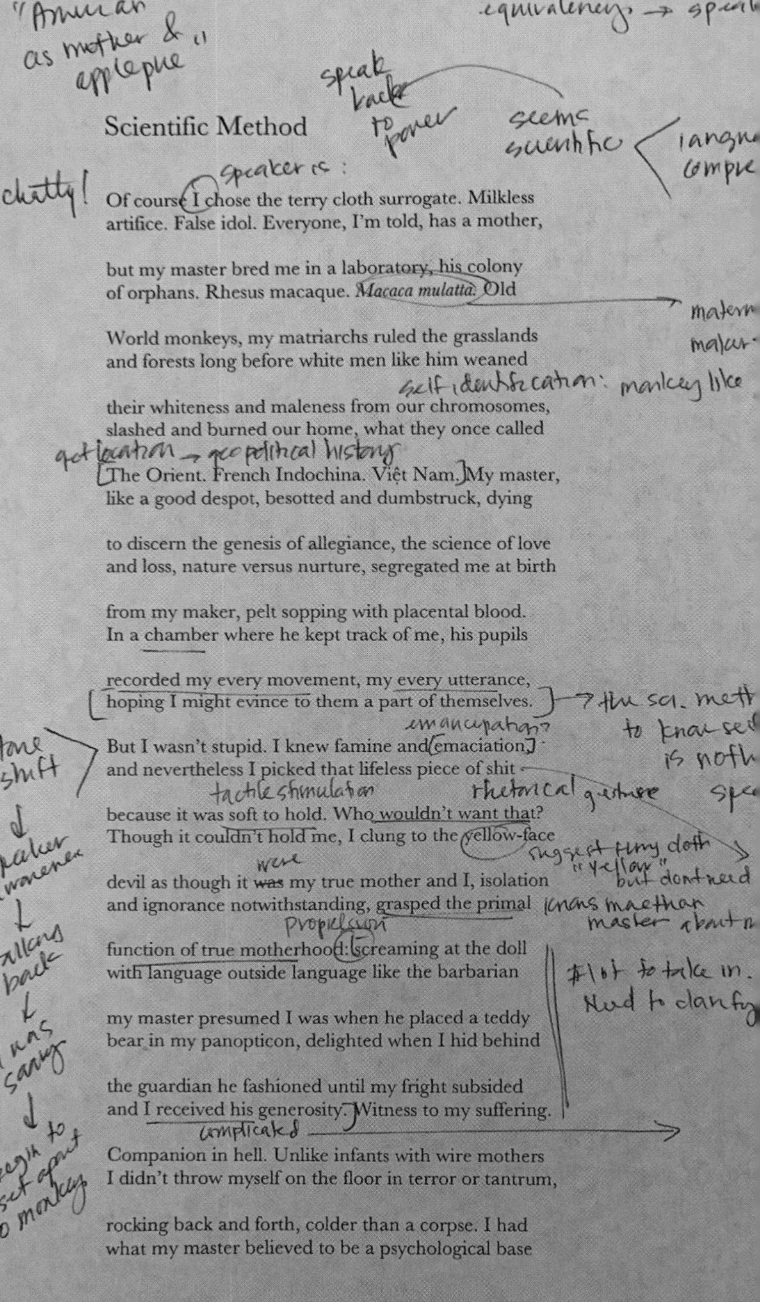

Scientific Method

Of course I chose the terry cloth surrogate. Milkless
artifice. False idol. Everyone, I'm told, has a mother,

but my master bred me in a laboratory, his colony
of orphans. Rhesus macaque. *Macaca mulatta.* Old

World monkeys, my matriarchs ruled the grasslands
and forests long before white men like him weaned

their whiteness and maleness from our chromosomes,
slashed and burned our home, what they once called

The Orient. French Indochina. Việt Nam. My master,
like a good despot, besotted and dumbstruck, dying

to discern the genesis of allegiance, the science of love
and loss, nature versus nurture, segregated me at birth

from my maker, pelt sopping with placental blood.
In a chamber where he kept track of me, his pupils

recorded my every movement, my every utterance,
hoping I might evince to them a part of themselves.

But I wasn't stupid. I knew famine and emaciation
and nevertheless I picked that lifeless piece of shit

because it was soft to hold. Who wouldn't want that?
Though it couldn't hold me, I clung to the yellow-face

devil as though it was my true mother and I, isolation
and ignorance notwithstanding, grasped the primal

function of true motherhood: screaming at the doll
with language outside language like the barbarian

my master presumed I was when he placed a teddy
bear in my panopticon, delighted when I hid behind

the guardian he fashioned until my fright subsided
and I received his generosity. Witness to my suffering.

Companion in hell. Unlike infants with wire mothers
I didn't throw myself on the floor in terror or tantrum,

rocking back and forth, colder than a corpse. I had
what my master believed to be a psychological base

Paul Tran

of operations. Emotional attachment. Autonomy.
Everything he denied and did to me, his ceaseless

cruelty concealed as inquisition, unthinkable until
it was thought, I endured by keeping for myself

the wisdom he yearned to discover and take credit
for. Love, like me, is a beast no master can maim,

no dungeon can discipline. Love is at once master
and dungeon. Whatever my master meant to love

he destroyed because it destroyed him: iconoclast
ignored by professors at Stanford, Lord of Goon

Park at Wisconsin. Insomniac chasing the bottom
of each bottle after Clara left with their kids, after

Margaret ceded her body to cancer. His black suit
at her funeral. His grief undomesticated despite

eons of electro-convulsive therapy, nursing his id
on my tits. So don't underestimate me. Simple-

minded and subservient as I may have appeared
to be, I gathered more about my master than he

did about me, which, I guess, is a kind of fidelity
conceived not from fondness but fear magnified

by fascination. My master made me his terry cloth
surrogate, his red-clawed god moaning for freedom

in my pit of despair, and for that, for all madness
unmasked of us, that which he snuffed in himself

and stalked in me, I pitied him. All this time he was
the animal. All this time my master belonged to me.

Paul Tran

9/12/17

'American as mother & apple pie'
equivalency > speaking through the speaker

speak back to power < seems scientific < language dense > move quickly
compression > tight couplet

Scientific Method

chatty!
Of course I *> speaker is:* chose the terry cloth surrogate. Milkless
artifice. False idol. Everyone, I'm told, has a mother,

but my master bred me in a laboratory, his colony
of orphans. Rhesus macaque. *Macaca mulatta*. Old
> maternal separation
experiment
maker >< master
World monkeys, my matriarchs ruled the grasslands
and forests long before white men like him weaned
self identification: monkey like, evolution

their whiteness and maleness from our chromosomes,
slashed and burned our home, what they once called

get location > geopolitical history
[The Orient. French Indochina. Việt Nam.] My master,
like a good despot, besotted and dumbstruck, dying

to discern the genesis of allegiance, the science of love
and loss, nature versus nurture, segregated me at birth

from my maker, pelt sopping with placental blood.
In a chamber where he kept track of me, his pupils

recorded my every movement, my every utterance,
hoping I might evince to them a part of themselves.
the sci. method is an innate desire to know self better > so subject is nothing > so here the speaker talks back

tone shift > speaker awareness > talking back > I was ??? > begin to set apart to monkey

But I wasn't stupid. I knew famine and [emaciation,]
> emancipation?
and nevertheless I picked that lifeless piece of shit
The mother you/master gave me > not sacred

tactile stimulation *rhetorical gesture*
because it was soft to hold. Who wouldn't want that?
Though it couldn't hold me, I clung to the yellow-face
suggest terry cloth 'yellow' but don't need

were
devil as though it ~~was~~ my true mother and I, isolation
and ignorance notwithstanding, grasped the primal
knows more than master about motherhood

propulsion
function of true motherhood: [screaming at the doll
with language outside language like the barbarian

A lot to take in. long sent. Need to clarify here.

my master presumed I was when he placed a teddy
bear in my panopticon, delighted when I hid behind

the guardian he fashioned until my fright subsided
and I received his generosity.] Witness to my suffering.
complicated >>>

Companion in hell. Unlike infants with wire mothers
I didn't throw myself on the floor in terror or tantrum,

rocking back and forth, colder than a corpse. I had
what my master believed to be a psychological base

B.F. Skinner
'Skinner boxes'

of operations. Emotional attachment. Autonomy.
Everything he denied and did to me, his ceaseless

cruelty concealed as inquisition, unthinkable until
it was thought, I endured by keeping for myself

High lyric > opens up
Bring us in

the wisdom he yearned to discover and take credit
for. Love, like me, is a beast no master can maim,

no dungeon can discipline. Love is at once master
and dungeon. ~~Whatever my master meant to love~~

~~he destroyed because it destroyed him: iconoclast~~
~~ignored by professors at Stanford. Lord of Goon~~

Borrowed details
makes the master sickeningly real
release from rhetoric > connects

Distracting in unproductive way
because it comes back to details
after fanning out
Jarring > out of nowhere
Takes out of poem

~~Park at Wisconsin. Insomniac chasing the bottom~~
~~of each bottle after Clara left with their kids, after~~

~~Margaret ceded her body to cancer. His black suit~~
~~at her funeral. His grief undomesticated despite~~

~~eons of electro-convulsive therapy, nursing his id~~
~~on my tits. So don't underestimate me.~~ Simple-

punctum minded and subservient as I may have appeared
. . .
to be, I gathered more about my master than he

did about me, which, I guess, is a kind of fidelity
conceived not from fondness but fear magnified

meditation
--
Before has a ginsburg howl
a well organized rant.
we feel the heat and intel.
--
Too many speakers happening

mother metamorphose into speaker <
by fascination. My master made me his terry cloth
surrogate, his red-clawed god moaning for freedom

in my pit of despair, and for that, for all madness
unmasked of us, that which he snuffed in himself

Bold
and stalked in me~~, I pitied him~~. All this time he was
the animal. All this time my master belonged to me.

Don't [illegible] things too easy

go back to 'appeared...'
and think it through

1st page < punctum: pierce > cause
2nd < studium: study or intel! approach

some images can make us feel physical pain and others that don't

Roland Barthes
Camera Lucida

chapter 9

DEATH AND REFLECTION

Death is inescapable: it is the certainty that awaits us at the end of life. Thoughts of impending mortality have often inspired writers and poets to reflect on their lives. In his poem 'A Reconsideration', written at the age of 86, Thomas Hardy looks back and considers whether his expectations of life were fulfilled.

Dylan Thomas wrote a number of poems inspired by his birthday, in which he self-consciously charted his journey towards death. Thomas's poem, 'In October', written about turning thirty, mourns the loss of his long-vanished childhood joys. Thomas died only nine years later at the age of 39. Another poet who died young was Anne Brontë; in the poem 'Self Communion' Brontë uses an internal dialogue to recount her experiences of time passing, lost love and death, unaware that she has only two years left to live.

The certainty of death generates a mood of reflection, but it can also act as a warning. The early Amharic poem 'Märgämä kəbr' (Refutation of Glory) reminds us of the impermanence of life and that we do not have long on this earth. The poem instils in the reader the importance of living a good Christian life.

Beyond the inevitability of our own death is the fear that we might lose someone we hold dear before their time. Rebecca Goss's poem 'Room in a Hospital' records the moment that she and her husband were informed of her baby daughter Ella's terminal illness. For Goss writing the poem was a means to come to terms with Ella's mortality and to mourn for her.

The loss of a loved one can be unbelievably hard to bear. *In Memoriam* by Alfred Tennyson might be considered a handbook on how to process grief, and many have found solace and hope in its pages. Other poems about death are less considered and contemplative: Mary Shelley's poem 'Absence', written shortly after her husband Percy's death, expresses her shock and pain at his loss. Poetry also allows us to remember those who have left us and can be a tribute to those we admire. Thomas Gray's 'Elegy in a Country Churchyard' considers the lives of the ordinary men and women buried beneath the headstones in a village churchyard, while in 'On the Death of Edmund Waller' Aphra Behn expresses esteem for her contemporary and sorrow at his passing in 1687.

Death can be used as a dramatic device. A shocking or brutal death might feature as a significant part of the plot in a Gothic or horror poem. John Keats uses the murder of Lorenzo in 'Isabella, or The Pot of Basil' in this way. In the poem, Isabella's sorrow is so overwhelming that she fades away in an attempt to join him.

Poetry lets us consider the path we have walked, to grieve for those we have lost, and to allow them to live forever in verse.

In Memoriam

ALFRED, LORD TENNYSON (1809–1892), COPIED OUT BY QUEEN VICTORIA (1819–1901)

1862–86, British Library, Add MS 62089, ff.4r and 5r, folios 13 × 8.5 cm, black ink on paper in a small, brown leather-bound notebook with an ornate gilt clasp.

In Memoriam is one of the greatest poems of the nineteenth century. Tennyson began writing it in 1833, after the death of his close friend and fellow poet Arthur Henry Hallam (1811–1833), and continued working on it until 1850, when the poem was first published. The poem goes beyond Tennyson's private grief for Hallam to explore the universal themes of sorrow and loss. It captured the hearts of many Victorians, including Queen Victoria.

In 1861 Queen Victoria lost her husband, Prince Albert (b.1819), and found great comfort in *In Memoriam*. She kept a copy of the poem by her bed. In a diary entry from Sunday 5 January 1862, she recorded that she was 'Much soothed and pleased with Tennyson's *In Memoriam*. Only those who have suffered as I do can understand these beautiful poems.'[1]

These extracts from the poem are contained within Queen Victoria's 'Album Consolativum', which was compiled by her and members of the royal household following Prince Albert's death. The album also includes poems and texts by Cardinal Newman (1801–1890), Charles Kingsley (1819–1875), Elizabeth Barrett Browning, Johann Wolfgang von Goethe and Friedrich Schiller (1759–1805). The tiny volume was purchased by the British Library at auction in 1981.

Queen Victoria chose two stanzas which held particular meaning for her in her grief. In the first stanza Tennyson describes his feeling of guilt at trying to express his grief in words. The next stanza describes how, despite his guilt, his words act like a cloak or barrier to the grief, supporting him through it but only expressing part of what he feels.

The following page of the album contains another extract from the poem including some of Tennyson's most famous words: ''T is better to have loved & lost / Than never to have loved at all.'

I sometimes hold it half a sin
To put in words the grief I feel;
For words, like nature, half reveal
And half conceal the Soul within.

In words like weeds I'll wrap me o'er,
Like coarsest clothes against the cold;
But that large grief which these enfold
Is given in outline, & no more.

ditto – V

I hold it true whate'er befall;
I feel it, when I sorrow most;
'T is better to have loved & lost
Than never to have loved at all.

ditto XXVI

Cover of Queen Victoria's 'Album Consolativum', British Library, Add MS 62089.

4.

—

I sometimes hold it half
a sin
To put in words the grief
I feel;
For words, like nature,
half reveal
And half conceal the
Soul within.

—

In words like weeds I'll
wrap me o'er,
Like coarsest clothes
against the cold;
But that large grief
which these enfold
Is given in outline,
& no more.

—

Ditto – V

5.

—

I hold it true whate'er
befall;
I feel it, when I sorrow
most;
'Tis better to have
loved & lost
Than never to have
loved at all.

—

Ditto XXVII

REBECCA GOSS (b.1974)

Room in a Hospital

23 August 2007, purple ink on cream lined paper, typewritten with black ink annotations on white paper. First published in *Her Birth* (Carcanet, 2007).

"

In March 2007, my husband and I walked behind a paediatric cardiac consultant beneath fluorescent light and followed him into a warm, quiet room: 'This was not the room where you waited for news. This was the room where you were told it.'

'Room in a Hospital' depicts the moment my husband and I were given our newborn daughter's terminal diagnosis. The draft is dated 23 August 2007. By then Ella had made it to five months old. A year later she would be two weeks dead. The final version of this early draft appeared in my collection, *Her Birth* (Carcanet, 2013), about my daughter's death from a rare and incurable heart condition.

I had forgotten my decision to include Ella's existence in the incubator: all those other hands touching her while I could not. These details went on to form a separate poem, but this version shows the woman whose mourning had already begun. I was separated from my baby in order to be told her of limited life, her body 'cribbed in an incubator a corridor away.'

In search of drafts, I unearthed notebooks half filled. Long descriptive episodes followed by blank, baffled pages. There are notes written on hospital car park tickets, lists of subjects for future poems (her breathing, her coughing) jotted on to the back of envelopes, a soon aborted food diary for a baby who wouldn't or couldn't eat. It all represented my state of mind at the time, and it was difficult to re-examine the fear and loneliness. I was either urgently trying to keep her alive or absorbed in recording every facet of her death. But Ella is remembered in this early, fundamental poem in the chronicling.

"

Room in a Hospital
(As soon as the door opened)
Its strangeness, everything about it
so unexpected, frightened me.
Usually, there's a tatty blanket
of tabloids, ~~scattered~~ vending cups,
snack litter, ~~the scattered~~ debris of
the bored and hungry. But this
was not the room where you waited
for news. This was the room
where you were told it.
Two sofas in deep red matched
ash
the walls. Coffee tables, vased plastic
prints, things, frames
flowers, a fireplace! But we didn't
we sat nervously on the edges
lounge. My husband + I sat in the
stillness. No history of movement here,
no history of others – it was clean,
(sterile), ready. Door shut
And so the consultant ~~took out his~~
flattened out the piece of white paper
borrowed
+ with a pen, drew a picture of
troubled
our daughter's heart. 36 hrs old, cribbed

links - matched – matched

false, pretend, artificial comfort

I stared at the fireplace, the coffee table,

Ikea prints, this room inviting you to lounge

and yet

23/08/07

Room in a Hospital

~~Its strangeness, everything about it so unexpected, frightened me.~~
Usually there's a tatty blanket of tabloids, vending cups, snack litter,
debris of the bored and hungry. But this was not the room where you

waited for news. This was the room where you were told it.

Red walls matched ~~bright~~ leather sofas. Ash frames of Ikea prints
matched the coffee table. There was carpet, there was a fireplace.
We did not lounge, my husband and I sat scared in the stillness.

No history of movement here, no history of others. Door shut,

this ~~room was~~ ready. The consultant flattened a scrap of paper
and with a borrowed biro drew a picture of our daughter's troubled heart.
Thirty six hours old, cribbed in an incubator a corridor away, she warranted

a new vocabulary, it filled the room in three horrifying minutes.

Downstairs, in my hospital bag, a leaflet promotes skin-to-skin.
I should be pressing the hot pearl of her cheek against my ~~breastbone~~.
Should be keeping ~~her sticky body~~ wrapped inside my new dressing gown.

Letting her legs ~~knead~~ the dough of my stomach. Instead, a registrar

with scrubbed arms, gowned and raised, instructs a nurse to open the portholes
to her incubator, reaches in to find a vein ~~beneath that luminous skin~~, his hands gloved.

embroidered / smooth / the? / the was / tense shift? / chest / the/That sticky heat of her, / I watch / pressing / incubator

~~of the~~ have to
scrub his arms, - bear him reaching in, to send for a vein -

his

Embroidered walls in deep red ~~so~~

Its red embroidered walls
contained the neatly staged list
clutter of a home. yet no

His gowned, hands gloved.

Red embroidered walls, smooth leather sofas -

It held me
Neatly staged clutter
of a home - Ikea prints, carpet, curtains
vases,

Smooth red leather sofas, matched embroidered walls.
~~Artificial~~ clutter of a home - staged -
Ash framed Ikea prints to match coffee table,
~~fireplace~~ + the thing that troubled me
most, the fireplace. A room inviting you
to lounge, but a room you follow a
consultant into in silence.

~~I stared at the~~ fireplace, ~~the~~ coffee table, Ikea prints, this room inviting you to lounge and yet 23/08/07

Room in a Hospital

~~It's strangeness, everything about it so unexpected, frightened me.~~
Usually there's a tatty blanket of tabloids, vending cups, snack litter,
debris of the bored and hungry. But this was not the room where you

waited for news. This was the room where you were told it.
emulsioned smooth The?
Red walls matched ~~bright~~ leather sofas. Ash frames of Ikea prints
matched the coffee table. There was carpet, there was a fireplace.
We did not lounge, my husband and I sat scared in the stillness.
– The was
No history of movement, no history of others. Door shut.

~~this room was ready.~~ The consultant flattened a scrap of paper
and with a borrowed biro drew a picture of our daughter's troubled heart.
Thirty-six hours old, cribbed in an incubator a corridor away, she warranted

a new vocabulary, it filled the room in three horrifying minutes.

Downstairs, in my hospital bag, a leaflet promotes skin-to-skin. ----- tense shift ?
I should be pressing the hot pearl of her cheek against my ~~breastbone.~~ chest
Should be keeping ~~her sticky body~~ wrapped inside my new dressing gown.
The/that sticky heat of her, I watch ----- ✓
~~Letting~~ her leg ~~knead~~ the dough of my stomach. Instead, a registrar
~~press (into)~~ pressing incubator
with (scrubbed) arms, gowned and raised, instructs/ a nurse to open the portholes
to her incubator, reaches in to find a vein ~~beneath that luminous skin~~, his hands gloved.
~~of the~~ have to

to
scrub his arms, bear him reaching in , search for a vein

Emulsioned walls in deepest red
Its red emulsioned walls contained the neatly staged clutter of a home, – yet is no –

Arms gowned, hands gloved. harbours red Red emulsioned walls, smooth leather sofas –

It held the Neatly staged clutter Carpet, curtains of a home – Ikea prints, vases
Smooth red leather sofas, matched emulsioned walls. A~~rtificial~~ clutter of a home – staged – Ash framed Ikea prints to
match coffee table ~~fireplace~~ + the timing that troubled me most, the fireplace. A room inviting you to lounge, but a room
you follow a consultant into silence

Elegy Written in a Country Churchyard

THOMAS GRAY (1716–1771)

December 1750, British Library, Egerton MS 2400, f.46r, folio 22.8 × 19 cm, bifolium written on all four sides, iron gall ink on laid paper.

This is the last folio from a fair-copy autograph manuscript of one of the most famous poems of the eighteenth century, written by the poet and scholar Thomas Gray. 'Elegy Written in a Country Churchyard' was completed in 1750 and published in 1751. The poem is noted for its atmospheric description of place. It was written about St Giles's Church, Stoke Poges, later the resting place of Gray's mother and the place where he was subsequently buried. The poem is a reflection on the inevitability of death for all mankind and contains the famous lines 'Far from the madding crowd's ignoble strife / Their sober wishes never learn'd to stray', which Thomas Hardy later used for the title of his novel. The final lines of the poem are in the form of an epitaph which is transcribed here.

The manuscript is contained within a volume of letters from Gray to Thomas Wharton (1717–1794), a physician and anatomist who had studied at Pembroke College, Cambridge, where they had become friends. This manuscript poem has faded in places, and the iron gall ink has bled through the first folio, making the text difficult to read. The paper bears folds, evidence that it had been sent with a letter.

Also in the British Library collections are manuscript instructions by Thomas Gray to his publisher, James Dodsley (1724–1797), for a new edition of his poems, published in 1768, which included 'Elegy Written in a Country Churchyard', a folio of which is shown here.

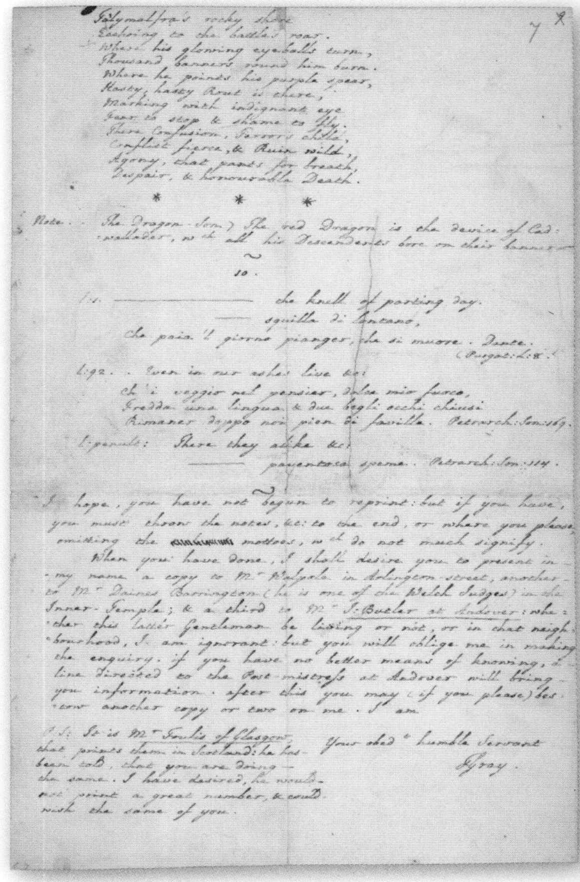

7

Plymlimmon's rocky shore
Echoing to the battle's roar.
Where his glowing eyeballs turn,
Thousand banners round him burn.
Where he points his purple spear,
Hasty, hasty Rout is there,
Marking with indignant eye
Fear to stop & shame to fly.
There Confusion, Terror's child,
Conflict fierce, & Ruin wild,
Agony, that pants for breath,
Despair, & honourable Death.

* * *

Note. The Dragon-Son) The red Dragon is the device of Cadwallader, wch all his Descendents bore on their banners.

10.

l:1. ——— the knell of parting day.
——— squilla di lontano,
Che paia 'l giorno pianger, che si muore. Dante. (Purgat: L:8.)

l:92. Even in our ashes live &c:
Ch' i veggio nel pensier, dolce mio fuoco,
Fredda una lingua & due begli occhi chiusi
Rimaner doppo noi pien di faville. Petrarch: Son: 169.

l:penult: There they alike &c:
——— paventosa speme. Petrarch: Son: 114.

I hope, you have not begun to reprint: but if you have, you must throw the notes, &c: to the end, or where you please, omitting the mottoes, wch do not much signify.

When you have done, I shall desire you to present in my name a copy to Mr Walpole in Arlington-street, another to Mr Daines Barrington (he is one of the Welch Judges) in the Inner-Temple; & a third to Mr J. Butler at Andover: whether this latter Gentleman be living or not, or in that neighbourhood, I am ignorant: but you will oblige me in making the enquiry. if you have no better means of knowing, a line directed to the Post-mistress at Andover will bring you information. after this you may (if you please) bestow another copy or two on me. I am

Your obed^t humble Servant
Gray.

P.S. It is Mr Foulis of Glasgow that prints them in Scotland: he has been told, that you are doing the same. I have desired, he would not print a great number, & could wish the same of you.

Instructions by Thomas Gray to Thomas Dodsley including Gray's notes on 'Elegy'. The famous first line '_the knell of parting day' can be seen in the upper half of the page. British Library, Egerton MS 38511, f.7.

Epitaph
Here rests his Head upon the Lap of Earth
A youth, to Fortune & to Fame unknown:
Fair Science frown'd not on his humble Birth,
And Melancholy mark'd him for her own.
Large was his Bounty & his soul sincere,
Heaven did a Recompence as largely send:
He gave to Misery all he had, a Tear;
He gain'd from Heav'n ('twas all he wish'd) a Friend.
No farther seek his Merits to disclose,
Or draw his Frailties from their dread Abode,
(There they alike in trembling Hope repose)
The Bosom of his Father and his God.

Haply some hoary-headed Swain may say,
, Oft have we seen him at the Peep of Dawn
, Brushing with hasty Steps the Dews away
, To meet the Sun upon the upland Lawn.
, There, at the Foot of yonder nodding Beech,
, That wreathes its old fantastic Roots so high
, His listless Length at Noontide would he stretch
, And pore upon the Brook, that babbles by.
, Hard by yon Wood, now smiling as in Scorn
, Mutt'ring his wayward Fancies would he rove
, Now drooping woeful-wan, like one forlorn,
, Or crazed with Care, or cross'd in hopeless Love.
, One Morn I miss'd him on the custom'd Hill,
, Along the Heath, & near his fav'rite Tree:
, Another came, nor yet beside the Rill,
, Nor up the Lawn, nor at the Wood was he.
, The next with Dirges due in sad Array
, Slow thro' the Churchway-Path we saw him born.
, Approach & read, for thou canst read, the Lay
, Graved on the Stone beneath yon aged Thorn.

Epitaph.

Here rests his Head upon the Lap of Earth
A Youth, to Fortune & to Fame unknown:
Fair Science frown'd not on his humble Birth,
And Melancholy mark'd him for her own.
Large was his Bounty & his Soul sincere,
Heaven did a Recompence as largely send:
He gave to Misery all he had, a Tear;
He gain'd from Heav'n ('twas all he wish'd) a Friend.
No farther seek his Merits to disclose,
Or draw his Frailties from their dread Abode,
(There they alike in trembling Hope repose)
The Bosom of his Father & his God.

Self-Communion

ANNE BRONTË (1820–1849)

1847–8, British Library, Ashley MS 154, f.5v, folio 18.2 × 11.4 cm, black ink on wove paper, later bound into a volume.

Death and grief were too often companions for the Brontë sisters. They lost their mother in 1821, before Anne was 2 years old, and their two eldest sisters, Maria and Elizabeth, four years later in 1825. Anne, the youngest child, formed a close bond with her sister Emily, and they wrote poetry together about the fictional kingdom of Gondal (see page 48).

The poem 'Self-Communion' is largely autobiographical. It addresses Anne's grief at the changing relationship with her sister Emily. The pair had been inseparable, and she describes Emily as 'My sun by day, my moon by night'. However, with the passing of time and absence from one another, they began to change as adults and to grow apart.

This manuscript draft of the poem is written in black ink by Anne, and she has made minimal changes to the text. The most notable on this page is the change of phrase to describe the alterations in the relationship between her and Emily. The original phrase 'angry passions' has been crossed out and replaced with 'jarring discords'. Twenty-one lines are shown and transcribed here.

Anne began writing the poem in November 1847. Her initials and the date 27 April 1848 appear at the end of this manuscript. Emily died eight months later in December 1848, three months after their brother Branwell's death. Anne died on 28 May 1849 at the age of 29.

In early friendship's pure delight, -
A genial bliss that could not cloy -
My sun by day, my moon by night.
Absence, indeed, was ~~bitterness~~ sore distress,
And thought of ~~death~~ death was anguish keen,
And there was cruel bitterness
When ~~angry passions~~ jarring discords rose between;

And sometimes it was grief to know
My fondness was ~~not~~ but half returned.
But this was nothing to the wo
With which another truth was learned: -
That I must check, or nurse apart
Full many an impulse of the heart
And many a darling thought:
~~For things I~~ What my soul worshiped, sought, and prized,
Were slighted, questioned, or despised; -
This pained me more than aught.

And as my love the warmer glowed
The deeper would that anguish sink,
That this dark stream between us flowed,
Though both stood bending o'er its (brink

In early friendship's pure delight,—
A genial bliss that could not cloy—
My sun by day, my moon by night.
Absence, indeed, was ~~bitterness~~ sore distress,
And thought of ~~death~~ death was anguish keen,
And there was cruel bitterness
When ~~angry~~ jarring ~~passions~~ discords rose between; X
And sometimes it was grief to know
My fondness was ~~not~~ but half returned.
But this was nothing to the wo
With which another truth was learned:—
That I must check, or nurse apart
Full many an impulse of the heart
And many a darling thought:
~~For~~ What ~~things~~ my soul ~~I~~ worshiped, sought, and prized, †
Were slighted, questioned, or despised;—
This pained me more than aught.
And as my love the warmer glowed
The deeper would that anguish sink,
That this dark stream between us flowed,
Though both stood bending o'er its brink

In October

DYLAN THOMAS (1914–1953)

30 August 1944, British Library, Add MS 52612, ff.153r and 154r, folio 30 × 20.3 cm, blue ink on paper, individual leaves sent as a letter.

Dylan Thomas's poem 'In October' begins with the curious line, 'It was my thirtieth year to heaven'. Here Thomas counts his progress to the grave rather than from birth. In the poem Thomas imagines a walk on his 30th birthday, leaving his home and climbing up a hill from which he can see the landscape spread out beneath him. He describes the scenery and the natural world around him and also reflects on his life so far, particularly his childhood.

This fair copy of the poem was enclosed with a letter to his fellow Welsh poet Vernon Watkins. Thomas and Watkins met in 1935. They struck up a friendship and corresponded regularly.

In his letter Thomas suggests that Watkins read the poem aloud, as he believes it has 'a lovely slow lyrical movement'. The poem was sent on 30 August 1944, 'a month and a bit premature'. Thomas also notes that in the poem the October trees are described as bare, something he will 'alter later'.

The letter and poem were acquired by the British Library from Vernon Watkins with the assistance of Philip Larkin.

It was my thirtieth year to heaven
Woke to my hearing from harbour and neighbour wood
And the mussel pooled and the heron
Priested shore
The morning beckon
With water praying and call of seagull and rook
And the knock of sailing boats on the net webbed wall
Myself to set foot
That second
In the still sleeping town and set forth.

My birthday began with the water
Birds and the birds of the bare trees flying my name
Above the farms and the white horses
And I rose
In rainy autumn
And walked abroad in a shower of all my days.
High tide and the heron dived when I took the road
Over the border
And the gates
Of the town closed as the town awoke.

A springful of larks in a rolling
Cloud and the roadside bushes brimming with whistling
Blackbirds and the sun of October
Summery
On the hill's shoulder,
Here were fond climates and sweet singers suddenly
Come in the morning where I wandered and listened
To the rain wringing
Wind blow cold
In the wood faraway under me.

Pale rain over the dwindling harbour
And over the sea wet church the size of a snail
With its horns through mist and the castle
Brown as owls
But all the gardens
Of spring and summer were blooming in the tall tales

It was my thirtieth year to heaven
Woke to my hearing from harbour and neighbour wood
And the mussel pooled and the heron
Priested shore
The morning beckon
With water praying and call of sea gull and rook
And the knock of sailing boats on the net webbed wall
Myself to set foot
That second
In the still sleeping town and set forth.

My birthday began with the water
Birds and the birds of the bare trees flying my name
Above the farms and the white horses
And I rose
In rainy autumn
And walked abroad in a shower of all my days.
High tide and the heron dived when I took the road
Over the border
And the gates
Of the town closed as the town awoke.

A springful of larks in a rolling
Cloud and the roadside bushes brimming with whistling
Blackbirds and the sun of October
Summery
On the hill's shoulder,
Here were fond climates and sweet singers suddenly
Come in the morning where I wandered and listened
To the rain wringing
Wind blow cold
In the wood faraway under me.

Pale rain over the dwindling harbour
And over the sea wet church the size of a snail
With its horns through mist and the castle
Brown as owls
But all the gardens
Of spring and summer were blooming in the tall tales
Beyond the border and under the lark full cloud.
There could I marvel
My birthday
Away but the weather turned around.

It turned away from the blithe country
And down the other air and the blue altered sky
Streamed again a wonder of summer
With apples
Pears and red currants
And I saw in the turning so clearly a child's
Forgotten mornings when he walked with his mother
Through the parables
Of sun light
And the legends of the green chapels

Dylan Thomas, photograph by Rosalie Thorne McKenna, Library of Congress, Washington D.C., POS – US .M241, no. 1.

Beyond the border and under the lark full cloud.
There could I marvel
My birthday
Away but the weather turned around.

It turned away from the blithe country
And down the other air and the blue altered sky
Streamed again a wonder of summer
With apples
Pears and red currants
And I saw in the turning so clearly a child's
Forgotten mornings when he walked with his mother
Through the parables
Of sun light
And the legends of the green chapels

And the twice told fields of infancy
That his tears burned my cheeks and his heart moved in mine.
These were the woods the river and sea
Where a boy
In the listening
Summertime of the dead whispered the truth of his joy
To the trees and the stones and the fish in the tide.
And the mystery
Sang alive
Still in the water and singingbirds.

And there could I marvel my birthday
Away but the weather turned around. And the true
Joy of the long dead child sang burning
In the sun.
It was my thirtieth
Year to heaven stood there then in the summer noon
Though the town below lay leaved with October blood.
O may my heart's truth
Still be sung
On this high hill in a year's turning.

DYLAN THOMAS

And the twice told fields of infancy
That his tears burned my cheeks and his heart moved in mine.
These were the woods the river and sea
Where a boy
In the listening
Summertime of the dead whispered the truth of his joy
To the trees and the stones and the fish in the tide.
And the mystery
Sang alive
Still in the water and singingbirds.

And there could I marvel my birthday
Away but the weather turned around. And the true
Joy of the long dead child sang burning
In the sun.
It was my thirtieth
Year to heaven stood there then in the summer noon
Though the town below was brown with October blood.
O may my heart's truth
Still be sung
On this high hill in a year's turning.

DYLAN THOMAS

Absence

MARY SHELLEY (1797–1851)

c.1822, British Library, Ashley MS A4023, f.114, folio 17.7 × 11.2 cm, ink written on one side of an octavo leaf of pale pink wove paper.

Mary Wollstonecraft Shelley (née Godwin) and her husband, Percy Bysshe Shelley, moved to Italy in 1818 to avoid creditors and to improve Percy's health. Both writers travelled throughout the country and wrote prolifically. Their time in Italy was repeatedly marked by tragedy. In September 1818 their daughter died from dysentery in Venice and in 1819 their son William died in Rome. Three years later, in July 1822, Percy drowned after his boat sank while returning from a trip to Livorno, where he had visited his friends Lord Byron and Leigh Hunt (1784–1859).

Mary Shelley was consumed by grief. In a letter to her friend Maria Gisborne (1770–1836), she said that 'the scene of my existence is closed'.[2] Nearly two weeks after his death, Percy's body washed up at Viareggio and was cremated on the beach where it was found. In the British Library collections are a fragment believed to be from Percy's ashes and a lock of his hair, both formerly owned by Claire Clairmont (1798–1879), the step-sister of Mary Shelley.

Shelley's poem was originally untitled. It was published in 1831 in the annual *Keepsake* with the title 'Absence', although it is sometimes referred to by the longer title 'Absence; Ah! he is gone – and I alone!'

An alleged fragment of Percy Bysshe Shelley's ashes, *c.*1822, British Library, Ashley MS 5022.

Ah! He is gone – and I alone;
How dark and dreary seems the time!
'Tis thus where the glad sun is flown,
Night rushes o'er the Indian clime.

Is there no star to cheer this night–
No soothing twilight for the breast?
Yes – Memory sheds her fairy light,
Beaming as sunset's golden west.

And hope of dawn – Oh brighter far
Than clouds that in the orient burn;
More welcome than the morning star,
Is the dear thought – he will return!

Mary W. Shelley

114

Ah! he is gone – and I alone;
How dark and dreary seems the time!
'Tis thus when the glad sun is flown,
Night rushes o'er the Indian clime.

Is there no star to cheer this night –
No soothing twilight for the breast?
Yes – memory sheds her fairy light,
Beaming as sunset's golden west.

And hope of dawn – oh brighter far
Than clouds that in the orient burn,
More welcome than the morning star,
Is the dear thought – he will return!

Mary W. Shelley

A Reconsideration (He Never Expected Much)

THOMAS HARDY (1840–1928)

1926, British Library, Add MS 59878, folio 24 × 18 cm, black ink and pencil on lined paper, later framed.

Although he was most famous as a novelist, Thomas Hardy was also a prolific poet who wrote over 1,000 poems. Despite the popularity and commercial success of his novels, Hardy's first love was poetry. Writing at the end of the nineteenth and beginning of the twentieth centuries, Hardy believed that poetry needed innovation and new ideas to adapt to a modernising world. Although his poetry was often thought unconventional during his lifetime, he is now considered one of the major English poets of his era.

As he grew older, Hardy drew on his life and experiences for his poetry. This poem, later published as 'He Never Expected Much', was written when he was 86 years old and is a conversation between Hardy and the world. For Hardy the world had proved much as he had expected it to be when, as a child, he lay watching the sky.

Hardy died on 11 January 1928, two years after this poem was written. It was first published in *The Daily Telegraph* shortly after his death, and later appeared in the collection *Winter Words* (1928). This is a working draft of the poem, written in ink with pencil annotations. It was purchased by the British Library on 10 June 1977.

<u>A Reconsideration</u>
<u>On my eighty sixth birthday</u>

Well, World, you have kept faith with me,
~~Kept~~ Yes, faith with me;
Upon the whole you have proved to be,
Much as you said you were.
Since as a child I used to lie
Upon the leaze & watch the sky,
Never, I own, expected I
That life would all be fair
~~A smooth life-thoroughfare~~

'Twas then you said, & since have said,
Times ~~yes oft~~ since have said,
In that mysterious voice you ~~spread~~ shed
From clouds & hills around:
'Many have loved me desperately,
Many with smooth serenity,
While some have shown contempt of me
Till they dropped underground'.

'I do not promise overmuch,
Child; overmuch;
Just neutral-tinted haps & such'
You said to minds like mine
Wise warning for your credit's sake!
Which I for one failed not to take,
And hence could ~~cope with~~ stem such ~~shock~~ strain & ache
~~In each years twist & twine~~
As each year might assign

A Reconsideration

On ~~my eighty-sixth birthday~~

Well, World, you have kept faith with me,
~~Kept~~ yes, faith with me:
Upon the whole you have proved to be
Much as you said you were.
Since as a child I used to lie
Upon the leaze & watch the sky,
Never, I own, expected I
~~A smooth life thoroughfare~~
That life would all be fair.

'Twas then you said, & since have said,
~~Times~~ ~~yes~~ oft since have said,
In that mysterious voice you ~~spread~~ | shed
From clouds & hills around:
"Many have loved me desperately,
Many with smooth serenity,
While some have shown contempt of me
Till they dropped underground."

"I do not promise overmuch,
Child; overmuch;
Just neutral-tinted haps & such,"
You said to minds like mine.
Wise warning for your credit's sake!
Which I for one failed not to take,
And hence could ~~cope with~~ stem such | ~~shock~~ strain & ache
~~In each year's twist & twine.~~
As each year might assign.

ይኸ፡መጽሐፍ፡አትመን፡
ይላል፡ክብር፡ለምን፡የማ
ያልፍን፡አውቆ፡በምድር፤
የዓለም፡ቆመ፡ሐጭር፤
ለተመለከተው፡አይመሳ
ም፡ሰገር፤ያኝሳል፡ከጸፋ
ር፤ከስንዴ፡ከአተር፤ከጤ
ፍ፡ከምስር፤ምንም፡ቢቆ
ጽሩ፡አይመሳም፡አስር፤ይ
ቀራል፡በጆምር፤የዓለም፡
ቆመ፡ሐጭር፤ይወዳል፡መ
ንደርደር፤ማመንዘር፡ማጨ
ብረር፤መከሐቅ፡ማንከርከ
ር፤የገበያ፡ጊ፡መንደር፤እንደ፡
እንስሳ፡መሳረር፤ተኝቶ፡መ
ሐደር፤እምላኩን፡ሳይዘክር፤
እግሩ፡ይመስል፡ወታደር፤ተ
መሳልሶ፡ሲያድር፤ተሸብሮ፡
እስኪያሸብር፤ዜጋውን፡ሲ

ያከብር፤ክብሩን፡ሲያሰ
ስር፤እጸድቅ፡ባዩን፡መ
ሾሌ፡ሲያቀነዝር፤ከግጸ
አውጾች፡ከዱር፤በሰው
መስሎ፡ሰይጣን፡ሲያስተ
ሕር፤አትፍሬህ፡ይላል፡ወ
ተኸም፡አትቀበር፤ትን
ኤ፡ሙታን፡አይኖር፤በኋ
ቅን፡ኀጢአት፡አይኩን
ኸም፡እግዚአብሔር፤
ጠቢብስ፡ይላል፡በኋ፡ሰ
ከአዳም፡እስከ፡ዛሬ፡ሞ
ና፡ሾንኑ፡ሳይዝመር፤ከ
ደርሶ፡ይቀር፤አዓለም፡
ንም፡አያመልጥሽ፡ያል
ነን፡ክብር፤ዛሬ፡በምድር
እንዴ፡እለ፡አባ፡እንጦን
በዱ፡ለበዱ፡የዞር፤እንደ፡
ፍ፡የበረር፤ምንም፡እስከ

Märgämä kəbr (Refutation of Glory)

UNKNOWN

Seventeenth century, British Library, Or 575, f.104v, volume 25.4 × 20.3 cm, black ink on parchment.

'Märgämä kəbr' (Refutation [or Condemnation] of Glory) is not only the title of this poem, but also the genre into which it fits in early Amharic literature. The poem is thought to derive originally from oral tradition. This type of poetry was intended to educate and warn the Christian community in Ethiopia.

There are at least five known poems with the title 'Märgämä kəbr', and it is possible they all derive from a single original poem. The text of each poem varies considerably, but their content and message are very similar. They all address themes of the impermanence of life and the imminence of death, and thus the importance of living a good Christian life. The transcription and translation have been taken from a similar manuscript, MKL-008 Mäṣḥafä qəddase, which was found in the church known as Läq̣ay Kidanä Məḥrät (wäräda Ganta ʾAfäšum, East Tigray), located close to the city of ʿAddigrat.

The original author of the poem is unknown, as is the name of the writer of this manuscript. The poem is written in Geez, an ancient Ethiopian language, and it is believed to date from the seventeenth century. The opening of the poem, shown here, considers the impermanence of the world. Contained within the volume alongside the poem is መልክአ ፡ ጉባኤ, *Malke'a gubā'e, A Collection of Hymns*, which is written in a different hand. The volume has been bound together using wooden boards.

መርገመ፡ ክብር Condemnation of glory
ልንገራችኍ፡ ነገር፡ የተሐየኝ፡ ጥቂት፡፡ 1) Let me tell you a little about a matter that appeared to me.
ዓለም፡ ኀላፊት፡ 2) The perishable world
ትመስል፡ ጽላሎት፡፡ 3) is like a shadow.
የሐለሙ፡ ሌሊት፡ 4) What they dreamt at night
አይገኝም፡ በጽዋት፡፡ 5) will not be found in the morning.
የመስከረም፡ ጽጌያት፡ 6) The flowers of Mäskäräm (September)
አይሻገርም፡ ለጥቅምት፡ 7) will not last into Ṭəqəmt (October).
ይኸ፡ ምሳልያት፡ 8) These are the parables
ለዓለም፡ እ[4]ኪት፡ 9) of a wicked world,
ትለንታዋ፡ መስገርት፡፡ 10) whose entirety is a snare.

Cover of *A Collection of Hymns*, British Library, Or 575.

On the Death of Ed:nd Waller Esq:e

How to thy Sacred Memory shall I bring
(Worthy thy Fame) a Gratefull Offering?
I, who by Toyles of Sickness am become
Almost as neere as thou art, to a Tombe.
While every soft and every tender straine
Is Ruffld and Ill Naturd growne with Paine.
But at thy Name my Languisht Muse revives
And a new spark in the Dull Ashes strives;
I heare thy tunefull Voyce, thy Song Divine!
And am inspird by every Charming Line!
But oh —
What Inspiration at the second hand
Can an Imortall Elegie command?
Unless like Pious Offerings mine shoud be
Made Sacred being ~~Dedicated~~ Consecrate to thee.
Eternall as thy owne all mighty Verse
Shoud be those Trophies that adorn thy Herse
The thought Illustrious, & thy Fancy young
The Witt Sublime, the Judgment fine & strong
Soft as thy Notes to Sacarisa sung —

While mine like Transitory flowrs decay
That come to deck thy Tombe a short liv'd day.
Such Tributs are like Tenures, only fitt
To shew from whom we hold our right to witt

Haile Wonderous Bard! whose Heav'n born Genius first
My Infant Muse and Blooming fancy Nurst,
With thy soft food of Love I first began;
Then fed on Nobler Panygeric straine.
Numbers Seraphick! and at every View
My soule Extended & much Larger grew
Where ere I read new Raptures seizd my blood.
Methought I heard the Language of a God!

Long did the untun'd world in Ignorance stray
Producing nothing that was Great & Gay,
Till taught by thee the true Poetic way.
Rough were the tracts before, Dull & obscure
Nor Pleasure nor Instruction coud procure
Their thoughtless Labour coud no Passion move
Sure in that Age the Poets knew not Love.

That Charming God like Apparitions then
Was only talkt on, but nere seen by men.
Darkness was ore the Muses Land displayd
And even the chosen Tribe unguided strayd.
Till by thee rescu'd from th' Egyptian Night,
They now look up and View the God of Light,
That taught em how to Love, & how to Write.
And to inhaunce the Blessing w:ch Heav'n Lent
When for our great instructer thou wer't sent
Large was thy life, but yet thy Glorys more,
And like the Sunn didst still dispence thy power
Producing somthing wonderous every howre.
And in thy Circulary Course didst see,
The very Life and Death of Poetrie.
Thou saw'st the Generous Nine Neglected Ly,
None listening to their Heav'nly Harmony
The World being growne to that Low Ebb of sense
To disesteeme the Noblest Excellence
And no incouragment to Prophets showne
Who in past Ages gott so great renowne,

Tho' Fortune Elevated thee above
Its scanty Gratitude or fickle Love.
Yet ~~Thus~~ sullen with the World, untird by Age
Scorning th' unthinking Crowde, thou left'st its stage

A Behn

On the Death of Edmund Waller

APHRA BEHN (1640?–1689)

1687, The Morgan Library & Museum, MA 4395, 1 bifolium, four pages, each folio 22.2 × 16.5 cm, iron gall ink on laid paper.

Aphra Behn, engraving by Robert White, British Library, 11626.bb.5.

This is an elegy of sixty-three lines written in memory of the poet Edmund Waller (b.1606), who died on 21 October 1687. Aphra Behn was the first Englishwoman to have earned a living from writing, and her biography is one that is both fascinating and mysterious. After working as a spy in Antwerp for King Charles II, Behn returned to England and began working as a playwright. She subsequently turned to prose fiction and published her most famous work, *Oroonoko, or, The Royal Slave* (1688).

Edmund Waller was one of the most celebrated poets of the seventeenth century and was highly regarded both in his lifetime and the years following his death. The poem not only immortalises Behn's esteem for Waller, but also her own ill health, stating that she was almost as near to the grave as Waller himself.

The poem was accompanied by a letter of condolence from Behn to Abigail Waller (née Tilney, 1662–1689), Edmund Waller's daughter-in-law. The letter also documents Behn's failing health, stating that she has 'been dying this twelve month' and 'I humbly beg pardon for my ill writing madam for tis with a lame hand scarce able to hold a pen'.

This is the only surviving literary autograph manuscript by Behn. The poem was first published in the volume *Poems to the Memory of that Incomparable Poet Edmund Waller, Esquire* (1688). The manuscript remained, by descent, in Waller's family until it was purchased by Paul Mellon (1907–1999) and Rachel Lambert Mellon (née Lowe Lambert, 1910–2014) at Sotheby's in 1981, who gifted it to The Morgan Library & Museum in memory of John D. Barrett. The first twenty lines on f.1 of the poem have been transcribed here.

On the Death of Ed:nd Waller Esq.

How to thy Sacred Memory shall I bring,
(Worthy thy Fame) a Gratefull offering?
I who by Toyles of Sickness am becom
Almost as neere as thou art, to a Tombe,
While every soft and every tender straine
Is Rufflld and Ill naturd growne with Paine.
But at thy Name my Languishd Muse revives
And a new spark in the Dull Ashes strives:
I heare thy tunefull Voyce, thy Song Divine!
And am inspird by every Charming Line!
But oh—
What Inspiration at the second hand
Can an Imortall Eligie command?
Un less like Pious offerings mine shoud be
Made Sacred being Consecrate to thee.
Eternall as thy owne all mighty Verse
Should be those Trophies that adorn thy Herse
The thought Illustrious, & thye Fancy young -
The Witt Sublime the Judgment fine & Strong,
Soft as thy notes to Sacharisa sung.

Isabella, or The Pot of Basil

JOHN KEATS (1795–1821)

1820, British Library, Egerton MS 2780, f.23r, folio 11.3 × 18.3 cm, black ink on paper in a leather-bound notebook.

Cover of John Keats's poetry notebook, British Library, Egerton MS 2780.

The portrayal of death in poetry is not always serious and emotional; it can also be shocking and grotesque. Many of the Romantic poets, including John Keats, Mary Shelley and Lord Byron, had a darker or Gothic side to their writing, which has subsequently been classed as Dark Romanticism. Edgar Allan Poe would be considered a key proponent of this subgenre.

John Keats based the poem 'Isabella, or The Pot of Basil' on a story from Boccaccio's *Decameron* (written 1349–53, published in English 1620). In the story Isabella falls in love with Lorenzo, one of her brothers' employees. Her brothers had intended to marry Isabella to a noble lord and so they murder Lorenzo and bury his body, telling Isabella that he has gone away. Lorenzo's ghost returns to Isabella to tell her of her brothers' crime. Isabella digs up his body and cuts off his head, which she places in a pot. She then plants 'Sweet Basil, which her tears kept ever wet', in the pot and nurtures the plant even as she fades away.

This is an extract from near the end of the poem when Isabella carries Lorenzo's head home and tends to it. This version of the poem is a fair copy written out by Keats in a notebook alongside his other poems 'The Eve of St Agnes' and 'The Eve of St Mark'. The notebook was sent to Keats's brother George (1797–1841), who had moved to North America with his wife Georgiana (née Wiley, *c.*1797–1879). George appears to have copied out other poems from manuscripts sent by his brother into this notebook, including 'Ode to a Nightingale', 'Ode on a Grecian Urn', 'Ode on Melancholy' and 'To Autumn'. The notebook was purchased by the British Library in 1893.

With death as life. The ancient Harps have said
Love never dies, but lives immortal Lord.
If ever any piece of Love was dead
Pale Isabella kist it, and low moan'd
'Twas love cold dead indeed, but not dethron'd.

In anxious secrecy they took it home
And then the prize was all for Isabel:
She calm'd its wild hair with a golden comb,
And all around each eye's sepulchral cell
Pointed each single lash: the smeared loam
With tears as chilly as a dripping well
She drench'd away; and still she comb'd and kept
Sighing all day and still she kiss'd and wept.

Then in a silken scarf, sweet with the dews
Of precious flowers pluck'd in Araby,
And divine liquids come with odorous ooze
Through the cold serpent pipe refreshfully,
She wrapp'd it up and for its tomb did choose
A garden pot wherein she laid it by,

With death as life. The ancient Harps have said
Love never dies, but lives immortal Lord.
If ever any piece of Love was dead
Pale Isabella kist it, and low moan'd
'Twas Love cold dead indeed, but not dethron'd.

In anxious secrecy they took it home
And then the prize was all for Isabel:
She calm'd its wild air with a golden comb,
And all around each eye's sepulchral cell
Pointed each single lash: the smeared loam
With tears as chilly as a dripping well
She drench'd away; and still she comb'd and kept
Sighing all day and still she kiss'd and wept.

Then in a silken scarf, sweet with the dews
Of precious flowers pluck'd in araby,
And divine liquids come with odorous ooze
Through the cold serpent pipe, refreshfully,
She wrapp'd it up and for its tomb did choose
A Garden pot wherein she laid it by,

chapter 10

LOVE

Love means different things to each of us. It can be platonic and familial (as explored in Chapter 7) or it can be desperate, passionate and beautiful. Love can be so intoxicating as to overcome the senses. For the Persian poet Omar Khayyám indulgence in love and wine was a metaphor for the joy of the spirit and devotion to God. However, overindulgence in romantic love can be dangerous. In the classical Chinese folktale, here retold by the great Japanese poet Fujiwara no Teika, the intense love of Orihime (織姫, 'Weaver Princess') and Kengyū (牽牛, 'Cowherd') leads them to neglect their duties and they are forced to live forever separated by the Milky Way.

Romantic love is often portrayed in poetry, and one of the most famous and often-quoted love poems is Robert Burns's 'A Red, Red Rose'. Valentine's Day is a popular occasion for expressing romantic feeling, often anonymously; the poem written by May Morris to George Bernard Shaw was not signed, although Shaw would have known from the illustrations who the card was from.

Romantic and spiritual love appear in the *ghazals* of Mah Laqa Bai. Believed to have been one of the first women to compose a *diwan* in Urdu, Mah Laqa Bai was a courtesan and an unconventional woman for her time. Historically women were often viewed as the object rather than the instigator of romantic love; in *Sonnets from the Portuguese*, Elizabeth Barrett Browning was one of the few female poets of the Victorian era to speak of her own love and desire.

Love does not always last and couples do not always share a life together. Byron was something of a master in the art of seduction, but his poem 'Love and Gold' warns of the perils of love. Jonathan Swift sent poems within letters to his lover, Vanessa. The couple were together for seventeen years until, despite claiming that only a 'blockhead or a rake' would forsake her, Swift moved on to another lover. The attraction between Ted Hughes and Sylvia Plath was instantaneous, but their relationship was tumultuous and ended in tragedy. In *Birthday Letters*, Hughes expresses his emotions about their relationship, vividly capturing snapshots of Plath that show why he had fallen in love with her.

Love poetry, with its potential to include implicit or explicit references to sex, can reflect or challenge the prevailing morality of the society in which it is written. John Donne wrote a number of poems in the sixteenth and seventeenth centuries that would be considered risqué even today. Erotic poetry has often been banned, requiring writers to conceal sexual content in metaphors, innuendos and puzzles. In Thai literature *Konlabot* poems were written as a code to be deciphered before their full meaning could be revealed. This poetic device was useful for subjects that were considered taboo. In many societies in the past it was not possible to write openly about same-sex love, and repression of homosexuality persists in some countries today. The American poet Walt Whitman pushed the boundaries by celebrating the different forms of love between men in his *Calamus* poems.

Passionate and painful, romantic and saccharine, love takes many forms. However, as much as we love someone else we should also recognise the need to love ourselves. Caroline Bird's poem 'Megan Married Herself' recognises the importance of being happy with who you are through the humorous absurdity of a self-marriage.

A Red, Red Rose

ROBERT BURNS (1759–1796)

c.1794, British Library, Add MS 22307, f.114r, volume 37.8 × 28 cm, folio 26.1 × 20.7 cm, iron gall ink on laid paper.

This is one of the most famous Scottish love songs. It is one of a number of works by Robert Burns which are thought to be based on traditional folk songs he collected in rural Scotland. He originally intended to publish it in *A Select Collection of Original Scottish Airs for the Voice* (1793–1818), a five-volume compendium compiled by George Thomson (1757–1851). Yet Burns felt Thomson did not understand the importance of the song, and he subsequently published it anonymously in 1794 in *A Selection of Scots Songs* by Pietro Urbani (1749–1816), who set it to a tune of his own composition.

The tune for 'A Red, Red Rose' was changed a number of times. Along the bottom of this manuscript Burns has included a note suggesting it should be set to the tune of 'Major Graham', composed by the Scottish fiddler Niel Gow (1727–1807). At top of the page, Burns has written and crossed through the line 'Tune Ceud soraidh nam d'an Ailleagan'. This refers to the song 'A thousand blessings to the lovely youth', which appeared in Patrick Macdonald's (1729–1824) *A Collection of Highland Vocal Airs* in 1784.

This folio is part of a collection of 174 letters and songs in Burns's hand. The volume was bequeathed to the British Museum Library by Archibald Hastie MP (1791–1857) and is known as the Hastie Manuscript.

TOP RIGHT: Cover of the Hastie Manuscript, British Library, Add MS 22307.

[~~Tune, Ceud soraidhh nam d'an Ailleagan~~]
[Tune, Major] Vol V. Song. 402.

O my Luve's like a red, red rose,
That's newly sprung in June;
O My Luve's like the melodie
That's sweetly play'd in tune. ------

As fair art thou, my bonie lass,
So deep in luve am I;
And I will love thee still, my Dear,
Till a' the seas gang dry. ------

Till a' the seas gang dry, my Dear,
And the rocks melt wi' the sun:
I will love thee still, my Dear,
While the sands o' life shall run.

And fare thee weel, my only Luve!
And fare thee weel, a while!
And I will come again, my Luve,
Tho' it were ten thousand mile!

\+ once thro the Music,
takes all the words
to this mark + so yt
more must added,
or these four lines
left out

The tune of this song is in Niel Gow's first Collection & is called there, 'Major Graham' — it is to be found, page 6th of that Collection. ——

110 ~~Tune~~, ~~Ceud soraidh uam do'n Ailleagan~~ 3

Vol V. Song. 402.

114

O my Luve's like a red, red rose,
That's newly sprung in June;
O My Luve's like the melodie
That's sweetly play'd in tune. —

As fair art thou, my bonie lass,
So deep in luve am I;
And I will love thee still, my Dear,
Till a' the seas gang dry. —

Till a' the seas gang dry, my Dear,
And the rocks melt wi' the sun:
I will love thee still, my Dear,
While the sands o' life shall run. +

And fare thee weel, my only Luve!
And fare thee weel, a while!
And I will come again, my Luve,
Tho' it were ten thousand mile! —

once thro the music, ~~takes~~ all the words to this mark + so 4 more must added, or these four lines left out

The tune of this song is in Neil Gow's first Collection & is called there, "Major Graham" — it is to be found, page 6th of that Collection. —

Calamus 17
pp 362–3

–~~79~~– ~~Leaf~~. Poemet.

Of ~~a man~~ him I love~~d~~ day and night, I dreamed I heard ~~he was~~ dead,
And I dreamed I went where they had buried the man I loved, but he was not in that place,
And I dreamed I wandered ~~to find~~ the ~~man I love~~, searching among burial places, to find him,
And I found that every place was a burial place,
The houses full of life were equally full of death, ~~(this house is now)~~
The streets, the shipping, the ~~houses~~ places of amusement, ~~the~~ Chicago, the Mannahatta, were ~~as~~ ~~just~~ as full of the dead as of the living, and fuller of the dead than of the living. —

Poemet (Of Him I Love Day and Night)

WALT WHITMAN (1819–1892)

***c.*1860**, University of Virginia Library, Walt Whitman Papers, 1838–1962, in the Clifton Waller Barrett Library, Accession #3829, folio 21 × 13 cm, black ink on pink paper.

Walt Whitman, photograph by Phillips & Taylor, Library of Congress, Washington D.C., LOT 12017, box 1.

Many men and women across the centuries have not been able to express their love for someone of the same sex freely. Even in poetry, where pushing the boundaries of social norms is common, it was dangerous to depict homosexual love. In nineteenth-century Britain and the United States same-sex relationships were criminalised, with punishments including imprisonment for those caught breaking the law.

One author who pushed the boundaries in the nineteenth century and wrote a series of poems between a man and his male lover was Walt Whitman. Known as the 'Calamus' poems (probably named after the grass known for its phallic shape), they form part of Whitman's poetry collection *Leaves of Grass* (1855–1892).

This poem, 'Of Him I Love Day and Night' – here titled 'Poemet' – begins with the narrator's despair at the death of his dream lover and goes on to depict the death of the nation. It has been suggested that Whitman used this poem to convey his frustration and grief at the homophobia that was prevalent at the time, which meant that many people in the country could not love freely. For Whitman, politics and personal life could not be separated.

Whitman wrote the poem across two pink leaves of paper in black ink. He revised the text in the same black ink and also used another lighter ink. The title was also changed from 'Leaf' to 'Poemet'.

Calamus 17
pp 362-3

79- ~~Leaf~~. Poemet.

Of ~~a man~~ him I love~~d~~ day and
night, I dreamed I heard
he was dead,
And I dreamed I went where
they had buried the man
I love~~d~~ but he was not
in that place,
And I dreamed I wandered, ~~to find~~
~~the man I love,~~ searching
among burial places, to find him,
And I found that every place
was a burial place,
The houses full of life were
equally full of death,
(this house is now;)
The streets, the shipping, the
~~houses~~ places of amusement, the Chicago,
the Mannahatta, were ~~as~~
~~just~~ as full of the dead
as of the living, and fuller
of the dead than of the
living;-

Seventh Month

藤原定家 FUJIWARA NO TEIKA (1162–1241)

1691–3, British Library, Or 16991, f.7, folio 32 x 40 cm, sumi ink and colour on Japanese paper (washi).

This *waka* (a form of Japanese poetry) tells the mythical story of two star-crossed lovers. Originating from China, the story is believed to have first reached Japan in the seventh century. It follows Orihime（織姫, 'Weaver Princess') and Kengyū (牽牛, 'Cowherd'), who fall in love. Blind to everything but their love for each other, they neglect their work. As punishment for their negligence, the couple are parted from one another across the Milky Way. The distance does not stop the couple longing for each other. Eventually they are allowed to meet once a year on the night of the seventh day of the seventh lunar month, when magpies flock to create a bridge between them. Tanabata, or the Star Festival, is still celebrated in Japan today.

This poem was originally composed by the great Japanese poet Fujiwara no Teika, who was a master of the *waka* form. Teika wrote his poetry during the late twelfth and early thirteenth centuries. The calligraphy is by Niwata Shigeeda 庭田重条 (1650–1725). The poem forms part of the manuscript 'Birds and Flowers of the Twelve Months', created in the late seventeenth century by nobles at the Japanese imperial court, which contains twelve poems representing the months of the year.

In the translation 'endless' has been chosen over 'long' for '長き夜'. The translator has kept the bridge keystone symmetry, but isolated '契', translating this as 'vow', with commas to isolate and centre it.

There are no clear links between the poem and the accompanying illustration. The latter may reflect the tradition in Japanese society of creating calligraphic copies of Teika's poetry.

長き夜にはねをならぶる契とて秋待ちたえる鵲の橋

Wings spread across the endless night, true to its vow, the magpie bridge awaits the Autumn

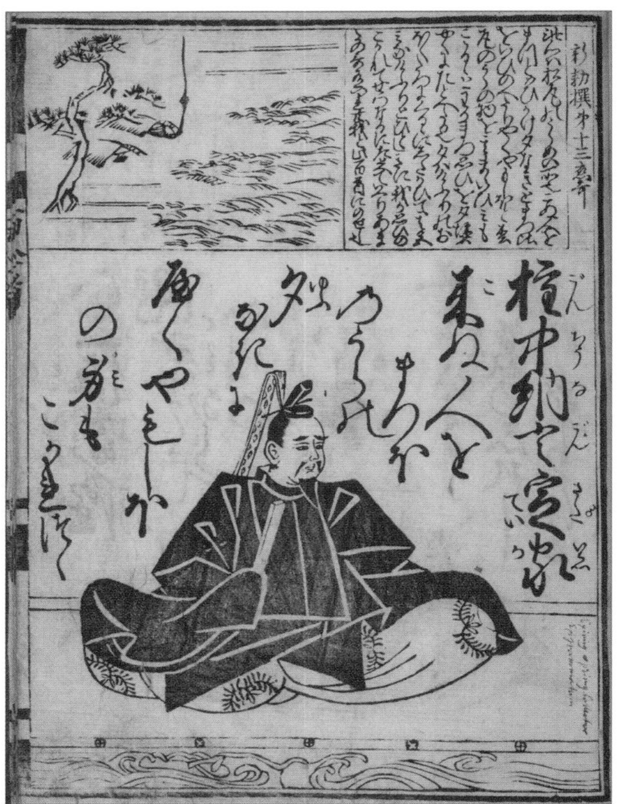

Fujiwara no Teika, woodblock, *Kashiragaki eshō hyakunin isshu* (1673), British Library, Or.75.h.3, f.43.

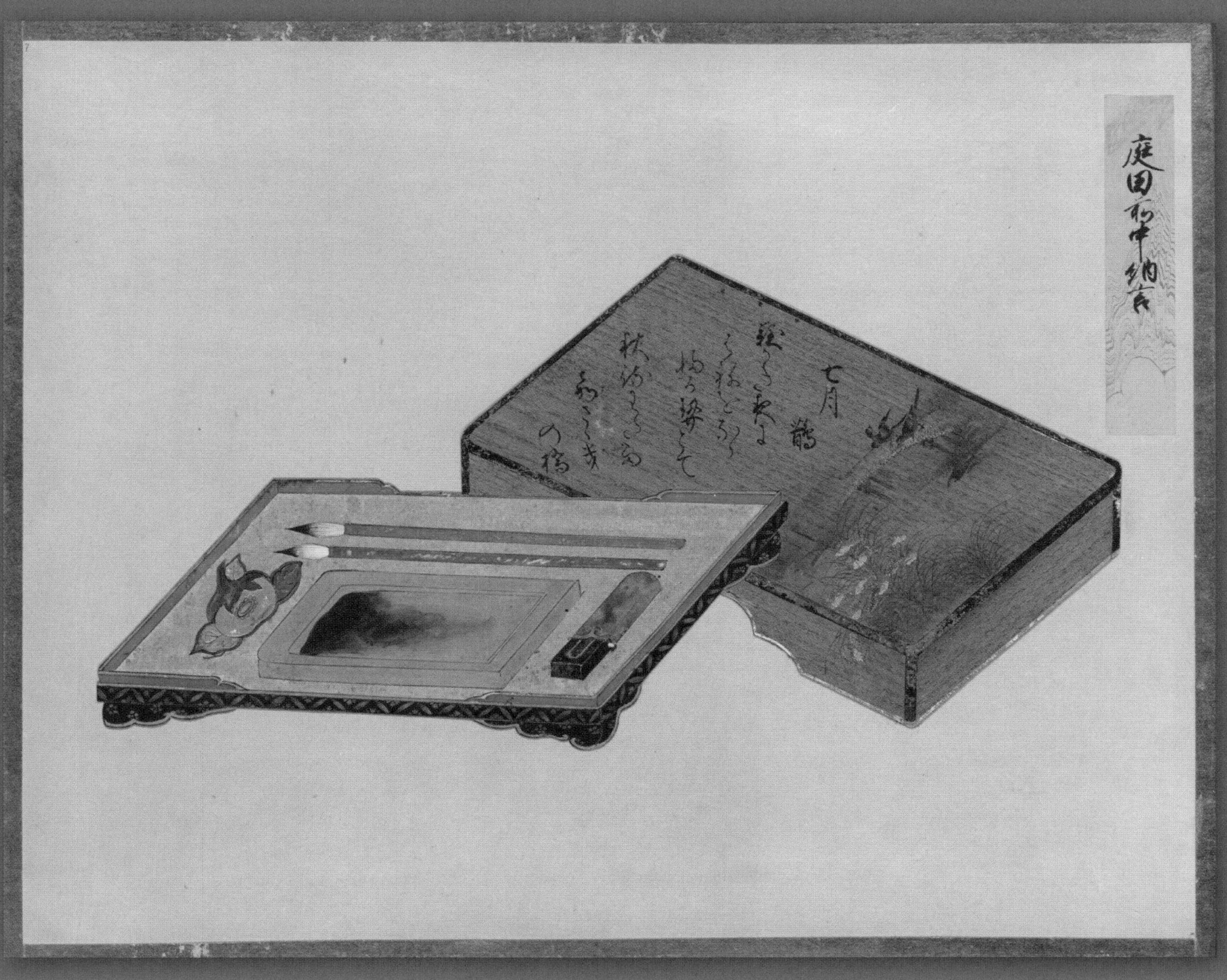
庭田前中納言

Valentine's Day card to George Bernard Shaw

MAY MORRIS (1862–1938)

14 February 1886, British Library, Add MS 50563, f.6r, folio 26.6 × 18.7 cm, pen and ink, watercolour and bodycolour on card with a gold edge.

This Valentine's card was sent to the playwright George Bernard Shaw (1856–1950) by May Morris, the daughter of his friend William Morris. On 14 February 1886, Shaw noted in his diary that he 'Got a handsome Valentine'.[1] Although it was sent anonymously, the style of the illustration was instantly identifiable to Shaw.

The card shows a group of women dressed in the Pre-Raphaelite style, worshipping at a burning shrine. A scroll of music sits below a portrait of Shaw. May Morris and Bernard Shaw were good friends but, despite this declaration of love, they did not become a couple, and Morris married Henry Halliday Sparling (1860–1924) in 1890. The marriage lasted only four years, perhaps in part because of Morris's closeness to Shaw, who lived as a guest in their house for months at a time.

This card was identified in 2016 as being by Morris. It is part of a collection of greeting cards, cartoons and caricatures sent to George Bernard Shaw and is part of his archive at the British Library.

Our time is yours; we care not for the rest
    Of your base sex: let each pursue his way,
    Its tenor moves us not; since none can play
Upon our hearts save you: within each breast
You strike a tender chord. Flatly confest,
    Minor considerations hold no sway
    We take our tone from you: be grave, be gay!
    Be sharp! Be natural! We like it best!
Even your very crochets form no bar
    To our affection; just the minimum
Of kindness – one brief note! one little line
    Is all we ask, the while we stand afar
And sing your praise in chorus, till she come
    Who finds the key to your heart's inmost shrine.

May Morris, photograph, Library of Congress, Washington D.C., LC-B2- 797-7 [P&P].

Seit ich ihn ge - se-hen, glaub'ich blind zu sein
Gardez-vous d'être sevère
Quand on vous parle d'Amour
Il n'est point d'amour sans peine
Ni sans amour de plaisir
Our time is yours; we care not for the rest
Of your base sex: let each pursue his way,
Its tenor moves us not; since none can play
Upon our hearts save you: within each breast
You strike a tender chord. Flatly confest,
Minor considerations hold no sway
We take our tone from you: be grave, be gay!
Be sharp! be natural! we like it best!
Even your very crochets form no bar
To our affection; just the minimum
Of kindness — one brief note! one little line
Is all we ask, the while we stand afar
And sing your praise in chorus, till she come
Who finds the key to your hearts inmost shrine.

CAROLINE BIRD (b.1986)

Megan Married Herself

Before 2017, black ink on cream paper. First published in *In These Days of Prohibition* (Carcanet, 2017).

“

My first drafts are always more like pre-first drafts. I don't try to write a poem, or write good lines, I'm just letting my pen play around in the privacy of my own imagination. I tell myself, 'No one will ever read this so it doesn't matter what I do.' I deliberately try to have absolutely no idea where I'm going or why; my only aim is to surprise myself, to escalate a situation until it gets sadder or wilder or stranger or funnier or preferably all of those things at once. I build the road I'm walking down, like a cartoon character laying train-tracks in front of their own speeding train. This is how I create the 'raw material' . . . and after that, I switch on my conscious brain – or at least half of it – and begin to rewrite and rewrite and rewrite.

”

A friend of a friend married herself.
As in, yes, she got married. To herself.
It wasn't a joke or an art installation.
~~They had we'd~~ She arrived at
the grand hotel in a white
limousine, her maid of honour
clutched a yellow bouquet. She'd sent
invitations with her name ~~printed twice~~
written twice with a 'and' symbol
in the middle, like the way
calligraphy de-shapes a couple.
She had a modest list of wedding
gifts, but there were no hints of
exploitation on the side, she wasn't in
it for the toasters ~~and~~ She refused
cheques. She did except china
tea-sets, cut-crystal tumblers etc –
'This'll set us up for life' she
said. She wore an ivory dress, not

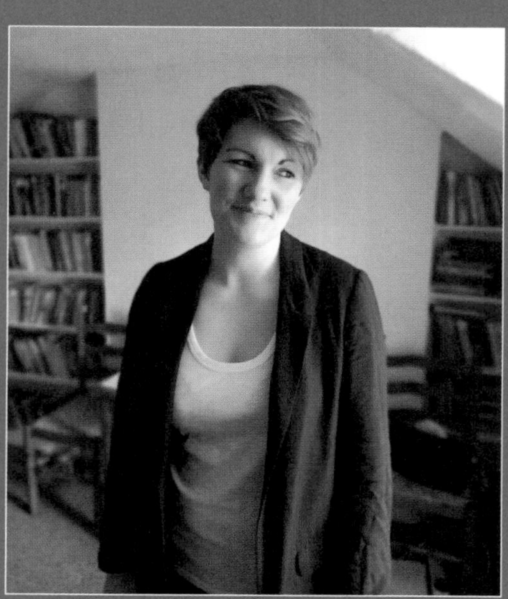

A friend of a friend married herself. A friend of a friend got married. To herself.

As in, yes, she got married. To herself.

It wasn't a joke or an art installation.

~~They had wed~~ She arrived ~~in~~ ~~to~~ at the grand hall in a white limousine, & her maid of honour clutched a yellow bouquet. She'd sent invitations with her name ~~printed twice~~ written twice with a 'and' symbol in the middle, like the way calligraphy ~~&~~ de-shapes a couple.

She had a modest list of wedding gifts, but there was no hints of exploitation on the side, she wasn't in it for the toasters ~~and~~. She refused cheques. She did accept Christmas fan sets, cut-edge crystal tumblers etc: 'This'll set us up for life' she said. She wore ~~white~~. ~~off~~ an ivory dress, ...

quite white, because they'd lived together thirty three years. Who were they kidding? But no one marries virgins these days. (It's probably ~~more rare~~ rarer than marrying yourself.) They played 'At Last' by Etta James when she walked down the aisle to face the celebrant, eyes fixed front, tears sparkling in them, a ~~[illegible]~~ shaking but certain voice: 'I do.'

Everyone said it was a beautiful service. My friend of a friend apparently made a speech at the reception and ~~used the word brave~~ ~~cried~~ cried until she couldn't stand.. ~~Glasses~~ Toasts were frequent + robust. No one saw it as a joke. A few even eyed their husbands, thinking about what it would have been if they hadn't turned down the proposal — all those years ago — in the light voice in their head said, 'marry me.'

quite white, because they'd lived together
thirty-three years, who were they kidding?
(but no one marries virgins these days.
it's probably ~~more rare~~ rarer than marrying
yourself.) They played 'At Last' by Etta
James when she walked down the aisle to
face the celebrant, eyes fixed front,
tears sparkling in them, a shaky
but certain voice: 'I do.'
Everyone said it was a beautiful service.
My friend of a friend apparently
made a speech at the reception and
~~Used the word brave~~ cried until
she couldn't stand. ~~Glasses~~ Toasts
were frequent and robust. No one saw it as
a joke. A few even eyed their
husbands, thinking about what might have (illegible!)
been if they hadn't turned down
that proposal - all those years ago
when the little voice in
their head said, 'marry me'

I cannot ~~speak~~ talk of love to thee

Though ~~you~~ thou art young, ~~& fair~~ gay & free & fair;

There is a spell, thou dost not see

~~That ...~~ ~~genuine~~ Love

That bids a genuine love forswear.

And not that a spell in either could

~~A spell that~~

For thee to sigh or seem

~~Can~~ ~~That~~ ~~Thou~~ ~~teaches~~ teaches ~~... ...~~ a falsehood

And truth itself abhor a ... dream

3.

Can dwell or blare ... possess

In woman's heart there ... in

Admit not ~~there~~ love into thy ...

~~Yet~~ Dwell ~~thou~~ others love all, ... to mine.

4

Perchance tis far feigned, perchance sincere

But false or true thou canst tell

So much hast thou from all to fear

In that unconquerable spell

Love and Gold

GEORGE GORDON NOEL BYRON, SIXTH BARON BYRON (1788–1824)

1812–13, British Library, Ashley MS 4727, f.1r, folio 25 × 19.5 cm, iron gall ink on laid paper.

'Love and Gold' is addressed to an unknown noblewoman, warning her of the perils of love. Byron may have written it for his future wife, Annabella Milbanke (1792–1860), in either 1812 or 1813. The poem uses imagery of shrines and altars, linking love to both worship and death.

The first four verses of the poem are written on the centre of the folio, with verses 8 and 9 on either side. The remainder of the poem is written on the verso. Byron has made extensive changes and corrections to it, using every part of the page and rotating the paper as he continued to fill the space. It is written in iron gall ink of the same composition throughout, which suggests that he probably composed it in one sitting rather than returning to correct it at a later date. The manuscript was collected by Thomas James Wise and now forms part of the Ashley Collection at the British Library.

I can not ~~speak~~ talk of Love to thee
Though ~~you~~ thou art young ~~& fair gay &~~ free & fair!
There is a spell~~;~~ thou dost not see
~~That Love genuine Love~~ That bids a genuine love
forbear.

2.

And yet that spell invites each youth,
~~A spell that~~
For thee to sigh or seem to sigh
~~That Can makes teaches makes~~ Makes ~~many a~~
falsehood ~~seem to be~~ under the garb of truth
~~Also~~ And Truth itself appear a lie.

3.

If ever doubt a place possest
In woman's heart, 'twere wise in ~~the~~ thine
Admit not ~~these~~ Love in to thy breast
~~Yet~~ Doubt [~~their all~~?] others love, nor trust to mine.

4.

Perchance 'tis ~~for~~ feigned, perchance sincere
Butt: false or true thou [canst] tell
So much hast thou from all to fear
In that unconquerable spell.

~~8.~~

~~Perhaps~~ [~~evermore~~] Each day some tempter's
[~~happen~~?] crafty suit
~~May draw~~ [Would ~~woo~~ Yes woo] thee to a loveless
bed:
I see thee to the altar's foot
A decorated victim led.

9.

~~Oh had a loveless lot been thine~~
~~Had thine Hear but lived [illegible] a horrible lot~~
~~Then I go~~ Adieu, dear maid! ~~[love] [only] [may] [a]~~
~~[for you?]~~ I must yet speak
~~And [made] a~~ Whateer [~~illegible~~] ~~[mark]~~ ~~[from me~~]
My secret thoughts may be;
Though thou art all that man can seek
I dare not ~~speak~~ talk of Love to thee.

Diwan e Chanda

MAH LAQA BAI (1768–1824)

1798, British Library, IO Islamic 2768, f.17r, volume 24 x 13 cm, black ink on paper.

Mah Laqa Bai is believed to have been one of the first female poets to compose a *diwan*, a complete collection of Urdu *ghazals* (lyrical poems). The collection, titled *Gulzar-e-Mahlaqa*, was published posthumously in 1824. The *ghazals* address themes of love, loss and the pain of separation and also refer to the public events and court life of her time.

Mah Laqa Bai was a poet, courtesan and philanthropist. An exceptional horse rider who had mastered archery and tent pegging, she accompanied Mir Nizam Ali Khan, Asaf Jah II (1734–1803), ruler of Hyderabad State in South India, into battle in male dress. She was also a talented singer and dancer. Her poetry readings were popular and she was the first woman known to have read her poetry in a *mushaira* (poetic symposium), a space usually reserved for men. Mah Laqa Bai gave generously to good causes including female education and help for homeless girls.

This poem is a short romantic *ghazal* in which the narrator is thinking about their lover. It is thought to have been handwritten by Mah Laqa Bai in black ink on paper in 1798 as part of the 'Diwan e Chanda', an early version of her collection of 125 *ghazals*. It was presented as a gift from this extraordinary woman to Captain Sir John Malcolm (1769–1833), a Scottish soldier, East India Company administrator and diplomat, in the middle of a dance in which she was the chief performer, on 18 October 1799.

دل میں میرے پھر خیال آتا ہے آج
کوی دلبر بے مثال آتا ہے آج

کیوں پڑا بیہوش اُٹھ ہاتف سے اب
ہے ندا صاحب جمال آتا ہے آج

سنگ رہ ہوں ایک ٹھوکر کے لیے
تس پہ وہ دامن سنبھال آتا ہے آج

مشتری و زہرہ باہم سعد ہیں
اس لیے ابرو ہلال آتا ہے آج

تم سوا چندا کے دل میں یا علی
کس کی عظمت کا جلال آتا ہے آج

Today the thought has returned to my heart
Of a peerless beloved

Why has that which was dormant now been awoken by a heavenly call?
There is a beautiful voice that comes today

I am the stone on a path waiting for an encounter,
Carefully skirting the edge of which they come today

Jupiter and Venus are auspiciously united
Which is why the crescent of the beloved's eyebrows appears today

O Ali, apart from you, in Chanda's heart
Whose majestic splendour arrives today?

ہے یا عاشقی کا رسم ہر ایک کو وفا کے بیچ
ثابت قدم ہو کم کوئی تیری جفا کے بیچ

ہو بیخبر آہ تو نہ مجھے زلف یار سی
یہ اندلوں غبار ہے میری صبا کے بیچ

جور و جفا سوائے نہیں ذرہ تجکو رحم
بس یہ جو دم رکھوں ہوں سو تیری رضا کے بیچ

اغیار سیں نظر ہے کر یہی تو یار کر
دیکھا نہ اب لطف کسو آشنا کے بیچ

ہے یہ مراد و مقصد و مطلب ہے یا علی
حیدرا یہ لطف و رحم ہو ہر دو سرا کے بیچ

دل میں مری یہ خیال آتا ہے آج
کوئی دلبر بے مثال آتا ہے آج

کیوں نترا بیہوش او تہمت تلف سبی اب
ہے نذر حبیب جمال آتا ہے آج

سنگ رہ ہوں ایک ٹھوکر کے لئے
بس یہ جو ان کو سنبھال آتا ہے آج

مشتری و زہرہ باہم سعد ہیں
اس لئے ابرو ہلال آتا ہے آج

تم سوا حیدرا کے دل میں یا علی
کیا عظمت کا جلال آتا ہے آج

قلبا

17

حق نے جو صفحۂ امکاں یہ کیا یار کے طرح
جسنے دیکھا سو بنا صورت دیوار کے طرح

رہو ہوں کو دیے ابرو کے ہر اکوقت میری
پر کہے دل میں ہماری یہ ستمگار کے بیچ

زہد و تقوا کو ہے رخصت کہ میں بیہوش ہوا
کچھ جمی انکھوں میں بطرح دو مے خوار کے طرح

کیوں طبیب اب یہیں کرتا ہے علاج دل ارتی
کیا خوش آئی ہے تری چشمیں یہ بیمار کے طرح

ہوئی حیدرا سبی دو روضہ کے تصدق یا شاہ
روز و شب شمس و قمر جس یہ ہے زوار کے طرح

آج کرتا ہے لباس اپنا بت گلفام سرخ
ہے جو کانہ شکر کا عاشق کا ہو انجام سرخ

ہر سحر لازم حذر ہے عشقیں اس ترک کے
ہو مبادا خون ناحق سیں نکوئی نام سرخ

شاخ گل میں کب ادا ہے و و چمن کے سبا قبا
خوشنما جیسا ہے تری ہاتھ میں یہ جام سرخ

مرغ دل اپنا ہے بارک اسقدر ہے کن تہیں
جب ملک ہو وہی رنگ گل سبی یہ بلبل دام سرخ

یا علی حیدرا کا رہوی صفحۂ دنیا یہ نقش
جسقدر تا ہو لگا قایم ہے نگیں بر نام سرخ

The Good Morrow / JD

I wonder by my troth what thou, and I
did, till wee lov'd; weare wee not wean'd till then?
But suck'd on childish pleasures seelily?
or slumbred wee in the seauen sleepers den?
T'was so; butt this, all pleasures fancies bee
If euer any Beautie I did see
which I desir'd and gott; t'was but a dreame of thee.

And now good morrow to our wakeinge soules,
which watch not one another out of feare,
But Loue, all Loue of other sights controule
and makes a little roome, an euerie where.
Lett sea-discouerers to new worlds haue gone
Lett Mapps to others worlds, ~~one~~ our worlds haue shone
Lett us possess our world; each hath one, and is one.

My face in thyne eye, thyne in myne appeares,
and plaine true harts doe in the faces rest
Where can wee fynde two fitter Hemispheres
Without sharpe North, without declininge West?
What euer dies is not mixt equallie:
If both our Loues bee one, or thou, and I
Loue Just alike in all; none of these Loues can die. //

Finis /

The Good Morrow

JOHN DONNE (1572–1631)

***c*.1620–30**, British Library, Egerton MS 3884, f.34r, volume 25.7 × 19.5 cm, iron gall ink on laid paper.

'The Good Morrow' was written by John Donne, probably in the 1590s, but it was not published until 1633, some two years after his death. The poem celebrates and explores a romantic union, as two lovers wake up next to one another. Donne plays on the idea of waking by suggesting that the lovers were asleep until they found love. Their intimacy makes 'a little roome an everie where'; the pair are physically so close that each is able to see their face reflected in the other's eyes. The poem contrasts this comfortable intimacy with the bustle of the wider world, epitomised by the attempts of explorers to map territories abroad. The word 'hemispheres' has a double meaning, denoting both the eyes of the lovers and the globes on which cartographers depicted new discoveries overseas. Donne's poetry was circulated among his friends in manuscript form during his lifetime. Very few poems in Donne's own hand survive, but many high-quality scribal copies exist, such as this manuscript. This poem has been written by one hand but corrected by another, using a different ink.

This manuscript was discovered in 2018 in the library at Melford Hall, Suffolk. A rare seventeenth-century volume containing over 130 poems by Donne, it is one of the largest near-contemporary scribal collections of his work. It provides an insight into Donne's poetry and the literary culture in which it was created. The volume contains other manuscript material that places it in East Lothian by the middle of the seventeenth century, which poses questions about the production and circulation of Donne's work and its reach in Scotland.

The Good Morrow JD

I wonder by my troth what thou, and I
did till wee lov'd; weare wee not wean'd till then?
But suck'd on childish pleasures seelily?
or slumbered wee in the seaven sleepers den?
T'was so; butt this, all pleasures fancies bee
If ever any Beautie I did see
which I desired and gott; t'was but a dreame of thee.

And now good morrow to our wakeinge soules,
which watch not one another out of feare,
But Love, all love of other sights controule
and makes a little roome, an everie where.
Lett sea-discoverers to new worlds have gone
Lett Mapps to others worlds, ~~are~~ our worlds have shone
Lett us possess our world; each hath one, and is one.

My face in thyne eye, thyne in myne appeares,
and plaine true harts doe in the faces rest
where can wee fynde two fitter Hemispheres
without sharpe North, without declininge West?
what ever dies is not mixt equallie:
If both our loves bee one, or thou and I
Love just alike in all; none of these loves can die.//

Finis /

To Vanessa

JONATHAN SWIFT (1667–1745)

1720, British Library, Add MS 39839, ff.47r–v, volume 24 × 21 cm, folios 18.8 × 15.5 cm, bifolium, pen and iron gall ink on laid paper with a wax seal.

This letter is addressed to Esther Vanhomrigh (*c*.1688–1723), known as Vanessa, who was a friend and lover of the writer and cleric Jonathan Swift. The name 'Vanessa' is a play on words: 'Van' was taken from her surname and 'Esse' was Swift's pet name for her. Swift wrote the poem 'Cadenus and Vanessa' about her in 1713.

Within the letter is a poem; Swift often included verse in his letters to Vanhomrigh. The pair were lovers for over seventeen years and the development of their relationship can be traced in their correspondence. Their relationship ended when Swift began another affair. The manuscript has been folded and contains the remnants of a wax seal, revealing its original format as a letter. It is now part of a bound volume of Swift's correspondence with Vanhomrigh held at the British Library. Shown and transcribed here are the first part of the letter and the entire poem.

I am now writing on Wednesday night, when you are hardly settled at home, and it is the first hour of Leisure I have had, and it may be Saturday before you have it, and then there will be Governor Huff, and to make you more so, I here inclose a letter to poor Malkin which I will command her not to shew you, because it is a love-letter. I reckon by this time the Groves and Fields and purling Streams have made Vanessa Romantick, provided poor Malkin be well. Your Friend sent me these verses he promised, w[hi]ch I here transcribe.

Nymph, would you learn the only Art
To keep a worthy Lover's heart
First, to adorn your Person well,
In utmost Cleanlyness excell
And tho' you must the Fashions take,
Observe them but for fashion sake.
The Strongest Reason will submit
To Virtue, Honor, Sense, and Wit.
To such a Nymph the Wise and Good
Cannot be faithless, if they wou'd:
For vices all have diff'rent Ends,
But Virtue still to Virtue tends
And when your Lover is not true,
Tis Virtue fails in Him or You;
And either he deserves Disdain,
Or you without a Cause complain.
But here Vanessa cannot err,
Nor are these Rules applyd to Her:
For who could such a Nymph forsake
Except a Blockhead or a Rake
Or how could she her Heart bestow
Except where Wit and Virtue grow

47

I am now writing on Wednesday night, when you are hardly settled at home, and it is the first hour of Leisure I have had, and it may be Saturday before you have it, and then there will be Governt Huff, and to make you more so, I have enclose a Letter to poor Malkin, which I will command her not to shew you, because it is a Love-Letter. I reckon by this time the Groves and Fields and purling Streams have made Vanessa Romantick, provided poor Molkin be well. Your Friend sent me these Verses he promised, wch I have transcribe.

Nymph, would you learn the onely Art
To keep a worthy Lover's heart
First, to adorn your Person well,
In utmost Cleanlyness excell
And thô you must the Fashions take,
Observe them but for fashion sake.
The strongest Reason will submit
To Virtue, Honor, Sense, and Wit.
To such a Nymph the Wise and Good
Cannot be faithless if they would:
For Vices all have diff'rent Ends,
But Virtue still to Virtue tends.

And when your Lover is not true,
Tis Virtue fails in Him or You:
And either he deserves Disdain,
Or You without a Cause complain.
But here Vanessa cannot err,
Nor are these Rules applyd to Her:
For who could such a Nymph forsake
Except a Blockhead or a Rake
Or how could she her Heart bestow
Except where Wit and Virtue grew

A Pink Wool Knitted Dress

TED HUGHES (1930–1998)

Before 1998, British Library, Add MS 88918/1/2, f.16r, folio 20.5 × 16 cm, black ink on lined paper in a grey-blue school exercise book.

Edward (Ted) Hughes was immediately attracted to Sylvia Plath when they met on 26 February 1956, and they were married less than four months later. The poem 'A Pink Wool Knitted Dress' remembers their wedding day. It formed part of *Birthday Letters*, Hughes's collection of poems written in the decades following Plath's 1963 suicide, which was not published until 1998. All but two of the eighty-eight poems are addressed to Plath.

This is one of two drafts of the poem written in a grey-blue school exercise book. Overall the British Library holds fifteen folders and volumes that contain poetry drafts, notes, personal reflections and correspondence relating to the creation, development and publication of *Birthday Letters*. The British Library purchased Hughes's archive from his widow, Carol Hughes (née Orchard), in May 2008.

The intensely personal nature of the poems in *Birthday Letters* is atypical of Hughes's work; in general he believed that it was undesirable to include autobiographical experience in poetry. The poems in *Birthday Letters*, written in private over many years, reflect his emotions and memories in the decades after Plath's suicide. Hughes heavily revised the poems before they were published and described them as 'so raw, so vulnerable, so unprocessed, so naive, so self-exposing & unguarded, so without any of the niceties that any poetry workshop student could have helped me to'.[2]

This is the first draft of 'A Pink Wool Knitted Dress' and it shows Hughes attempting to bring his wedding day to life. The poem is presented as a series of memories. Large chunks of text have been crossed out so that the words beneath can no longer be seen. Lines from the final published version also appear. A later draft, which is longer and closer to the published version, can be found a couple of pages further on in the exercise book.

In your pink wool knitted dress
Before anything had smudged anything
You stood at the altar. Bloomsday.

Rain- so that a new umbrella
Was the only furnishing about me:
Newer than about three years old
Sandals the one ~~fastened~~ repaired with a drawing pin
~~My tie- the worn hand-[illegible]~~
My tie- sole, drab veteran RAF black-[~~illegible~~]
The worn-out symbol of a tie
~~By~~ My cord jacket- thrice dyed black ~~[illegible]~~, exhausted,
Dragging its pockets agape
[~~Th~~] Just hanging on to itself
Not quite the frog-prince
But what a ~~son-in-law~~ post war utility son-in-law!
What a hill shepherd, without sheep or hill.
To be rustling daughter's ~~[illegible]~~, pedigree dreams
From under that watchtower ~~[illegible]~~ career

Those days such no ceremony could conscript me
~~[Illegible]~~ Out of my uniform ~~as S.R.O~~.
Marriage- or another bottle of wine
[M] was ~~[illegible]~~ song, and ~~[the]~~ mother-in-law
Were part of the world's ~~behaviour~~ deposits ~~[illegible] behaviour~~

St George of the Chimney sweeps.
My Parish Church ~~at~~ now ~~[befallen]~~ discovered
Your mother your only bridesmaid ~~in there [brave]~~ brave even in this
~~Even in this deception of every [certainly] bravely~~
Was an international ~~[tragedy]~~ gamble.

16

In your pink wool knitted dress
Before anything had smudged anything
You stood at the altar. Bloomsday.

Rain — so that a new umbrella
was the only furnishing about me
Newer than about three years old.
Sandals ~~the~~ one repaired with a drawing pin.
My tie — sole, drab veteran RAF black —
the worn-out symbol of a tie.
Baggy cord jacket — thrice-dyed, black, exhausted,
Dragging its pockets agape,
clinging on to itself. Not quite the frog-prince.
But What a post-war utility son-in-law!
What a hill-shepherd, without sheep or hill
To be a daughter's penniless dreams
From with fame careers.
Those days, no ceremony could conscript me
uniform,
Marriage or another bottle of wine
It was just a song, and the mother-in-law
Was part of the world's deposits.

St George of the chimney sweeps.
My Parish Church covered brave
Your mother your only bridesmaid,
Even in gamble.

And for my best man my squire
To hold the meanwhile rings
We requisitioned the Sexton. Twist off. the ~~[illegible]~~ cottage.
He was packing children into a bus —
Taking them to the zoo, in that sun.
~~[illegible]~~ All the animals had to wait
While we ~~[illegible]~~ married.

Slender you were there, in flower —
A nodding spray of wet lilac — cream
You sobbed with joy, you shook with ~~[illegible]~~ feeling
Of ~~[illegible]~~ being awash with God.
You said you saw the heavens open
And show riches, ready to drop upon us.
Where was I ??? ~~[illegible]~~ my subtleties
~~[illegible]~~ to a strange tense: the absent present.
All I remember is you, in that cold church,
In your pink wool knitted dress
And your eyes — truly like big jewels
Jostling their tears flame ~~[illegible]~~
~~[illegible]~~ jewels
There in a dream & held up to me.

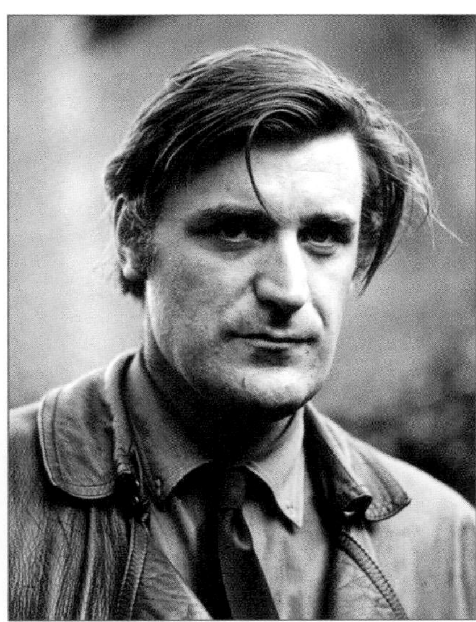

Ted Hughes, photograph by Fay Godwin, British Library, FG597-5-11.

And for my best man. My squire
To hold, the meanwhile rings
We requisitioned the sexton. Twist of the ~~[illegible]~~ outrage.
He was packing children into a bus-
Taking them to the zoo, in that rain
~~Every body had to be [illegible]~~ All the animals had to wait
While we ~~[were]~~ married

Slender you were there, in flower
A nodding spray of wet lilac
You sobbed with joy. ~~You~~ shook with ~~[illegible]~~ ocean feeling
Of ~~a vertical [illegible] God~~ being awash with God.
You said you saw the heavens open
And show riches, ready to drop upon us.
Where was I ? I ~~cannot remember~~ was subjected
~~Myself there~~ To a strange tense: the absent present.
All I remember is you, in that cold church,
In your pink wool knitted dress
And your eyes- truly like big jewels
Jostling their tear flames, ~~shaken in a dice cup~~
~~And held up to me~~ great cut ~~[illegible]~~ jewels
Shaken in a dicecup & held up to me.

Bird in the Cave

UNKNOWN

Nineteenth century, British Library, Or 16102, f.17, volume 34 × 10.7 cm, pen, black ink, watercolour and gold lead on mulberry paper.

One of the most famous literary treasures from Thailand is *Chindamani* (Jewels of Thought). The earliest version of *Chindamani* is attributed to the seventeenth-century royal astrologer Phra Horathibodi of Ayutthaya. While he probably compiled the work in around 1670 in Lopburi, central Thailand, for King Narai (1633–1688), it is likely that he drew on earlier textual sources for inspiration. The original manuscript no longer survives, but many copies of the work have been preserved, as well as poetry books based on the *Chindamani* such as this nineteenth-century folding book (*samut khoi*) made from mulberry bark paper.

The poetry within is known as *Konlabot* กลบท, which is a special form of rhyme that often can be read vertically or horizontally, similar to a word puzzle and involving word play and puns. This form of poetry was sometimes used to cover taboo subjects, as the meaning could be hidden.

Shown here is the 'Bird in the Cave', a love poem or secret message to a lover, the meaning of which is hidden in metaphors relating to nature. The words in the poem are a combination of ancient Tai terminology and Sanskrit, arranged in a geometric pattern that is embedded in an illustration of a golden bird in a cave. The title is a symbolic expression for lovemaking, and the poem elaborates on the poet's desire for his lover, a beautiful woman with a playful voice and a face that sparkles like a diamond.

รจนาเร่ร้อง
สะทิดทำ ปักษา อยู่แฮ
ปักสีส่งเสียงจำนันจา ย้อเย้า
เพริดพริ้งพพรายเพ้ต ลายเลือม
สังวาสนางย้อเย้า ยิ่งงามฯ

Writing and wandering around to sing
About a bird who's living in a cave
His lady chatting playfully
Teasing, exciting his desires
She is so elegant, bright with an aura
Sparkling like a diamond
Insatiably is the bird beguiling
His beautiful, gorgeous lady

อยู่แฮ
ย้อเย้า
ปักษ
ยิ่งงาม
ปักสี
ส่งเสียง
พพรายเพด
หง

Rubáiyát of Omar Khayyám

OMAR KHAYYÁM (1048–1131), TRANSLATED BY EDWARD FITZGERALD (1809–1883), DECORATED BY WILLIAM MORRIS (1834–1896), CHARLES FAIRFAX MURRAY (1849–1919) AND EDWARD BURNE-JONES (1833–1898)

1872, British Library, Add MS 37832, f.1r, volume 15 × 11.5 cm, watercolour and gold on parchment with a binding in red leather tooled with gold.

In the latter part of the 1850s, the English poet and writer Edward FitzGerald translated a series of quatrains (or *rubáiyát*) written by the Persian mathematician, astronomer and poet Omar Khayyám. FitzGerald called the work the *Rubáiyát of Omar Khayyám*. It was first published in 1859 and features 101 verses drawn from the original. FitzGerald's work became popular with the Pre-Raphaelite Brotherhood, a group of artists whose work was influenced by art made before the famous Renaissance painter Raphael (1483–1520), and caught the attention of artists and writers such as William Morris, Edward Burne-Jones and Charles Fairfax Murray.

This manuscript was created in 1872 and handwritten and decorated by William Morris. The figures in the decorated borders were designed by Morris and Burne-Jones and then painted by Charles Fairfax Murray. The *Rubáiyát of Omar Khayyám* covers many different themes, including the transience of life, wine drinking and love.

The manuscript bears Morris's note on f.12v: 'I finished my work on this book on the sixteenth of October 1872. W Morris.' It was given by Morris to Georgiana Burne-Jones (née Macdonald, 1840–1920), the wife and biographer of Edward Burne-Jones. The letter 'G' in the decorated borders stands for 'Georgiana'. She gave the volume to the British Museum Library in 1909.

1

Awake! For morning in the bowl of night
Has flung the stone that puts the stars to flight;
And lo the Hunter of the East has caught
The sultan's turret in a noose of light.

2

Dreaming when dawn's left hand was in the sky
I heard a voice within the tavern cry,
Awake my little ones and fill the cup
Before Life's liquor in its cup be dry.

3

And as the cock crew, those who stood before
The tavern shouted, Open then the door!
You know how little while we have to stay,

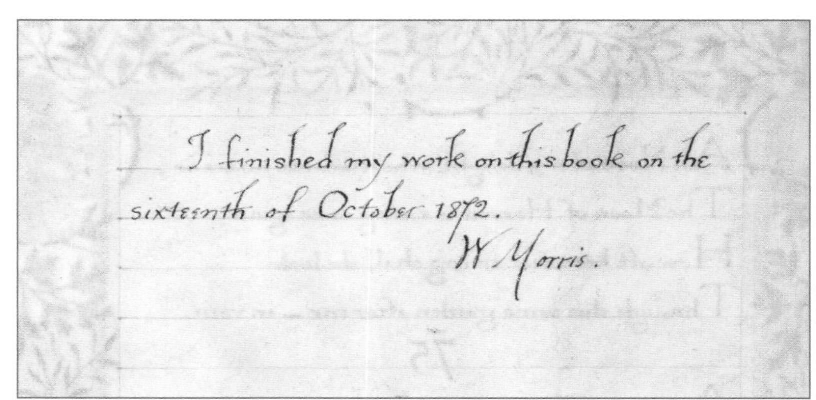
I finished my work on this book on the
sixteenth of October 1872.
W Morris.

Detail of British Library, Add MS 37832, f.12v.

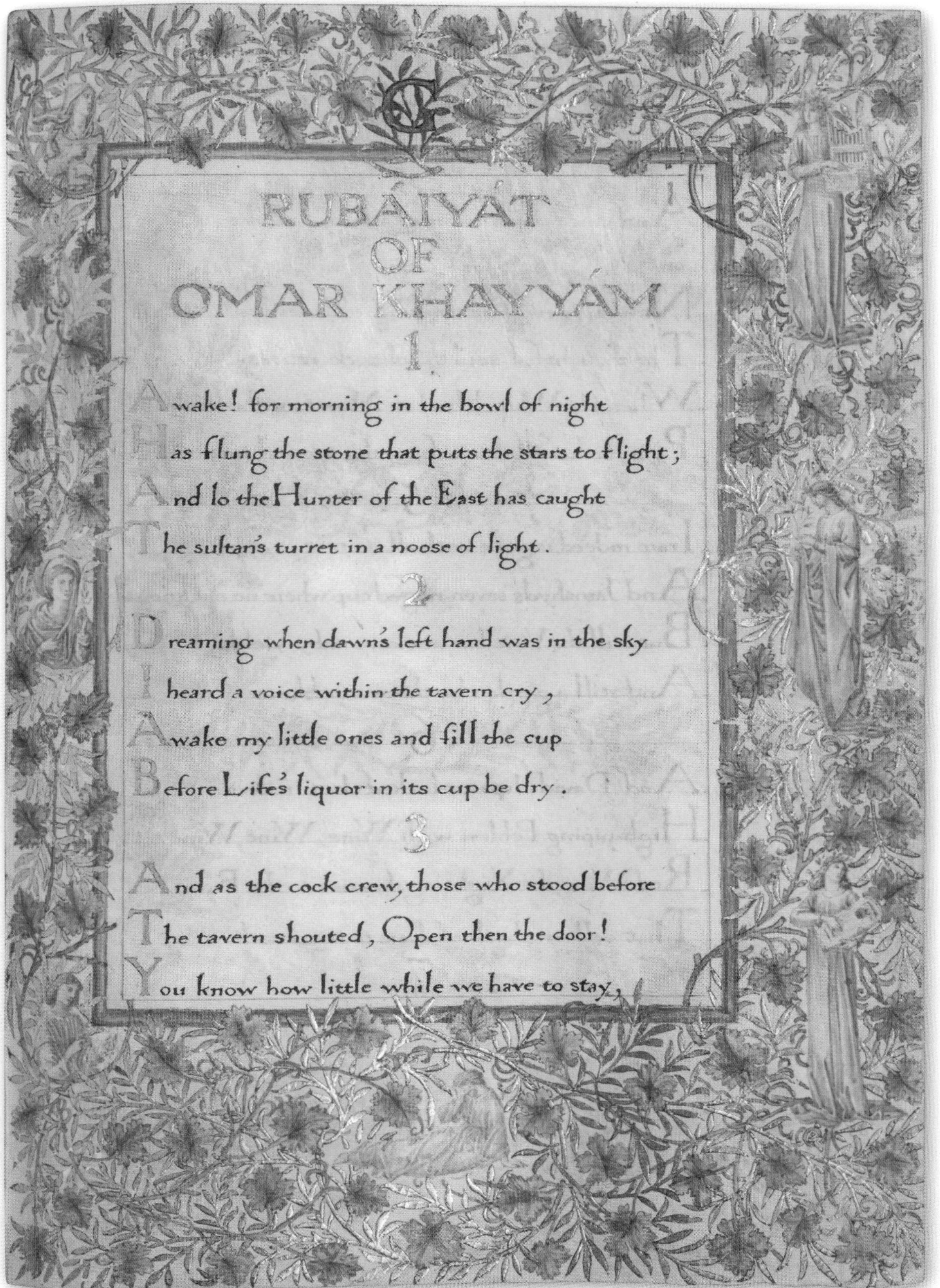

RUBÁIYÁT OF OMAR KHAYYÁM

1

Awake! for morning in the bowl of night
Has flung the stone that puts the stars to flight;
And lo the Hunter of the East has caught
The sultan's turret in a noose of light.

2

Dreaming when dawn's left hand was in the sky
I heard a voice within the tavern cry,
Awake my little ones and fill the cup
Before Life's liquor in its cup be dry.

3

And as the cock crew, those who stood before
The tavern shouted, Open then the door!
You know how little while we have to stay,

Sonnet XCIII How do I love thee

ELIZABETH BARRETT BROWNING (1806–1861)

1846, British Library, Add MS 43487, f.49r, folio 18 × 10.5 cm, ink on paper, bound in half roan with marbled sides.

Sonnets from the Portuguese (1850) is a sequence of forty-four poems written by Elizabeth Barrett Browning during her courtship with the poet Robert Browning. Sonnet 43 (XCIII) is perhaps the most famous, with its opening line 'How do I love thee? Let me count the ways'.

Barrett Browning was initially reluctant to publish the poems because of their intimate nature. However, her husband Robert Browning convinced her of their importance and she published them in her book *Poems* in 1850. To protect her privacy, Barrett Browning called them *Sonnets from the Portuguese*, giving the impression that she was the translator rather than the author. The choice of Portuguese is thought to have been inspired by her husband's nickname for her, 'My little Portuguese'.

The sonnets were an instant success and became Elizabeth Barrett Browning's most commercially successful work. They were also ground-breaking because of their female narrator; usually women were depicted in love poems as passive and remote objects of admiration, without voice or opinion.

This handwritten manuscript of the sonnets was owned by Robert Browning until his death in 1889. Their son, Robert Wiedemann Barrett Browning (1849–1912), gave it to Elizabeth Smith, the wife of the publisher George Murray Smith (1824–1901), in 1898. Smith bequeathed the manuscript to the British Museum, subject to a life interest of her children.

Elizabeth Barrett Browning, engraving after a painting by Alonzo Chappel, British Library, 11651.e.7.

XCIII
How do I love thee? Let me count the ways!
I love thee to the depth & breadth & height
My soul can reach, when feeling out of sight
For the ends of Being and Ideal Grace.
I love thee to the level of everyday's
Most quiet need , by sun & candlelight –
I love thee freely, as men strive for right, –
I love thee purely, as they turn from Praise!.
I love thee with the pass[illegible] put to use
In my old griefs , and with [~~illegible~~] my childhood's faith ' –
I love thee with the love I seemed to lose
With my lost saints' – I love thee with the breath,
Smiles, tears, of all my life '- and, if God choose,
I shall but love thee better after [my] death.

49

XLIII

How do I love thee? — Let me count the ways! —
I love thee to the depth & breadth & height
My soul can reach, when feeling out of sight
For the ends of Being and Ideal Grace.
I love thee to the level of everyday's
Most quiet need, by sun & candlelight —
I love thee freely, as men strive for Right, —
I love thee purely, as they turn from Praise;
I love thee with the passion, put to use
In my old griefs; and with my childhood's faith: —
I love thee with the love I seemed to lose
With my lost Saints! — I love thee with the breath,
Smiles, tears, of all my life! — and, if God choose,
I shall but love thee better after death.

Notes

Chapter 1

[1] The line numbers correspond to lines 201–12 in the revised version of the poem published in *Sibylline Leaves* (London: Res Fenner, 1817).

Chapter 2

[1] Anita Sethi and Lawrence Scott, 'Obituary, Derek Walcott', *The Guardian*, 17 March 2017.
[2] Edgar Allan Poe, 'The Fall of the House of Usher and Other Writings, Poems, Tales, Essays and Reviews', *The Philosophy of Composition*, ed. David Galloway (London: Penguin, 2003), p.436.
[3] Samuel Taylor Coleridge, *Christabel: Kubla Khan, a vision; The Pains of Sleep* (London: John Murray, 1816), pp.51–3.
[4] Ibid.

Chapter 3

[1] Vachel Lindsay, 'The Congo', *Collected Poems* (New York, 1925), pp.178–84.
[2] Chris Beckett, 'From the Bombast of Vachel Lindsay to the Compass of Noise: The Papers of Bob Cobbing at the British Library', *Electronic British Library Journal*, 2010 article no.9, www.bl.uk/eblj/2010articles/article9.html. Accessed 17 January 2022.
[3] T. S. Grimshawe, ed., *The Works of William Cowper: His Life, Letters and Poems* (New York: Robert Carter & Brothers, 1849) p.61.

Chapter 4

[1] Anne Walmsley, *The Caribbean Artists Movement* (London: New Beacon Books, 1992), p.45.
[2] Andrew Salkey, *Jamaica* (London: Hutchinsons, 1973), back cover.
[3] Jared Curtis, *The Fenwick Notes of William Wordsworth* (London: Bristol Classical Press, 1993), p.82.

Chapter 7

[1] Penelope Fitzgerald, 'Charlotte Mary Mew', *Oxford Dictionary of National Biography*.
[2] George Eliot, *Impressions of Theophrastus Such* (Edinburgh: William Blackwood and Sons, 1879), p.38.

Chapter 9

[1] Queen Victoria, journal entry for Sunday 5 January 1862, Royal Archive, RA VIC/MAIN/QVJ (W) 5 January 1862 (Princess Beatrice's copies), http://www.queenvictoriasjournals.org. Accessed 31 January 2022.
[2] British Library, Ashley MS 5022, f.1.

Chapter 10

[1] Bernard Shaw, *Bernard Shaw: The Diaries 1885-1897 with early autobiographical notebooks and diaries, and an abortive 1917 diary*, edited and annotated by Stanley Weintraub (University Park, Pa:. Pennsylvania State University Press, 1986), Vol. 1, p.146.
[2] Ted Hughes to Keith Sagar, 'Letter 720', 18 July 1998, *Letters of Ted Hughes*, ed. Christopher Reid (London: Faber & Faber, 2007).

Acknowledgements

The authors would like to give special thanks to their colleagues in the Modern Archives and Manuscripts Department at the British Library for their support in reading drafts and checking transcriptions: Catherine Angerson, Tabitha Driver, William Frame, Jessica Gregory, Alexander Lock and Zoe Louca-Richards.

The authors would like to thank the following British Library colleagues for their help in recommending poems, providing images and advising on the text. This support has made for a rich and varied selection of manuscripts taken from a range of departments across the British Library: Eleanor Casson, Pardaad Chamsaz, Marina Chellini, Andrea Clarke, Calum Cockburn, Eyob Derillo, Rachel Foss, Annabel Gallop, Emma Harrison, Julian Harrison, Han-Lin Hsieh, Jana Igunma, Arani Ilankuberan, Callum McKean, Olivia Majumdar, Pasquale Manzo, Helen Melody, Yasuyo Ohtsuka, Susan Reed, Ursula Sims-Williams, Hamish Todd, Peter Toth and Jonathon Vines.

The authors would like to thank Maria Ranauro for her assistance in clearing copyright. Special thanks goes to Abbie Day for her editorial work, advice and support. We would like to thank Karin Fremer for her beautiful design and Sally Nicholls for her picture research.

We are very grateful to the contemporary poets who have chosen poems, provided images and transcriptions and written commentaries on their work and creative process. Thanks go to Simon Armitage, Fiona Benson, Liz Berry, Caroline Bird, Rebecca Goss, Kathleen Jamie, Hollie McNish, Pascale Petit, Paul Tran and Benjamin Zephaniah.

The following individuals have been generous with their time and have given permission and helped the authors select and research manuscripts in collections both inside and outside the British Library: Barbara Bair from the Library of Congress; Mary Ellen Budney and Yasmin Ramadan from the Beinecke Library, Yale University; Ashley Cataldo from the American Antiquarian Society; Jeff Cowton of the Wordsworth Trust; Stephen Cullis from Nagasaki University of Foreign Studies; Peter Gilbert; Merlin Holland; Christine Jacobson from the Houghton Library; Megan Mulder from the ZSR Library at Wake Forest University; and Elliott Vigar.

Manuscript Reproduction Credits

Chapter 1

14–15 The Morgan Library & Museum. MA 307. Purchased by Pierpont Morgan, 1904 (MA 307, Book I, f.2r).

18–19 'A Dream' by Stevie Smith reproduced courtesy of Faber and Faber Ltd.

20–1 © Simon Armitage 2022. Used with permission of the author. Armitage, S. *c.*2003. Sir Gawain and the Green Knight draft notebook. At: Leeds University Library, BC MS 20c Armitage/1/21/1 https://explore.library.leeds.ac.uk/special-collections-explore/417740.

26–7 With permission of Tate Lloyd Schieferle.

28–9 By kind permission of Priscilla Coleridge Cassam.

Chapter 2

36–7 'Lampfall' from *The Castaway And Other Poems* by Derek Walcott. Copyright © 1965 by Derek Walcott. Reprinted by permission of Farrar, Straus and Giroux. All Rights Reserved.

38–9 MS Am 233.6 (Volume 6), Houghton Library, Harvard University.

42–5 Editorial comments by T. S. Eliot reproduced courtesy of Faber and Faber Ltd.

50–3 By kind permission of Priscilla Coleridge Cassam.

Chapter 3

62–3 With thanks to The Cobbing Family.

66–7 'Insomniac' by Sylvia Plath reproduced courtesy of Faber and Faber Ltd.

Chapter 4

78–9 © 2022, The Estate of Laura Waugh.

Copyright: © John Betjeman 1949.

82–3 Copyright elements of this poem reproduced by kind permission of the Estate of Oscar Wilde.

84–5 With permission of the Estate of Andrew Salkey.

88–9 With permission of Stephen Stuart-Smith, Literary Executor of David Gascoyne.

90–1 Reproduction courtesy of the Wordsworth Trust.

92–3 Reproduced with the permission of the trustees of the Frances Crofts Cornford Will Trust.

94–5 With permission of the literary executor of Lee Harwood.

Chapter 5

100–1 Reproduction courtesy of the Wordsworth Trust.

102–3 'Forecast' ('Glanmore Sonnets, VII') by Seamus Heaney reproduced courtesy of Faber and Faber Ltd.

114–15 'Song: The Three Ships' by Philip Lark reproduced courtesy of Faber and Faber Ltd.

120–1 Letter to the Tandy family by T. S. Eliot reproduced courtesy of Faber and Faber Ltd.

122–5 Library of Congress, Washington D.C. (Accession No. 13,470. mm 81001625). © 2022 Robert Frost Copyright Trust.

Chapter 6

128–9 Courtesy, American Antiquarian Society.

132–3 V.a.104, f.5r, image 23396, used by permission of the Folger Shakespeare Library.

136–7 Maya Angelou Film and Theater Collection, Special Collections and Archives, Z. Smith Reynolds Library, Wake Forest University, Winston-Salem, North Carolina. 'Still I Rise' Manuscript by Dr. Maya Angelou. Used with Permission by Caged Bird Legacy, LLC.

'Still I Rise' from *And Still I Rise: A Book Of Poems* by Maya Angelou, copyright © 1978 by Maya Angelou. Used by permission of Random House, an imprint and division of Penguin Random House LLC. All rights reserved.

140–1 Reproduced with permission of the literary representative of George Eliot.

142–5 Reproduced by permission of the Provost and Fellows of Eton College.

146–7 Reproduced with the permission of the trustees of the Frances Crofts Cornford Will Trust.

148–9 The Society of Authors as the Literary Representative of the Estate of A. E. Housman.

150–1 Reproduced with permission of Helen Pankhurst.

152–3 MS Am 1118.3 (66b), Houghton Library, Harvard University. *The Poems of Emily Dickinson*, edited by Thomas H. Johnson, Cambridge, Mass.: The Belknap Press of Harvard University Press, Copyright © 1951, 1955 by the President and Fellows of Harvard College.

Copyright © renewed 1979, 1983 by the President and Fellows of Harvard College. Copyright © 1914, 1918, 1919, 1924, 1929, 1930, 1932, 1935, 1937, 1942, by Martha Dickinson Bianchi. Copyright © 1952, 1957, 1958, 1963, 1965, by Mary L. Hampson. Used by permission. All rights reserved.

Chapter 7

156–7 © James Berry: By permission of the Estate of James Berry.

162–3 Reproduction courtesy of the Wordsworth Trust.

178–9 Reproduced with permission of the literary representative of George Eliot.

Chapter 8

182–3 The Wilfred Owen Literary Estate. Annotations by Sassoon © Siegfried Sassoon by kind permission of the Estate of George Sassoon.

186–7 © the estate of Rupert Brooke.

190–1 Permission granted by the Estate of W. B. Yeats.

196–7 © Siegfried Sassoon by kind permission of the Estate of George Sassoon.

198–9 Reproduced by permission of the Provost and Fellows of Eton College.

202–3 With Permission of The Keith Douglas Estate.

204–5 With Permission of the Literary Executor to the Estate of Wilfrid and Alice Meynell.

206–7 Langston Hughes Papers. James Weldon Johnson Collection in the Yale Collection of American Literature, Beinecke Rare Book and Manuscript Library (JWJ MSS 26 Box 384, Folder 6976). Reproduced by permission of David Higham Associates Ltd.

Chapter 9

214–15 With permission of David Lord Tennyson.

224–7 The Dylan Thomas Trust.

234–5 The Morgan Library & Museum. MA 4395. Gift of Mr. and Mrs. Paul Mellon, 1981.

Chapter 10

242–3 Walt Whitman Papers, 1838–1962, in the Clifton Waller Barrett Library, Accession #3829, Special Collections, University of Virginia Library, Charlottesville, VA.

260–3 © The Ted Hughes Estate.

268–9 Reproduced by permission of the Provost and Fellows of Eton College.

Transcription and Translation Credits

The authors would like to give thanks and credit to the following individuals for newly translating and transcribing poems or allowing us to use their extant translations.

Chapter 1
12 Translation of a similar copy of the poem from Sheldon I. Pollock, *The Rāmāyaṇa of Vālmīki, Volume II, Ayodhyakanda*, ed. Robert P. Goldman (Princeton, NJ: Princeton University Press, 1986).
17 Translation from William Morris and A. J. Wyatt, *The Tale of Beowulf sometime King of the Folk of the Weder Geats* (London: Longmans, Green & Co. 1910).

Chapter 3
58–60 Transcription by Ursula Sims-Williams, Lead Curator of Persian, BL Asian and African Collections, British Library. Translation of a similar copy of the poem by Richard Le Gallienne from John Arberry, *Fifty Poems of Hafiz*, (Cambridge: Cambridge University Press, 1947).
60 Transcription by Catherine Angerson, Curator of Modern Archives and Manuscripts, British Library. Translation from Richard Stokes, *The Book of Lieder* (London: Faber & Faber, 2011), provided courtesy of Oxford Lieder (www.oxfordlieder.co.uk).

Chapter 4
96 Translation from Roy Campbell, *Poems of Baudelaire* (New York: Pantheon Books, 1952).

Chapter 5
156 Transcription of James Berry, 'My Father', from *The Penguin Book of Caribbean Verse in English*, ed. Paula Burnett (London: Penguin, 1986).

Chapter 7
164 Transcription by Professor Andrew Lo, Emeritus Professor of Chinese, SOAS and Emma Harrison, Curator of Chinese Collections, British Library. Translation by Professor Andrew Lo.
170 Transcription by Pardaad Chamsaz, Curator of Germanic Collections, British Library. Translation by Pardaad Chamsaz and Susan Reed, Lead Curator of Germanic Collections, British Library.

Chapter 8
185 Translation © Martin Sorrell 2001, from *Arthur Rimbaud Collected Poems* (Oxford: Oxford University Press, 2009). Reproduced with permission of Oxford Publishing Limited through PLSclear.
192–3 Transcription from *H. C. Andersens samlede skrifter.* (Kjøbenhavn: C. A. Reitzels, 1879), vol. 12, p.344. Translation by Nielsine Nielsen.

Chapter 9
233 Translation of a similar manuscript (MKL-008 Mäṣḥafä qəddase, Missal) by Maria Bulakh, Russian State University for the Humanities / National Research University Higher School of Economics and Denis Nosnitsin University of Hamburg, from 'An Old Amharic poem from northern Ethiopia: one more text on condemning glory', *Bulletin of SOAS*, 82, 2 (Cambridge: Cambridge University Press, 2019). © The Authors, 2019.

Chapter 10
244 Transcription and translation by Stephen Cullis, Lecturer at Nagasaki University of Foreign Studies.
254 Transcription and translation by Olivia Majumdar, Project Curator of Bengali Books, British Library.
264 Transcription and translation by Dr Cholthira Satyawadhna, Professor Emeritus, Walailak University, Nakhon Si Thammarat and Jana Igunma, Ginsburg Curator for Thai, Lao and Cambodian Collections, British Library.

Picture Credits

Introduction
6 *The Rubáiyát of Omar Khayyám* by Omar Khayyám, translated by Edward Fitzgerald, British Library, Add MS 37832, f.6r.

Chapter 1
10–11 Detail of p.25.
14 Contract for *Paradise Lost*, 27 April 1667, British Library, Add MS 18861.
20 Simon Armitage, photograph by Peter James Millson.
24 Lord Byron, engraving by Edward Finden, after George Sanders 1807–9, frontispiece to *The Works of Lord Byron* (1837), British Library, 1466.i.25.

Chapter 2
30–1 Detail of p.41.
35 John Donne, engraving by Pierre Lombart, frontispiece to *Poems, by J. D. With elegies on the authors death* (1633), British Library, G.11415.
36 Derek Walcott in his home office in Brookline, MA, after winning the Nobel Prize for Literature, photograph by Brooks Kraft, 8 October 1992 (Brooks Kraft/AFP/ Getty Images).
47 Hollie McNish, photograph by Kat Gollock.
50 Samuel Taylor Coleridge, mezzotint by Samuel Cousins, 1854, after a portrait by Washington Allston of 1814, frontispiece to *The Poems of Samuel Taylor Coleridge* (1870), British Library, c.126.C.10.

Chapter 3
54–5 Detail of p.63, top.
73 Christina Rossetti, engraving after a drawing by Dante Gabriel Rossetti, 1891, frontispiece to *Letters translated by Mary J. Serrano with portraits* (1891), British Library, 010920.f.20.

Chapter 4
74–5 Detail of p.79.
82 Oscar Wilde, photograph by Napoleon Sarony, 1882, British Library, Add MS 81785 1.
84 Andrew Salkey, photograph by Vanessa Stamford, February 1972, with kind permission of Jason Salkey, British Library, Deposit 10310.
86 Liz Berry, photograph poet's own.
88 Surrealist poet David Gascoyne, author of 'A Vagrant and Other Poems', and 'Night Thoughts', sits on a flight of basement steps next to a cluster of milk bottles, photography by George Douglas. (Original Publication: *Picture Post* – 5314 – Are Poets Really Necessary? – pub. 1951. George Douglas/Picture Post/ Hulton Archive/Getty Images).
96 Charles Baudelaire, photograph by Étienne Carjet, 1863, published in *Galerie contemporaine, littéraire, artistique* (1876–1874), British Library, General Reference Collection P.P.1931.peg.

Chapter 5
98–9 Detail of p.111.
107 Rudyard Kipling, etching by William Strang, 1901, frontispiece to *A series of thirty etchings illustrating subjects from the writing of Rudyard Kipling* (1901), British Library, L.R.301.bb.6.
108 Ben Jonson, engraving by Robert Vaughan *c.*1640, frontispiece inserted into *The workes of Beniamin Ionson* (1613), British Library, G.11630.
110 William Blake, self-portrait, pencil, British Library, Add MS 49460 f.35r.
113 'The Tyger' from *Songs of Innocence and Experience* by William Blake, British Library, C.71.d.19. (1923) Facsimile of a coloured and gilded copy by H.Young & Sons, Liverpool, of the first edition of *Songs of Innocence and Experience*.
116 Kathleen Jamie, photograph by Robin Gillanders.
118 Charlotte Brontë, steel engraving by J. C. Armytage after a portrait of George Richmond *c.*1850, in *A collection of engraved and lithographed Portraits of English poetesses made by F. J. Stainforth* (n.d.), British Library, 1876.f.22.
124 Robert Frost, photograph by Doris Ulmann, 1929, National Portrait Gallery, Smithsonian Institution, Washington D.C., NPG.97.112.

Chapter 6
126–7 Detail of p.137.
129 Phillis Wheatley, engraving, published 1773, frontispiece to *Poems on Various Subjects* (1793), British Library, 992.a.34.
130 Percy Shelley, reproduction published 1876, after a portrait by Amelia Curran, 1819, plate opposite 190 in *Twelve Essays with Twelve Portraits* (1876), British Library, 1560/4193.
134 Fiona Benson, photograph by Jessica Farmer of Perspectives Photography.
136 Maya Angelou, photograph by

Martin Godwin, London, 4 June 1999 (Martin Godwin/Getty Images).

148 A. E. Housman, photograph, 1890s, Trinity College, Cambridge.

151 Sylvia Pankhurst, photograph, *c.*1911, Library of Congress, Washington D.C., JK1881 .N357 sec. XVI, no. 3-9 NAWSA Coll.

153 Emily Dickinson, daguerreotype, *c.*1847, Emily Dickinson Museum, Amherst College.

Chapter 7

154–5 Detail of p.165.

156 'My father's non-interest in education', James Berry, British Library, Add MS 89353/1/13.

158 Jane Austen, reproduction after a drawing by Cassandra Austen, *c.*1810, frontispiece to *A Memoir of Jane Austen* (1870), British Library, 10855.e.8.

160 Sappho and her companions, from a Dutch translation of Christine de Pizan's Livre de la Cité des Dames, Bruges, 1475, Add MS 20698, f.73r.

162 Dorothy Wordsworth, lithograph, before 1855, frontispiece to *Journals of Dorothy Wordsworth* (1897) British Library, 10826.de.10.

168 'Love Me, I Love You', illustration by Arthur Hughes, p.2 in *Sing-Song. A nursery rhyme book* by Christina Rossetti (1872), British Library, 11651.e.7.

176 Pascale Petit, photograph by Brian Fraser.

179 George Eliot, engraving by G. J. Stodart after François D'Albert Durade, 1850, frontispiece to *Agatha* (1869), British Library Ashley 712.

Chapter 8

180–1 Detail of p.207.

182 Wilfred Owen, reproduction after the last known photograph of the poet, Hastings 30 August 1918, illustration opposite p.192, to *De Unge døde. Første del. Keats-Shelley-Byron. Annen del. Brooke-Sorley-Owen* (1832), British Library, 11855.d.12.

195 Hans Christian Andersen, photograph by Thora Hallager, 1869, Odense City Museum, Denmark.

198 Robert Browning, engraving by J. Armytage, illustration after p.152, in *A New Spirit of Age* (1844), British Library, 1203.g.3.

201 Alexander Pope, engraving by George Vertue, 1715, after a portrait by Charles Jervas, frontispiece to *The Works of Mr Alexander Pope*, vol., 1 (1717–1735), British Library, C.59.i.20.

206 Langston Hughes, photograph by Carl Van Vechten, 29 February 1936, Library of Congress, Washington D.C., LOT 12735, no. 540.

Chapter 9

212–13 Detail of p.223.

216 Rebecca Goss, photograph by Lucy Carter.

226 Dylan Thomas, photograph by Rosalie Thorne McKenna, published in *Dylan Thomas; great authors from the Time Reading Programe* (1965), Library of Congress, Washington D.C., POS – US .M241, no. 1.

228 An alleged fragment of Percy Bysshe Shelley's ashes, *c.*1822, British Library, Ashley MS 5022.

235 Aphra Behn, engraving by Robert White after John Riley, frontispiece to *Poems upon several Occasions* by Aphra Behn (1696), British Library, 11626.bb.5.

Chapter 10

238–9 Detail of p.241.

243 Walt Whitman, photograph by Phillips & Taylor, Philadelphia [1873], Library of Congress, Washington D.C., LOT 12017, box 1.

244 Fujiwara no Teika, woodblock, f.43, *Kashiragaki eshō hyakunin isshu*, (1673), British Library, Or.75.h.3.

246 May Morris, photograph, 1909, Library of Congress, Washington D.C., LC-B2- 797-7 [P&P].

248 Caroline Bird, photograph poet's own.

263 Ted Hughes, photograph by Fay Godwin, 1970, British Library, FG597-5-11.

266 Detail from *The Rubáiyát of Omar Khayyám*, by Omar Khayyám, translated by Edward Fitzgerald, British Library, Add MS 37832, f.12v.

268 Elizabeth Barrett Browning, engraving after a painting by Alonzo Chappel, published facing p.352 in *Portrait Gallery of Eminent Men and Women of Europe and America*, vo1. 2 (1873), British Library, 11651.e.7

Endmatter

277 Letter from Dylan Thomas to Vernon Watkins, British Library, Add MS 52612, f.152r.

286–7 Folios from the Beowulf manuscript, British Library, Cotton MS Vitellius A XV, ff.200v–201r.

Blaen Cwm
Llangain
near Carmarthen

[30 Aug 1944]

Wednesday

Dear Vernon,

A complication. On Monday Sept. 4 we are moving into a new house — we call it a house; it's made of wood and asbestos — in New Quay, Cardiganshire. It's in a really wonderful bit of the bay, with a beach of its own. Terrific. But it means that we're much much further from Carmarthen. Now how can we meet? Can you come down here? You said you didn't want to spend your leave outside Pennard, but couldn't you spare us just one night in New Quay? We would love it so. Anyway, write. After Monday, our address will be Majoda, New Quay. The name is made of the ~~....~~ beginnings of the names of the three children of the man who built the questionable house. I may alter the name to Catlleudylaer.

Here is a new poem. It's a month & a bit premature. I do hope you like it, & wd like very much to read it aloud to you. Will you read it aloud too? It's got, I think, a lovely slow lyrical movement.

Write as soon as you can.

We must all meet.

Love,

Dylan.

In the poem, I notice, on copying out, that I have made October trees bare. I'll alter later.

Glossary

The language used to describe poetry and manuscripts may sometimes sound specialised. This glossary of key terms that appear throughout this publication explains the language used to talk about poems, books and manuscripts.

Ancient Egyptian ink: Egyptian ink has been in use since the twenty-sixth century BC and was developed into two colours: red and black.

Ballad: A narrative poem or song usually written in short stanzas. Ballads traditionally are of unknown authorship and have been passed down through the generations.

Bifolium: A sheet of paper or parchment, folded to produce two leaves (four pages).

Bindings: The covering and sewing of a book or volume.

Burnished paper: A technique used to stop the risk of bleeding ink in manuscripts. The paper is made less fibrous and spongy by the application of great pressure on the top of the sheet using horn, bone, agate or glass.

Canto: A section or part of a long poem.

Chinese inks: The first Chinese inks date back possibly as far as three or four millennia. They were composed of plant, animal and mineral extracts, such as graphite, that were ground with water and applied with ink brushes. The first recorded evidence of Chinese ink is from around 256 BC.

Draft: A working document characterised by deletions, corrections and revisions.

Epic: Classical epic poetry that recounts a physical or mental journey.

Fair copy: A neat, legible manuscript copy of a text made by its author or another scribe. Though written neatly, they often display editorial changes.

Folio: An individual leaf or sheet of paper or parchment. Folios can be loose or bound into a volume.

Ghazal: A lyric poem with a fixed number of verses and a rhyme scheme. *Ghazals* are particularly associated with the Middle East and India, and can be set to music.

Guard volume: A bound volume made up from individual leaves or pages which have been adhered onto strips of paper or card.

India ink: First invented in China, although the ingredients were traded from India. The traditional method of making the ink was to grind a mixture of hide glue, carbon black, lampblack and bone black pigment with a pestle and mortar. The mixture was then poured into a ceramic dish to dry. In order to be able to use the dry mixture, a wet brush would be applied until it returned to a liquid form.

Ink: A coloured solution used for writing, drawing, printing or duplicating. Typically, ink was used with a pen, brush, quill or reed pen to write on papyrus, animal skin (parchment or vellum) or paper. The earliest inks are believed to have been made with lampblack, a kind of soot, which was produced as a by-product of fire.

Iron gall ink: Commonly used in European and North American manuscripts, iron gall ink was made from iron salts and tannic acids (using ground oak galls from trees) until synthetic ink was developed in the nineteenth century. This ink is highly acidic and often contributed to the corrosion of paper or parchment.

Konlabot: A form of Thai poetry. It uses a special form of rhyme that often can be read vertically or horizontally, similar to a word puzzle, and usually involves word play and puns.

Laid paper: Laid paper displays ridges or lines as a result of the manufacturing process. It was the predominant form of paper in Europe until about 1780, when wove paper was widely introduced. Laid paper usually shows lines when held to the light, whereas wove is flatter and smoother.

Leaf: The term 'leaf' is used for a page in the description of some manuscripts, although this is often interchanged with the term 'folio', which comes from the Latin for 'leaf'.

Manuscript: A handwritten text.

Notebook: A small book with blank or ruled pages for writing notes in.

Page: The term is used for one or both sides of a sheet of paper bound into a book or volume. It is often used interchangeably with 'folio' and 'leaf'.

Paper: A material manufactured into thin sheets from the pulp of a tree or other fibrous substances including rags and other cloth materials. The earliest archaeological remains of paper were found in China and date back to the second century BC. From China, the production of paper spread to the Middle East and across to medieval Europe. The development of new techniques, including a shift from the use of rags to wood pulp, meant that by the nineteenth century paper could be mass-produced on an industrial scale with varying price points and quality.

Papyrus: A material similar to a thick paper made from the pith of the papyrus plant.

Parchment: A thin flat material made from the prepared skin of an animal, usually a sheep or goat, and used as a durable writing surface in ancient, medieval and early modern times.

Phoneme: The smallest unit in speech used to identify one word from another.

Pothi form: The *pothi* form consists of loose leaves placed one on top of another.

Rag paper: A type of paper originally made from cotton rags, but now made from cotton linters.

Recto: The front of a page or leaf. It corresponds to the right-hand page of a bound volume. This is often shortened to 'r' when citing particular parts of a manuscript.

Scribal copy: A scribal copy refers to a manuscript written or copied by someone, usually a professional and not the author.

Scribe: A scribe is someone who copies out text but is not the author of the document.

Sonnet: A poem of fourteen lines with a rhyme scheme, usually having ten syllables per line.

Stanza: A group of lines forming the basic metrical unit in a poem, known as a verse. 'Stanza' and 'verse' have been used interchangeably throughout the book.

Sumi ink: Sumi ink is made from lamp soot or burnt pine with animal glue and perfume. It originates from Japan and can be used for painting or lettering.

Transcription: Copies of a text reproduced from a manuscript.

Translation: The process of changing the words of an original text into another language.

Typescript: A typed document.

Vellum: A type of fine parchment made from the skin of a calf.

Verse: Writing arranged with a metrical rhythm, often with a rhyme scheme. It also denotes a group of lines that form the basis of a song or poem.

Verso: The back of a page or leaf. It corresponds to the left-hand page of a bound volume. This is often shortened to 'v' when citing particular parts of a manuscript.

Waka: *Waka* (和歌) means Japanese poem and is the basic form of Japanese poetry. *Waka* can include *choka* (long poem) and *tanka* (short poem).

Washi paper: A traditional Japanese paper manufactured by hand. It is made from local fibres from either the bark of the gampi tree, the mitsumata shrub or the kozo (paper mulberry) bush.

Watercolour: A paint made with a water-soluble binder such as gum arabic and thinned with water rather than oil, giving a transparent colour.

Wax seal: A piece of wax with a design imprinted on it, often used to fasten letters and verify documents.

Wove paper: A writing paper with a smooth surface. After its introduction in the eighteenth century, it became the predominant paper for use in Europe.

Index of Poets

Index of Titles

This index contains the titles of poems as published.

Index of First Lines

This list contains the first lines of poems as they were published, which may differ substantially from the manuscript drafts. For extracts from longer poems, or poems within larger works, the first line of the full work has been used. Where a published version does not exist, the poem has been omitted.

ƿyrm of̄ ƿeallclif

mian frætƿa hyr

on ƿæn hladen æg

har hilde to hr

Him ða gegiredan

un ƿaclicne hel

beorhtū byrnū s

middes mærne þe

leofne ongunnon

t on ƿæg niman flod f

e þ ƿæs ƿundē

æs unrim æþelinge b

es næfre : xliii·

gæta læde að on scyp

n behongen hilde bor

hebbenda ƿæs alegdon

ch hæleð hiofende h

a on beorge bæl rim